# GET RICH
## LIKE INSTANT COFFEE

# GET RICH
## LIKE INSTANT COFFEE

Unlocking Your Purpose
for Financial Freedom

## CLEMER LEGGETT

Library of Congress Control Number: 2024922840

ISBN:   979-8-89228-184-3   (Paperback)
ISBN:   979-8-89228-185-0   (Hardcover)
ISBN:   979-8-89228-186-7   (eBook)

Printed in the United States of America

*The Journey of Clemer Leggett: A Transformational Personal Development Entrepreneur's Accurate Measure of Power*

*Clemer Leggett's journey started with modest beginnings, marked by limited literacy and numerous challenges. Despite facing various obstacles and setbacks, his unwavering persistence and commitment to self-improvement enabled him to surmount these difficulties and achieve success as an entrepreneur. However, despite his business accomplishments, Leggett felt a deep sense of unfulfillment and aspired to make a meaningful impact on the lives of millions.*

*This drive led him to develop his techniques for personal transformation and to become an inspirational speaker, author, and trainer. His core message of self-improvement through personal responsibility and purpose-led motivation resonates with individuals and corporate audiences.*

*His book, Get Rich Like Instant Coffee: Unlocking Your Purpose for Financial Freedom, has been a catalyst for transformation in countless lives, empowering people to achieve greater success and happiness. Leggett envisions himself as a leading figure in self-improvement and manifestation, a vision that has now become a reality, thanks to over a decade of dedication to personal development and corporate training.*

*His journey is a testament to the power of perseverance, a burning desire for success, and the crucial role of finding purpose in life.*

## The 41-word prayer

I am open and ready to accept the cup of blessing that the universe holds for me. I am worthy of expanding my steps. I am deserving of an abundance of wealth and prosperity. This abundance should come in all areas of my life.

# DEDICATION

To all the young souls and seasoned hearts who've walked this journey with me, I want to take a moment to express my deepest gratitude. Your support means everything, and this moment is for you. This isn't just a lighthearted reflection; there's something much deeper at play. Perhaps, just perhaps, you've found a piece of yourself in these pages—something that resonates beyond the surface. While humor might not always be my strong suit, what we share here is no laughing matter. It's real, it's raw, and it's ours. Thank you for being a part of this story with me.

First and foremost, I extend a huge thank-you to my incredible wife, Donna Leggett. Donna, you've been my rock and my partner in both life and business. From the early days of *Get Rich Like Instant Coffee: Unlocking Your Purpose for Financial Freedom* to the growth of our successful company, your unwavering support and selfless dedication have propelled every achievement. I deeply cherish your commitment and the strength you bring to our shared journey.

To my siblings, Darrell Leggett, Monier Leggett, and Keisha Leggett, I am going to say the big one: Thank you for your steadfast encouragement and support. Your belief in me has been a constant source of strength and motivation.

I am profoundly grateful to my friends, Toni Shah and Timothy Pitts. Your encouragement and insights were invaluable throughout the writing process. Your dedication to proofreading, providing feedback, and offering unwavering support shaped this book into its best form.

Your belief in my vision has fueled my drive to overcome challenges and stay laser-focused on my goals. I feel truly blessed to have friends who not only inspire me but also invest so deeply in my success. A special heartfelt thanks goes out to each of you, especially my beloved grandmother, Mrs. Bama Hobbs, and my incredible parents, my father, Mr. Clemer Leggett, and my mother, Helen Barlametta Leggett. Their unwavering support and constant push for tenacity echo in my heart and mind every day, not only shaping this book but also transforming the person I've become.

To everyone within my community where I grew up in Fairhope, Alabama, and to all the people I met on my journey along the way, your collective support has been extremely valuable and priceless, as your encouragement has made this journey even more rewarding. To those who have crossed my path during this journey, whether briefly or for a season, your presence has been a meaningful part of this process. Your support, even if only for a moment, has been deeply appreciated.

Lastly, I dedicate this work to my mentor, Percy Ford, who has become like family to me. His lessons on integrity and excellence in business have profoundly impacted my approach and success.

Thank you, all, for being part of this remarkable journey.

# ACKNOWLEDGMENTS

Another key figure in my success is my lawyer, Kenneth Funderburk, who showed me that success is not just about material wealth but also about satisfying one's soul. I also want to express how happy and deeply grateful I am for my children and friends who believed in me and stood by me even when others doubted my abilities. They have always been a constant source of joy, motivation, and support; and I cannot thank them enough.

Additionally, I want to express my gratitude to Rico Goodloe, Janet G. Williams, and the Hobbs families, who have inspired me greatly. A special thanks goes to Laron Smith and Charles Mitchell, the talented photographers at Ultimately Expression Photographer Studio. Their work captured my best angles and created a stunning book-cover photo that perfectly represents my book and its message. Their dedication and artistic skills have contributed greatly to the success of this project.

# CONTENTS

# FOREWORD

## Get Rich Like Instant Coffee: Unlocking Your Purpose for Financial Freedom

As you hold this book in your hands, you are about to embark on a transformative journey. You are invited to uncover a wellspring of meaningful insights and genuine empowerment. Influential voices have contributed to this work, not merely to present ideas but to offer a clear pathway toward personal transformation as well. Within these pages, you will find practical tools and exercises designed to tap into the limitless potential of your subconscious mind, an essential component of personal growth and financial success.

I want you to know that this is not just a book about money, nor is it a vague blueprint without clear guidance. While it may appear focused on wealth, its true purpose is to help you build a life rooted in fulfillment, clarity, and intention. This guide draws from universal wisdom, offering valuable resources to anyone committed to elevating their life and reaching their highest potential.

Within these pages, you'll learn to harness the immense power of your subconscious mind to manifest the life you envision.[1] Inspired by thinkers like Napoleon Hill,[2] Earl Nightingale,[3] Raimon Samso,[4]

---

1   Joseph Murphy, *The Power of Your Subconscious Mind* (Prentice Hall, 1963).

2   Napoleon Hill, *Think and Grow Rich* (The Ralston Society, 1937).

3   Earl Nightingale, *The Strangest Secret* (Nightingale-Conant, 1956).

4   Raimon Samso, *The Manifestation Code* (Self-published, 2016).

and Gabrielle Bernstein,[5] the insights shared here are designed to strengthen your belief in your abilities and prepare you for meaningful change. It incorporates wisdom from influential figures such as Esther and Jerry Hicks,[6] Leo Tolstoy,[7] Robert T. Kiyosaki,[8] Joseph Murphy,[9] Jack Canfield,[10] Frederick Douglass,[11] T. Harv Eker,[12] Rhonda Byrne,[13] W. E. B. Du Bois,[14] Carter G. Woodson,[15] Phillis Wheatley,[16] Oscar Micheaux,[17] and many others. Together, they provide a comprehensive guide to mastering your financial well-being and living a purpose-driven life.

As someone deeply immersed in personal development, I am profoundly grateful to the authors whose wisdom has shaped my thoughts and beliefs. Their teachings have illuminated my path to

---

5    Gabrielle Bernstein, *The Universe Has Your Back: Transform Fear to Faith* (Hay House, 2016).

6    Esther and Jerry Hicks, *Ask and It Is Given: Learning to Manifest Your Desires* (Hay House, 2004).

7    Leo Tolstoy, *The Kingdom of God Is Within You* (Dodd, Mead, 1894).

8    Robert T. Kiyosaki, *Rich Dad Poor Dad* (TechPress, 1997).

9    Murphy, *The Power of Your Subconscious Mind.*

10    Jack Canfield, *The Success Principles: How to Get from Where You Are to Where You Want to Be* (HarperCollins, 2005).

11    Frederick Douglass, *Narrative of the Life of Frederick Douglass, an American Slave* (Anti-Slavery Office, 1845).

12    T. Harv Eker, *Secrets of the Millionaire Mind: Mastering the Inner Game of Wealth* (Harper Business, 2005).

13    Rhonda Byrne, *The Secret* (Atria Books/Beyond Words, 2006).

14    W. E. B. Du Bois, *The Souls of Black Folk* (A.C. McClurg & Co., 1903).

15    Carter G. Woodson, *The Mis-Education of the Negro* (Associated Publishers, 1933).

16    Phillis Wheatley, *Poems on Various Subjects, Religious and Moral* (Archibald Bell, 1773).

17    Oscar Micheaux, *The Conquest: The Story of a Negro Pioneer* (The Western Book Supply Company, 1913).

success, and this guide is my way of giving back by sharing my own stories and insights with the world, just as they did for me.[18]

In "Get Rich Like Instant Coffee," prepare for a journey that offers profound transformation. The knowledge within these pages has the potential to reshape every part of your life. The real impact, however, comes not from reading alone but from deliberately applying the insights you discover. When I began writing this book, I knew I was sharing ideas that could create meaningful change. Your presence here shows that you have drawn this information into your life—not only the physical book but also the wisdom it carries. Life unfolds according to a greater design, so engage deeply with each page. Spending an hour on a single page is not only acceptable, but it is often essential as well. The depth of your understanding will influence the magnitude of your transformation.

Immerse yourself fully in the material. Reflect on how these principles apply to your current reality and actions. Identify areas for improvement, and weave this newfound wisdom into your daily routine. The goal is to internalize these powerful insights and act upon them, realizing the promises made by these teachings. By the time you finish this journey, you will emerge as a liberated and dynamic individual, fully harnessing your innate power. Expect a profound shift in your beliefs, a richer self-awareness, and an elevated state of consciousness.

Let us revisit the origins of this transformative knowledge. My pivotal shift began at the age of twenty-four, awakening a deep curiosity about meaningful change. That curiosity fueled more than twenty-five years of focused research into human behavior and success. During this

---

18    Mitch Horowitz, *The Miracle Club: How Thoughts Become Reality* (Rochester, VT: Inner Traditions, 2018).

journey, I have studied the philosophies and life patterns of many of history's most influential thinkers.

My mentor, Percy Ford, immersed himself in the teachings of influential thinkers and used a scientific approach to analyze and apply their ideas. The principles you are about to explore have been tested and refined over many years, demonstrating their lasting strength. These principles have guided me in building businesses, traveling widely, and inspiring others to achieve meaningful financial success.

You hold a repository of transformative wisdom in your hands, yet its true value is unlocked only through consistent practice. To make the most of these insights, it is helpful to share them with those who are open to receiving them. As I reflect on my journey, I remember a defining seminar in Atlanta, Georgia, that reshaped my direction and deepened my commitment to teaching these principles. That moment fueled my dedication to passing on the powerful lessons I gained. This work stands as a testament to my desire to share the knowledge that has profoundly influenced my life.

Influenced by mentors such as Minister Louis Farrakhan and Bishop T. D. Jakes, I learned to live in alignment with universal principles, even though I initially struggled to explain the reasons behind my success. This guide is written to help you gain that same clarity and to pursue fulfillment and prosperity in your own life with confidence.

As you explore these ideas, I hope they inspire meaningful growth in your life, just as they have in mine. I leave you with a powerful insight from Dick Gregory: "If all you can do is judge a person by their appearance because you lack the spirit to judge someone from within, you are in trouble." Embrace this wisdom as you move through the concepts in this guide, and let it support your journey toward greater understanding and lasting success.

# PREFACE

Welcome to ***GET RICH LIKE INSTANT COFFEE***. This book is crafted to inspire and equip you with the tools needed to unlock your full potential. While it will not solve every challenge overnight, it offers a clear and practical roadmap to help you begin and sustain your journey toward success and a joyful, meaningful life.

Within these pages, you will find insights drawn from real experiences of overcoming adversity and breaking free from limiting circumstances. This guide emphasizes the power of mindset transformation and personal development, helping you recognize your own strengths and abilities.

This is more than a guide to financial success. It is an invitation to discover and cultivate the untapped potential within you. By embracing a growth mindset, setting clear goals, and investing your time and energy in personal development, you position yourself for a fulfilling and successful life.

This book is designed not only to help you understand your habitual patterns of thinking and imagined limitations but also to support you in creating your own destiny. Let these pages be your first step toward realizing your dreams and building the life you truly desire.

# INTRODUCTION

GET RICH LIKE INSTANT COFFEE explores the incredible potential of the subconscious mind and the influence of infinite intelligence. Through my personal experiences, I offer insights into the mind's capabilities in a way that is both practical and transformative. A word of caution: If you are not yet ready to explore your higher self and the presence of the "I am" within, you may choose to pause before beginning this journey.

By immersing yourself in these pages and completing the exercises as instructed, you can deepen your understanding of how your subconscious mind shapes your thoughts, words, emotions, and actions. My view of abundance as an inner driving force introduces a new level of awareness and empowerment. This guide provides practical tools that support meaningful personal growth and success, making it a valuable resource for anyone committed to improving every area of life.

2 Corinthians 10:5 reminds us that we can control our thoughts and use our God-given imaginations without limits.

In the beginning, there was an infant intelligence and imagination stemming from an infinite source. Over time, this intelligence evolved and created various things. But as humans became focused on their own creations, many forgot the original source of all wisdom. They began to believe that new discoveries were entirely original, even though much of what we call innovation is simply a rediscovery of what has always existed.

The principles and laws of infinite wisdom have always been available to anyone willing to explore their potential. Understanding this helps us appreciate the depth of knowledge that has existed since the beginning of time. We are uncovering what was already placed before us. When people drifted into ignorance, they became disconnected from this understanding. Yet even now, in the twenty-first century, new ideas are being revealed, although they have always been present.

Everything we experience has existed in some form before, and these principles were always accessible. Only by awakening from ignorance can we reconnect with these forgotten truths and tap into the infinite intelligence and imagination within us. Negative emotions such as hatred, envy, jealousy, selfishness, and war distract people from what truly matters, causing them to lose sight of the lessons of the past.

I was fortunate to have a mentor who taught me how to manifest the life I desired. His teachings on the theology of science explained how the mind shapes ideas and creation. By applying these teachings each day, my life changed for the better. I now build upon his timeless principles, adding my own insights as I continue learning and growing.

For many years, I lived with disabilities, scarcity, fear, and negative labels such as "loser"—until I discovered the power of words. Our words can strengthen or weaken us, shape our identity, and influence our success. It is vital to pay attention to our emotions and beliefs because they guide the subconscious mind and shape the reality we experience.

Mr. Percy Ford planted the ideas of prosperity and abundance in my mind, guiding me toward personal growth, spiritual completeness, and financial freedom. His teachings were a blessing, and they left a lasting impact on everyone who knew him. His life was his greatest sermon, demonstrating what it means to pursue one's dreams with purpose and conviction. I believe his principles will continue to transform lives for generations.

Born on June 9, 1940, Percy Ford grew up in Columbus, Georgia, and graduated from William H. Spencer High School in 1958. After earning a degree in agronomy from Tennessee State University, he returned home and became a successful entrepreneur, establishing Ford and Son's Landscaping and Nursery. His work beautified homes and businesses across Georgia, Florida, Alabama, and Tennessee; and he helped former inmates learn the landscaping trade so they could build new careers. His legacy lives on in the landscapes he created, the crepe myrtles that line the highways, and the projects he completed for major companies and cities.

Percy's nursery on Buena Vista Road was the first African American–owned nursery in Georgia. He contributed to projects for the Aflac corporate headquarters and other significant landmarks, leaving an enduring mark on the communities he served. He was known for his storytelling, his humor, and his generous spirit. Percy lived by principles that emphasized setting clear goals, adapting to change, continuous learning, and maintaining a strong work ethic.

Percy Ford's commitment to integrity, honesty, and respect, combined with his drive for excellence, continues to inspire me. Like Percy, I believe it is our duty to use our success to uplift others and support our communities. His life stands as a powerful reminder of the value of hard work and ethical conduct. By embracing these principles, we can encourage others to live with purpose and contribute to a more compassionate world. Thank you for considering these values as guidance in your own journey.

# SUMMARY

Embark on a transformative journey with *Get Rich Like Instant Coffee*, a guide that blends practical advice with meaningful insights on mindset, subconscious influence, and manifestation. Each chapter offers actionable strategies to help you recognize your potential, move beyond limiting beliefs, and create a life aligned with your highest aspirations. With its combination of timeless wisdom and modern techniques, this guide serves as a key to unlocking greater abundance, happiness, and purpose.

*Chapter 1: Setting the Stage, Your Journey to Manifestation Begins*

This chapter introduces your journey by focusing on the powerful spirit within you. By connecting with this inner source, you begin to understand your limitless potential and your natural ability to shape your reality. This foundation sets the tone for deeper self-discovery and a stronger connection with the universe.

*Chapter 2: Starting the Adventure Path*

This chapter explores the influence of the subconscious mind and infinite intelligence, offering tools for personal growth and success. Drawing from personal experience and teachings from figures such as Napoleon Hill, it highlights the importance of desire, faith, and imagination in creating your reality. By aligning your thoughts and actions with clear intentions and releasing limiting beliefs, you can move toward greater wealth, health, and fulfillment.

*Chapter 3: Limiting Beliefs and Subconscious Barriers*

This chapter highlights the role of self-awareness, self-concept, and the mind in shaping personal reality. It explains how consciousness and beliefs influence external circumstances and shows how shifting internal patterns can lead to meaningful change. The chapter also examines the limitations of traditional goal setting and introduces transformational coaching, a method that focuses on awareness, alignment, and intentional thinking to help individuals break free from limiting beliefs. By embracing your potential and recognizing the connection between your inner and outer worlds, you can create a purposeful and fulfilling life.

*Chapter 4: Commitment to Delve Deeper into Consciousness*

This chapter explores how consciousness and self-awareness contribute to prosperity and fulfillment. Drawing on teachings from Dr. David Hawkins, Napoleon Hill, Neville Goddard, and others, it explains how thoughts, beliefs, and emotions shape your experience. The chapter emphasizes moving beyond ego-driven desires to reach higher levels of awareness, where collaboration, compassion, and inner trust support lasting growth. Through practices such as positive reaffirmation, constructive thinking, and disciplined focus, readers can align with their purpose and unlock greater personal potential, transforming their inner world to create outer success.

*Chapter 5: The Path to Personal Growth, Intuition, and Self-discovery*

This chapter examines how the laws of attraction and assumption shape our experiences. It explains how aligning beliefs, thoughts, and emotions with our aspirations can influence reality and support personal success. Drawing from the teachings of Neville Goddard,

Albert Einstein, and others, it highlights how thought and imagination can direct the outcomes we attract. The chapter encourages aligning desires with a deeper spiritual purpose and reinforces the idea that through belief, assumption, and intentional living, we participate in creating a life of abundance and fulfillment.

*Chapter 6: Mastering the Laws of Attraction, Assumption, and the Power of the Word*

This chapter explores how words, thoughts, and beliefs influence the results we experience. Drawing on ideas from Napoleon Hill, Neville Goddard, Earl Nightingale, and others, it explains how intentional inner dialogue supports personal transformation. The concept of the law of the word emphasizes the power of language and encourages using it with clarity and purpose. Techniques such as decrees, visualization, and affirmations are offered as tools to build a mindset of abundance. The chapter also shows how prosperity grows from both disciplined habits and spiritually aligned intentions, guiding readers to overcome fear, embrace joy, and unlock their potential for a meaningful and prosperous life.

*Chapter 7: Consciousness and the Symphony of Subconscious Manifestation*

This chapter explains how consciousness and the subconscious work together in shaping experience. Using the metaphor of a symphony, the conscious mind serves as the conductor and the subconscious becomes the orchestra, expressing the patterns we hold within. The chapter focuses on aligning inner patterns with intentional goals and shows how practices such as visualization, affirmations, and emotional awareness support this process. It also highlights how clearing limiting beliefs, cultivating inner harmony, and maintaining persistence help create lasting personal transformation.

*Chapter 8: Faith and the Alchemy of Thought*

This chapter examines how decisions rooted in faith can transform personal and financial outcomes. Drawing on examples from Napoleon Hill and other successful individuals, it shows how aligning thoughts and emotions with a deeper conviction helps overcome challenges. The chapter also discusses capital creation, mindset barriers, and the role of consistent self-reflection and visualization in strengthening belief. By integrating faith with strategic action and gratitude, readers can build lasting success while staying aligned with their core values.

*Chapter 9: Unlocking the Hidden Wealth Through Godly Wisdom*

This chapter explores the relationship between divine wisdom and authentic abundance. It explains how connecting with infinite intelligence opens the door to spiritual, emotional, and material growth. Readers are encouraged to align thoughts, beliefs, and actions with higher principles through practices such as prayer, reflection, and faith. By trusting divine guidance, the chapter reframes wealth as both inner fulfillment and purposeful living, showing how true prosperity arises from spiritual clarity and connection.

*Chapter 10: The Triad of Self*

This chapter explains how consciousness, conscience, and the subconscious work together in shaping a person's experiences. Using symbolic examples, it emphasizes how thoughts and beliefs influence reality and how inner mind programming supports the manifestation of desired outcomes. Techniques such as mindfulness, visualization, and goal mapping are introduced to help align inner patterns with intentional goals. The chapter concludes by highlighting the importance of imagination, spiritual awareness, and emotional well-being in supporting personal and financial growth.

*Chapter 11: Genius and Creating Your Desired Reality*

This chapter explores how individuals can unlock their inner genius by aligning beliefs, thoughts, and attitudes with their highest potential. It explains how faith, focused intention, and positive thinking shape outcomes and offers practical methods, including the 369 technique, to help direct energy toward desired results. Drawing on lessons from influential thinkers, the chapter shows how self-awareness, visualization, and consistent belief support the process of manifesting personal success and abundance.

*Chapter 12: The Power of Detachment and Universal Principles of Fulfillment*

This chapter explores detachment as a powerful principle for creating inner peace, personal growth, and authentic living. Through examples such as Donna's and Latrice's experiences, it shows how releasing attachment, fear, and the need for control opens the way to deeper clarity and higher levels of consciousness. The chapter explains how trusting the process, embracing uncertainty, and maintaining a positive mental attitude help align one's inner state with desired outcomes, supporting a life of purpose and fulfillment.

*Chapter 13: True Measure of Power*

This chapter examines manifestation as a process of aligning inner belief, emotional clarity, and purposeful action with the reality one intends to create. It highlights how guided visualization, prayer, and self-hypnosis can help reprogram the subconscious and strengthen personal conviction. The chapter also discusses how releasing self-sabotaging patterns and adopting gratitude, trust, and patience support lasting transformation. Ultimately, it encourages readers to use their innate creative power to shape a purposeful, abundant life.

*Chapter 14: The Abundance Mindset*

This chapter focuses on developing an abundance mindset as the foundation for personal and financial fulfillment. It explains how shifting from scarcity to appreciation and self-worth strengthens one's ability to manifest success. Through visualization, clear goal setting, and inspired action, readers learn to align their thoughts with their desired outcomes. The chapter also encourages releasing fear and dependence on external approval while building a supportive environment. Additional practices such as feng shui, crystal healing, and gratitude journaling are presented as complementary tools for cultivating inner peace and a prosperous mindset.

*Chapter 15: The Ultimate Insight: Your Path to Manifestation Mastery*

This final chapter brings together the core insights of the book and encourages readers to apply what they have learned. Rather than viewing this as an ending, it invites readers to see this moment as the beginning of a renewed and empowered version of themselves, equipped with the tools to manifest a purposeful and abundant life.

## CHAPTER 1

---

# SETTING THE STAGE: YOUR JOURNEY TO MANIFESTATION BEGINS

This may sound simple, but it is rarely taught in schools. Wealth exists within, through self-awareness and contentment, we begin to mobilize the power of our thoughts to shape the lives we desire. Rather than obsessing over negative thinking, this work invites us to cultivate a mindset that keeps us moving forward with intention, confidence, and purpose. Its focus is not merely on what we want, but also on who we are becoming because lasting success grows from inner alignment. The universe neither excludes nor denies; it responds. When we anchor our focus in gratitude and possibility, we position ourselves to move steadily along a path of growth, fulfillment, and expansion.

Embarking on a path to manifestation is both exhilarating and transformative. This journey begins the moment you recognize that real change starts within. When intention aligns with belief, clarity follows, purpose sharpens, and opportunity reveals itself.

This is not a passive experience; it is an active decision to engage your inner power and step into a deeper awareness of who you are and what you can create.

By choosing to be here, you are acknowledging that something more is possible. Growth does not arrive by chance; it unfolds when we commit to understanding ourselves at a deeper level. This commitment opens the door to alignment, expansion, and the realization that the life you desire is shaped first within your own consciousness. The moment you recognize that your inner world is the creator of your reality and everything you touch, you stop waiting for permission and begin moving as the one that is entitled to move as whom it already belongs to. You stop entertaining doubt and start operating from the place of emotional feeling of certainty that what you're reaching for is simply the outer expression of what you've already claimed within. Life stops feeling like something you chase and becomes something that rises to meet you because you're finally standing in the place it was always trying to find. My path in life has never been easy, and I know that many of you may have gone through something very similar. From all this, I learned that there is much more to this world than what our physical senses may perceive.

This learning is important because tapping into deeper layers of awareness allows you to manifest and attract specific outcomes. With spiritual insight, you can align your thoughts and actions with intention. Open your mind as we journey together, the power of manifestation lies within us.

Clarity and understanding emerge when we take time to be present, quiet the mind, and listen to our inner voice. Throughout this book, key ideas are repeated intentionally because repetition strengthens understanding and embeds important truths into the subconscious mind. Presence allows us to recognize intuitive signals, deepen our awareness, and connect more fully with the universe's guidance. When we slow down and truly listen, we gain insight that helps us align our conscious decisions with our deeper purpose.

This presence to self is strong and may make us aware of things we would not have known, such as intuitively sensing when someone is thinking about us.

From my own experience, learning to remain present changed everything. It revealed patterns I had overlooked and insights I could not have accessed otherwise. Presence has a way of uncovering truths that logic alone cannot reach, reminding us that intuition is not accidental but an inherent ability waiting to be trusted.

Hundreds of books have explored manifestation, yet many fail to deliver lasting results. While dreaming and visualization are valuable, they are not enough on their own. True fulfillment comes from understanding oneself and recognizing the inner power that drives belief, action, and persistence. When self-doubt interferes, the subconscious mind cannot respond effectively. Alignment between conscious intention and inner belief is essential for meaningful results.

Let me share my story with you. I once navigated life with limited education and a timid personality. I lacked self-belief and simply went along with whatever life threw my way. Then, one evening at 8:00 p.m., something miraculous happened.

Alone in my bedroom with my alarm clock set in front of me and looking in the mirror, for the first time, I had a moment of clarity where I saw my weaknesses and how I had been holding myself back from the life I really wanted to live. Like the transformative experience of Apostle Paul, that was, for me, an overwhelming self-realization. I understood that my lack of confidence was sabotaging my success.

In that moment, I delved deep and identified the root of my insecurity. I recognized why I had convinced myself that I wasn't capable of success and why I allowed myself to dream without truly believing. I decided to confront my fears and build my confidence. I began exploring ways to pursue my dreams with determination and resilience. Growing up, I often felt I lacked the qualities needed for success and believed that the life I desired was reserved for others deemed worthy. This belief made me feel unworthy of greatness.

I discovered that many people, including myself, unknowingly sabotage their own success through negative self-talk. I learned that our subconscious mind is always listening, and negative self-talk only reinforces self-doubt, impacting every aspect of our lives.

To boost my confidence, I began crafting affirmations and quotes, reciting them daily. I recorded them to listen to throughout the day and night. One morning, I experienced a surge of power and faith, feeling as if I could conquer the world. This shift was significant, transforming me from someone sensitive to criticism into a person ready to face challenges with newfound confidence.

With this newfound self-worth and determination, I created opportunities and demanded the pay I deserved. I pursued education and joined the fraternal order of Freemasonry while launching multiple successful companies. Each accomplishment strengthened my confidence, revealing that there were no limits to what I could achieve.

My story illustrates that dedication makes what once seemed impossible achievable. Although my family and community initially opposed my pursuits, I continued to believe in myself and achieved milestones others thought impossible. I am proud of my journey and achievements that affirm my choice was right for pursuing success at my own pace. I hope that my story will inspire you to pursue your dreams, come hell or high water, despite any doubts or criticisms.

I am setting ambitious goals for the coming year. First, it is to reach more than two hundred thousand email subscribers, demonstrating the growth of my audience and the ever-growing impact of my work. I anticipate exciting business opportunities and keynote speaking engagements at top companies and conferences worldwide where I'll discuss the science of tapping into the subconscious for manifestation, visualization, imagination, habit formation, behavior change, and continuous improvement.

God has given us the power to control our own destiny by empowering us with free will to make choices. Unfortunately, so many people do not realize the true potential of their free will. Now, it's time for us to take matters into our hands and use the power that has been bestowed upon us. We should not allow others to derail or abandon the planning of our future and the manifestation of our wishes; this is the essence of free will.

*"Therefore, let us stop passing judgment on one another. Instead, make up your mind not to put any stumbling block or obstacle in your brother's way"* (Romans 14:13). Imagination, as it were, is one of the most powerful forces backed by our highest faculties. Our conscious mind, akin to prophets in the Bible, conveys messages with regard to God's consciousness and how to make use of imagination.[19] The inner mind, as exemplified by Christ Jesus, holds immense power. As King David said, "As a man believes, so is he."[20] Similarly, thinkers like James Allen and Shakespeare emphasized the influence of our thoughts. Allen stated, "No man is hindered by another; he is only hindered by himself,"[21] while Shakespeare noted, "There is nothing either good or bad, except that thinking makes it so."[22] This highlights the power of our thoughts and beliefs in shaping our reality.

---

19  Neville Goddard, *Feeling is the Secret* (Martino Publishing, 2012), 18. Originally published in 1944.

20  Proverbs 23:7, The Holy Bible, King James Version (KJV).

21  James Allen, *As a Man Thinketh* (Arc Manor, 1903), 22.

22  William Shakespeare, *Hamlet*, Act 2, Scene 2, various editions.

David J. Schwartz, PhD, believed that thinking big leads to a fulfilling life.[23] He emphasized living large in terms of happiness, accomplishments, income, friendships, and respect. Schwartz encouraged taking bold actions and starting now.[24] We can do miraculous things by listening to our inner voice and connecting with our subconscious mind to unleash our unlimited potential.[25] Schwartz's philosophy of thinking big motivates us to reach our full potential and create our best lives.

## WOO HOO! YOU'VE DONE IT!

Together, we have explored the power of the inner mind and the role awareness plays in shaping your reality. This is not about perfection or immediate mastery but about willingness. When you begin to trust your intuition and remain open to the guidance within, the path ahead becomes clearer and more purposeful.

Self-doubt may still surface at times, and that is part of being human. What matters is how you respond to it. With intention, patience, and consistency, belief begins to replace uncertainty, and confidence strengthens naturally. This journey is just beginning, and with an open heart and mind, there is no limit to where it can lead you.

Many people find it helpful to anchor these ideas through simple, meaningful practices. These are not requirements or rules but tools that can support awareness and reinforce belief as you move forward.

Daily affirmations, when spoken or written with intention, can help reinforce confidence and strengthen belief in your vision. They

---

23　David J. Schwartz, *The Magic of Thinking Big* (Simon and Schuster, 1959), 15.

24　Schwartz, *The Magic of Thinking Big*, 20.

25　Murphy, *The Power of Your Subconscious Mind*, 112.

serve as gentle reminders of who you are becoming and what you are aligning with.

Visualization allows you to imagine your goals with clarity and emotion. Taking even a few quiet moments to picture the life you are working toward can deepen focus and strengthen commitment.

Gratitude, when practiced consistently, shifts attention toward abundance. Reflecting on moments of appreciation, whether written or simply acknowledged, helps attune the mind to growth, possibility, and balance.

As you continue, allow these practices to support you in whatever way feels natural. There is no rush. Progress unfolds through awareness, intention, and trust. When you are ready, we will move forward together into the next chapter.

# CHAPTER 2

## STARTING THE ADVENTURE PATH

Your subconscious mind is the architect of your reality—what you plant within it will manifest in your life.

—Anonymous

I n 2015, my life started to change dramatically when my wife gave me a very special gift, a book entitled *Think and Grow Rich* by Napoleon Hill.[26] His principles inspired me to delve deeper, leading me to other influential works, including Joseph Murphy's *The Power of Your Subconscious Mind*.[27] These teachings revealed that desire, faith,

---

26 Hill, *Think and Grow Rich*.

27 Murphy, *The Power of Your Subconscious Mind*.

daily affirmations, and specialized knowledge are critical components of success.

Through sustained desire, focused faith, daily affirmations, continual learning, and imagination, I came to understand that these outcomes were achievable. I began to make courageous decisions, no longer afraid of defeat, and directed my focus toward the deliberate pursuit of my goals.

Imagination and visualization became crucial tools in igniting my drive and prompting action.[28] History shows that success begins with purposeful intent, strategic goal setting, and the creation of ideas or services that benefit society, a blueprint for potential fortune. As Napoleon Hill aptly stated, "A goal is a dream with a deadline."[29]

Effectively tapping into the subconscious mind requires practical tools and techniques that will serve as a means to long-lasting personal growth. Visualization is all about creating a detailed mental picture of what is desired. Regular visualization strengthens your bond with the subconscious, aligning it with your desired outcomes and enhancing your focus on relevant goals.

Another powerful way to reprogram the subconscious is through affirmations. Consistently repeating positive statements reinforces desired beliefs and outcomes, replacing negative thought patterns and self-doubt with empowering beliefs. This practice gradually shifts our inner mind to align with our desired reality.

Focused intention, another key technique, involves aligning our actions with our goals. This requires taking deliberate steps toward our objectives and ensuring that each action supports the outcomes we desire. Focused intention requires the highest level of awareness and

---

28   Hill, *Think and Grow Rich*.

29   Hill, *Think and Grow Rich*.

commitment because, quite simply, we consciously direct our efforts and resources to achieve specific goals.

My personal journey highlighted the importance of these techniques. Initially, I felt a sense of discontent, realizing that my subconscious beliefs weren't aligned with my aspirations. The teachings of Napoleon Hill,[30] Joseph Murphy,[31] and other influential figures provided invaluable insights into the workings of the subconscious mind. Applying Hill's principles helped me understand that desire, faith, and imagination are essential for success.[32] I learned that genuine transformation requires more than superficial changes; it demands a profound internal shift in mindset and belief.

I initially believed it would take around five years for an idea to manifest. However, I chose to apply this concept differently. Rather than focusing solely on accumulating wealth, I aimed to develop an idea that would positively impact others financially within a shorter time frame. Through spiritual growth, I realized that our world reflects consciousness; and our thoughts, beliefs, and actions are pivotal in shaping our reality.[33] I began to view spirituality as the power of imagination within the subconscious mind. By harnessing this power, I understood that I could create and effect real change in my life and the lives of others.[34]

The journey to unlocking the magic of the subconscious mind starts with recognizing its immense potential. The subconscious mind is both a passive repository of experiences and an active force shaping

---


30    Hill, *Think and Grow Rich.*

31    Murphy, *The Power of Your Subconscious Mind.*

32    Nightingale, *The Strangest Secret.*

33    David R. Hawkins, *Power vs. Force: The Hidden Determinants of Human Behavior* (Hay House, 1995).

34    Goddard, *Feeling is the Secret.*

our reality. It responds to our thoughts and emotions, turning them into tangible experiences.

Influential figures like Napoleon Hill have emphasized the importance of desire, faith, and imagination in shaping our reality. Hill's teachings highlight that unlocking the subconscious's power involves effectively harnessing these elements. According to Hill, desire is the starting point of all achievements. It fuels our ambitions and motivates us to pursue our goals. Faith reinforces our determination and keeps us focused on our goals, even in the face of challenges.

Imagination is another essential component. We can access and consolidate our subconscious mind by developing our visualization skills. Using our imagination helps make our goals and desires seem more real and attainable. Imagination bridges the gap between our current reality and our desired future, allowing us to mentally rehearse and prepare for achieving our goals. This mental rehearsal is not mere fantasy but is also a crucial step in programming our subconscious mind to align with our aspirations.

As Luminary Clemer Leggett, I have always focused on practical application rather than writing how-to guides or delivering motivational speeches. As a business owner and transformational personal development mentor, I am dedicated to helping others envision their ideal lives through prayer, visualization, and effective manifestation management. I specialize in guiding individuals in generating ideas that lead to creating and managing multimillion-dollar companies with numerous employees. I thrive in the business trenches and embrace the challenges that come with it.

I understood that maintaining an open mind and being receptive to infinite intelligence within the subconscious could reveal everything I needed to know. Most people mistakenly misuse their subconscious minds, but author Joseph Murphy, PhD, observed, "There are no limits to the prosperity, happiness, perfect health, and peace of mind you can achieve simply by using the power of the subconscious mind."[35] If you are not living a brilliant, wonderfully fulfilling life, it is likely because you're not fully utilizing your imagination, visualization, and subconscious mind.[36]

Even with the success of several companies and a college degree, I often felt like a failure. Growing up in a challenging environment marked by violence and bullying, and later facing imprisonment, I yearned for greater wealth and prosperity but struggled to find the path.

At its core, the subconscious mind controls much of our daily behaviors and perceptions. It stores our beliefs, emotions, and deeply ingrained thought patterns, influencing our actions and decisions. It often works behind the scenes to manifest our inner state into our outer reality. Understanding and tapping into this power is essential for making fundamental changes in our lives.

Aligning our conscious desires with the power of the subconscious enables us to create significant changes in our lives. This process requires a deliberate synchronization of our thoughts, beliefs, and actions with our desired outcomes. When our desires are in harmony with our inner mind, a powerful sense of hope is created, propelling us toward our goals. By tapping into the vast potential of the subconscious, we can cultivate feelings of joy, exhilaration, and fulfillment. Aligning our thoughts, beliefs, and actions with our ultimate vision is crucial for unlocking our true potential. Success begins with purposeful intent, strategic goal setting, and creating products or services that foster personal growth and contribute to the well-being of others.

---

35    Murphy, *The Power of Your Subconscious Mind*, 7.

36    Goddard, *Feeling is the Secret*.

During this journey, I realized that I was the primary obstacle holding myself back. However, with determination and the right mindset, I was able to overcome these challenges and achieve my goals. I devoted myself to understanding the power of the subconscious mind, closely examining my thoughts, distinguishing between optimistic and pessimistic ones, and paying attention to how each thought made me feel. Success, I learned, lies in the alignment of our thoughts and emotional responses.

It all begins with a genuine desire to comprehend the power of the subconscious mind and how it influences our reality. I unlocked my full potential by connecting with my higher self and aligning my thoughts with positive beliefs. I even learned that illness often starts in our consciousness before manifesting in our bodies. Believing in good health and rejecting negative thoughts significantly improved my well-being.

Regarding finances, I shifted my focus from bills and debt to investing in assets. The inner mind operates based on our beliefs, emotions, and faith. Constantly dwelling on negative aspects of our financial situation reinforces limiting beliefs and fuels stress and anxiety. Instead, concentrating on positive financial goals and taking actionable steps, like using the snowball method to pay off debts, has proved more effective.

One of my most significant lessons was addressing inner-mind beliefs and thought patterns that held me back. These patterns hindered my progress and prevented me from reaching my goals.

Through active effort and self-reflection, I began to challenge and reframe these limiting beliefs. This process of self-discovery and transformation was essential for creating lasting change.

This journey also revealed another important lesson: the power of engaging with positive influences and seeking mentors to aid in personal growth. It was a collaborative effort, reinforcing that success is not a solo endeavor but is built within a network or tribe of like-minded individuals.

As I reflect, it is clear that the ways through which one can harness the subconscious mind involve continuous learning and self-improvement. Internalized positive affirmations and quotes became powerful tools for transformation.

My journey has also explored how the unconscious mind impacts various aspects of life, including health and finances. Cultivating a mindset of abundance led to better economic outcomes.

I want to support you as you illuminate your path to success, whether that means achieving prosperity, good health, happiness, financial independence, or a deeper relationship with God. That's why I wrote this handbook. Many people struggle with self-sabotaging beliefs and a fear-driven poverty mindset. My goal is to help you focus on your passionate desires, have faith in yourself, and train your inner mind to believe in success. By developing a clear, detailed plan, you can transform your life, just as I did. This journey isn't just about acquiring wealth; it's about becoming more loving, generous, grateful, and spiritual as well.

# Self-Awareness Activation:
## How to Recognize What You Have

When it comes to identifying your belongings and self-awareness, many people overlook how much the things in their lives reflect who they are.

This is an exercise that will help you think about the things that exist in your life and how you associate with them! This will help you empower yourself on your journey towards discovering more about yourself rather than giving you exact steps. Allow yourself to be patient as you complete this process as you will gain some insights that will start to flow naturally into your consciousness to be turned into your own personal realizations. I want you to also ask yourself as you embody these questions to remember:

Privilege invites gratitude.

Entitlement invites expectation.

Awareness transforms both into responsibility.

### Step 1 - Write Down 50 Items You Own

You own to begin with creating a thoughtful list of 50 items that you currently possess, think about the following: What do you own? What do you value? These items can be large or small; they could include:

Your home or apartment

Your car

Your phone

Your shoes

Your education

Your skills

Your family relationships

Your personal qualities, such as patience or creativity

Remember, this exercise is not intended to focus on material possessions; however, it should help you become more aware of what you already own in your life.

## Step 2 – Reflection Questions

Once you've completed your list, take a moment to reflect on the following questions:

Did I work for this? Or did it just happen to be given to me?

Did I want to have it before it became a "normal" part of my life?

How do I view that item: as a privilege, an entitlement, or just something I own?

What motivates me to attain that item?

These questions are to take you from a place of ownership to an active realization of everything you have been doing.

## Step 3 - Transitioning your Awareness

Now that you've accepted these things, think of them as a way to understand that every item you have on your list started out as an ideal, goal, dream, thought, desire. You have so much proof that you created your life! There are so many examples in your life that relate to your creative capacity as current realities!

Instead of simply saying, "You are not just an expression of Source Infinite Intelligence," I encourage you to consider:

"Your reality is not an accident; it has been created through your awareness, choices, and identity."

By using this method, you will come to your own conclusions while having a deeper relationship with the exercise.

## Why This Method Works

This process helps build gratitude within you without using religious or mystical phrases or meanings. You are encouraged to not look outside of yourself for validation and authorizing of your own self through your own creativity. Now, once you establish a clear connection between your desires, identity, and manifestation in a practical manner, you'll find it much easier and the ability to resist is decreased, and you will be guided in a gentle manner as opposed to being preached at.

## Balance is Important

Use the word entitlement with care when discussing it. Some people may connect it to being arrogant. Frame it more from a natural right, deserving of your own ability to accomplish, inherent value, and potential to create/authenticate whatever you want.

Using this type of language creates a positive outlook, while avoiding being negative.

The objective of this exercise is to get you to recognize that you are an expression of Source and to demonstrate the proof that you are a creator, you have a capacity to impact your world and you are creating that world every moment you are alive. Once you experience the evidence of your own creation, you will know in your soul that you have created your world and all of it is because of you. Now that you see all that you've created and recognize your privilege and entitlements, it's time to step into the person who naturally manifests these realities. Feel, think, believe, act, and walk like the creator of the life you desire, and watch how your reality responds.

So take time to enjoy this journey of self-discovery because as you reflect upon who and what you are, you will gain knowledge and understanding from the experience of who you really are.

# CHAPTER 3

- - - - - - - - - - - - - -

# LIMITING BELIEFS AND SUBCONSCIOUS BARRIERS

*When you judge another, you do not define them,*
*you define yourself.*

—Wayne Dyer

Through my experience leading, conducting research, and attending seminars and workshops, I have noticed a common theme among many speakers. While they often provide valuable insights, strategies, and direction, the focus frequently remains at the surface level of goal achievement. What is often overlooked is the deeper importance of understanding the "why" behind our goals and the necessity of listening closely to our inner conversation.

In today's world, as conscious-minded beings, it is natural to pursue goals and desires. We rush toward the next milestone, seeking fulfillment through achievement, recognition, or advancement. Yet in this constant pursuit, we often overlook the deeper purpose behind our ambitions. As a result, even when we accomplish what we set out to achieve, a sense of dissatisfaction can remain, reminding us that true fulfillment requires more than external success.

By listening with intention and reflection, we can better understand our desires and align our goals with deeper meaning.

The main obstacle in this process is our self-centered mindset. We often prioritize fulfilling our immediate desires and avoiding disapproval over pursuing personal growth or self-awareness. We focus on getting what we want rather than seeking truth. However, by actively listening and reflecting on the true meaning behind our goals, we can break free from this egocentric mindset and broaden our perspectives.

Our tendency toward egocentric thinking can limit how well we understand ourselves and others. This lack of self-awareness prevents us from reaching our potential for success and fulfillment.

Breaking free from this egocentric thinking means taking responsibility for our learning and actively seeking new perspectives. This helps us break away from simplistic thinking patterns and leads to a deeper understanding of ourselves and those around us.

Napoleon Hill pointed out seven primary negative emotions that can hinder success: fear, jealousy, hatred, revenge, greed, superstition, and anger. The key is to understand that positive and negative emotions cannot coexist in our minds simultaneously. So it is up to us to ensure that positive emotions dominate our thoughts and actions. Developing positive habits helps us overcome these negative feelings and build confidence to take action toward our goals.

True success isn't just about external accomplishments but is also about our inner selves and how we positively impact others. Prioritizing inner work alongside external achievements is crucial for a meaningful and successful life. This involves understanding ourselves and being empathetic toward others, which helps us create genuine connections and contribute positively to the world.

Reflecting on our behaviors and attitudes is essential for personal development. Unquestioningly accepting what we've been taught can lead to egocentric beliefs that distort our thinking and behavior. Instead, by intentionally mastering both our internal and external actions, we can express ourselves authentically and create a fulfilling life aligned with our true selves.

Self-examination allows us to recognize patterns that influence our behavior and align our actions with ethical and meaningful choices.

Society often holds us back with illusions that prevent us from being all that we could be. Awakening the higher mind enables us to break free from such shackles and build a life that truly reflects our authentic selves. This includes unlearning what society has taught us and tapping into our inner strength to create the life we envision.

Our thinking creates meaning around events, but again, we must sift through and distinguish the thoughts propelled by ego from those leading us to fair reasoning. Coupled with this, our emotions bring forth the value we place on these thoughts. Indeed, personal growth and success first begin with self-examination and then understanding the impact of internal reflections and external expressions. This level of awareness lets us be more deliberate with the choices we make, serving and benefiting our personal values and goals.

To do this, we need to get to know our mind and how it works: Thinking creates meaning, feeling weighs it, and wanting focuses our energy on our goals. Hard or easy, the fact is that we have to face our mind itself and see how it affects or informs our decisions. Awareness of the aforementioned functions allows us to take action on our choices so that growth and success can take place.

Although it may be difficult for some to understand, on a personal note, I've experienced the rewards of self-study and conscious choice. It's my trust in my mission that has taken me down a nonconventional path of growth and success. Through deep insight into my thoughts, feelings, and desires, self-reflection provided the insights that directed me toward fulfilling choices.

The self-discovery journey has been utterly transformative. Understanding the workings of one's mind and emotions has opened new horizons, enabling one to look forward to the future with excitement.

Although this might be a journey through less conventional norms, I am convinced of my purpose and the decisions made in life. The review of experiences justifies the decisions taken and encourages me to be further exploratory in order to enjoy my real self. I'm thankful for all that I've learned and the person I've become on this journey that has enabled me to break through limitations and embrace my authenticity.

I have found this expedition of self-discovery quite captivating and thrilling. It has pushed me out of my comfort zone, made me more vulnerable, and encouraged me to work on personal growth day in and day out. I have really learned that our emotions and ways of thinking are closely connected to the meanings we attach to experiences. More specifically, understanding how thoughts affect the way we interpret things has been a game-changer for me. I have become more aware of my thought process and how I perceive things in daily life, which leads to better judgment and a broader understanding of the world overall. The awareness of my reasoning has been one of the most important lessons I have derived from this course, through which evolution and growth have been experienced by me.

I appreciate everything I have learned and continue to learn along the way. Learning to manage my emotions and perceptions, evaluate information critically, and make sound decisions has helped me become more self-aware and mindful. This is the path of personal growth and fulfillment, and I am grateful for the experiences that shaped who I am today. The journey has been challenging, but the reward has been significant. I hope to move forward with this process and continue embracing all it has in store.

Thinkers like Napoleon Hill, Earl Nightingale, and Neville Goddard have put forth conscience as the most significant factor in shaping reality. According to them, everything in this world is a manifestation of one's conscience.

My wife and I share a very strong bond that allows both of us to appreciate almost all forms of activities, together or individually.

Those close to us know how dear the moments of quality spent with a loved one are the exploration of places, hobbies, or simply the quietness of home. Yet we understand that spiritual connection and intention are necessary for our deep desires to manifest.

The coaching profession has driven me to believe that many people enter the profession based on what they hear rather than what they experience. Too often, life coaching focuses only on material success, completely eliminating any spiritual development a person may want or need.

It would seem that most life coaching books believe, by and large, that most coaches approach their work from a strictly mental point of view, essentially stunting the growth of their clients. If one is serious about making a difference, then both of these, the mental and spiritual aspects, must be combined in coaching. This is how it becomes all-inclusive and an effective way to mentor someone. All aspiring life coaches should seek formal training in order to learn the technology of change and its proper application. However, as Raimon Samso states in *The Manifestation Code*, being a transformational coach does not necessarily imply an inner journey or self-realization.

In the future, we will continue to see these unproductive coaches, individuals deeply unhappy with their own lives and unable to manifest their desires. Lacking the essential skills to channel their inner potential, they will struggle to inspire meaningful change in others. The truth is clear: Coaches who cannot transform themselves are powerless to transform others.

I agree with Raimon Samso: It is the coaches themselves who must understand and apply the principles in order to be effective and bring change into their clients' lives. In coaching, and in all disciplines, the most that a coach can do to help others manifest their desires is to continuously improve themselves and practice what they preach.

Experience and understanding are the keys that will help an individual mentor or coach someone in life. With a strong moral compass, one can lead another during the journey to self-realization.

To truly aid others, we must first ensure our own growth. This involves striving for personal and professional excellence and setting an example for others.

Spiritual mentoring surpasses mere guidance in achieving personal and professional success. It involves devising intelligent, strategic paths that resonate with an individual's inner aspirations and values. Unlike traditional coaching, spiritual mentoring prioritizes the inner journey and personal growth over mere outward actions. It's rooted in the profound understanding of one's inner self, consciousness, and a heart-centered approach.

In the pursuit of self-discovery and personal growth, there are different approaches one can adopt. The first centers on making a difference in the world and striving for societal impact. Motivated by a strong sense of purpose, this approach seeks to create a better world for oneself and others alike. It demands a deep understanding of personal values and beliefs, coupled with steadfast action to effect change. Conversely, the second approach is related to self-transformation, wherein one needs to be truly introspective, self-reflective, self-critical, and above all, ready to get rid of the old self when it no longer serves growth. This requires a high degree of consciousness and a pledge to ceaseless betterment.

Both work as methodologies to change people's lives and society for the better. Be it oneself or society, the road to discovering oneself and building a better person is an ongoing process that requires introspection, will, and an open mind. At the end of it, both lead to a more enriching and meaningful life.

In that sense, self-awareness and personal growth are major keys to changing the world. It is through introspection that we realize our shortcomings and limitations, which then lead to further development of the self. However, true awakening is the third kind of approach, when one realizes that by changing ourselves, we change the world.

This step gives meaning to an important premise: Self-awareness and its acceptance are vital in meeting our objectives. It reminds us that more often than not, it is not the externals that need to shift; it is our insight into ourselves. The acknowledgment of this fact alone frees us from ego-sourced motivations to work for objectives that do not need perfectionism or external approval for their validation. This realization empowers us to let go of the necessity for constant comparison and invest instead in personal growth and improvement. If we adopt this state of mind, then we can approach our goals authentically and with self-compassion, and ultimately, both lead to a more fulfilling and meaningful life.

Given that, letting go of attachment to goals may seem quite counterintuitive because more often than not, we think holding on to desires and relentlessly pursuing them means getting what we want. Yet real accomplishment means letting go of the attachment so that one can recognize new opportunities and possibilities not yet seen.

By accepting the present and finding peace within us, we transcend the need for external validation and concentrate on personal growth and development. This third step in the journey toward goals involves a shift of the psyche from constant striving to surrender and trusting. In that process, the tentacles of attachment will fall away, paving the way for true growth and transformation to take place within and around us.

Creating positive change in the world is often associated with actions like activism or charity work. However, true change begins within ourselves. By taking time to deeply understand who we are, the development of a strong sense of self-awareness and compassion can take place. It is self-awareness that enables us to recognize our very own biases and negative behaviors, challenge them, and allow ourselves to be open to personal growth and transformation.

If we are doing the work continuously, then it takes us to a place where we do whatever we can to make sure the world is better. Within that process, we enter situations with more empathy and understanding, leading to healthier relationships and, hence, a better society. What this does is point to the fact that, actually, the journey within us does have the power to change the world outside. The effect of such an attitude creates a ripple of positive change. It reminds us that change cannot come from just external actions; it must begin with oneself. Giving importance to self-discovery and growth will eventually create a positive impact on our lives and the lives of other people too, for a better world.

It is often said that with much power comes great responsibility, and indeed, that can be held true for any of us who actually think that we are influential. Whether through money, authority, or social influence, power implies a heavy burden of responsibility. Where we might imagine power to be the magic that enables us to control situations and people, real life can sometimes turn out differently. The power, however, can be unpredictable, especially in cases where it has been misused or abused. It is, therefore, very important that the person holding the power makes wise and ethical use of it since the consequences of their actions could largely affect others and society at large.

It means that the infinite intelligent power within us is not determined by what we have or how big, strong, tall, or even short we are. It lies in our ability to manifest changes in the world. Exciting, maybe, but it comes with a key condition: We have to change ourselves first. Sometimes an individual may get psyched up by the whole idea of making a difference in the world. This calls for humility and a proper perspective on the self, couched in an openness toward constant learning and growth.

Before we seek external power and influence, we must first work on ourselves, for it is only through an inner transformation that we can hope to affect any real good in the world. Understanding is often seen as a mental exercise, but it really involves both the mind and the spirit. The mental perspective allows us to analyze and interpret information while the spiritual perspective dives deeper by exploring our inner selves to understand our thoughts, emotions, and beliefs. Mental understanding comes from external sources such as perception and observation, but true spiritual understanding comes from introspection and self-knowledge.

In this world full of constant external stimuli and information, it is important to take a step back and seek our spiritual nature within ourselves in order to understand both ourselves and the world. We can only then fully begin to develop the mental and spiritual aspects to gain insight into life from a well-rounded perspective. This balanced perspective allows us to sail through our lives with more fulfillment and meaning. Introspection and self-knowledge make us aware of the real meanings, values, and beliefs that constitute a person. A truly enlightened view of life seems only then possible. Both standpoints are complementary to our overall understanding of our existence.

Knowing the difference between what we know and who we actually are can make a huge difference in personal growth and real change. Knowledge involves gathering information and understanding while our being involves all those inherent qualities, beliefs, values, and actions. While perception shapes the interpretation of the world, true knowledge lets us take an active role in shaping our reality. Knowledge empowers us to evaluate that information and make positive choices in life, not only for our benefit but also for the good of everyone around us. The position of knowing is stronger than that of perceiving because knowing enables one to transcend beyond observation and participate actively in changing the world around them. It is, therefore, very necessary to acquire knowledge and unfold one's true nature for a positive impact on oneself and the world.

The deeper the understanding of self, the greater the realization of our power and positive influence in the world. All positive changes in the world begin with a true understanding of our strengths, weaknesses, values, and beliefs. Self-awareness, therefore, helps us apply our full potential and talents. It's impossible to contribute positively to the world without self-awareness. Self-reflection and introspection are the ways we find our passion and purpose, take action, and make choices based on what really honors us. The outcome will be a more fulfilling and impactful life. Further, to know oneself is to find one's way around difficult hurdles and to surmount them with firmness and determination. With a deeper realization of self-understanding and coming to grips with our identity, we can more fully leverage our power to better understand how to be a force for good and help create positive change in this world. Reflection helps us learn who we are and what we have to offer by considering our strengths, weaknesses, interests, and values.

This kind of self-awareness makes us more aware of our innate talents and the things that interest us the most, which we can develop into something worthwhile. By making use of such skills, we are able to give something back to society through our profession, volunteer work, or personal undertakings. Knowing ourselves will eventually help us make sure that our actions are aligned with our values and passions. When we use our talents to help others in some unique way, we are not only helping ourselves but also adding value to others in the process. In that sense, our ability to know ourselves allows us to make a dent on this earth and establish a legacy beyond our own lifespan. The ability to be self-aware is a very critical component of personal growth and development.

It means being aware of our thoughts, feelings, and actions, and how these shape our behaviors and choices. It allows us to notice our shortcomings and admit them, which is important for continuous improvement and growth. Understanding one's strengths and weaknesses enables constructive changes toward striving to become the best version of oneself. With deep self-awareness, we are able to base our actions upon our values and beliefs, living a life that is far more purposeful. This means living a life based on our core values and principles and being true to ourselves. We are at an advantage when continuously reflecting upon our thoughts and actions, thus making conscious choices that are in tune with our goals and aspirations.

Self-awareness helps us not only understand ourselves but, more importantly, also live a life that is far more meaningful and authentic. Personal growth and fulfillment become possible as we continue learning, evolving, and striving to be the best version of ourselves. At the same time, being confident in oneself makes it easier to deal with difficulties and failures, push forward, and create positive impact in the world.

When we have a strong sense of self-awareness and self-acceptance, it becomes a whole lot easier to go through painful times and not be deterred by challenging obstacles. It gives us inner strength to hold dear our values and beliefs despite all odds. As this understanding of oneself goes deeper, clarity also starts to develop about strengths and weaknesses, the areas that call upon making better decisions with a foremost willingness to take on challenges. This helps us personally while it allows us to give something positive to the world. So with confidence in ourselves, we are able to use our abilities to create a better world for ourselves and others. This makes us empathetic, compassionate, and resilient individuals who can create positive impacts on other people's lives. This journey provides, through self-discovery, the foundation of personal growth, enabling us to be a force for good in life. When we know ourselves well, we can unleash all our potential and use it for a higher good.

By "the second glance," Neville means realization of the true nature of the world and our actual standing in it. It is not a superficial observation or way of interpretation; it is an intrinsic knowing from deep inside the spirit. This second glance enables us to look beyond what we receive from the physical senses into a more advanced form of consciousness. It is a form of knowledge rooted in our conscience, allowing us to see the interconnectedness and oneness of all things. Through this second glance, we can access a deeper understanding of ourselves and the world, bringing us closer to our true purpose and fulfillment. This profound concept helps us comprehend the vastness and complexity of existence and embrace the divine, infinite wisdom within us. The second glance is both enlightening and transformative, allowing us to transcend our limited perspectives and connect with universal truth.

In a world where our self-concept is different, our entire life experience would change drastically. Our beliefs, values, and perceptions shape how we interact with the world around us. According to Neville, the biggest illusion is thinking external factors control our experiences. He argues that our thoughts and beliefs are the real creators of our reality. At first glance, we see the world as separate from ourselves. However, a closer look reveals how interconnected and dependent the world is on our own being.

By grasping this concept, we can break free from the illusion of our reality being at the mercy of the external world and take charge of our own lives. The power of such a "second glance" is immense for connecting us with our real potential and molding lives in the direction we want. By being conscious of the power of thought and belief, we can mold experiences and manifest our desires. This perspective calls us to be the full authors of our lives by realizing that success or failure does not come from outer circumstances but rather from our inner world. With this insight, we can overcome limitations and craft a life that truly aligns with our deepest desires. Neville's viewpoint reminds us that we have the power to shape our reality, starting with a shift in perception—from the first glance to a deeper, more insightful view.

The infinite intelligence of consciousness is a guiding force that is always accurate. It is the source of all wisdom and creativity, continuously offering us what we first envision in our minds. However, our lower self often strays by ignoring this divine guidance, leading to challenging situations. Rather than focusing on how we arrived at these circumstances or when they will be resolved, it is more beneficial to understand and learn from the situation. This approach fosters personal growth and helps prevent similar challenges in the future. Trusting in this infinite intelligence can bring peace and clarity, allowing us to move forward with confidence and a deeper self-understanding. By aligning with this creative force, we tap into a wellspring of wisdom and let situations evolve naturally for our highest good. This alignment enables us to live harmoniously with the universe and realize our true potential.

When facing difficult or tragic events, it's natural to seek reasons or justifications. However, being preoccupied with the "why" and "how" often results in further confusion and hurt. Rather, one should realize the lessons that can be learned from such experiences. Of course, understanding why something has happened can bring a certain realization, but true growth must come from deeper learning about the life purpose and meaning it really carries and trusting the infinite intelligence of consciousness to guide us toward a more fulfilling and purposeful life. By embracing life's lessons, we build strength and wisdom that carry us toward a more hopeful future. It is not an issue of looking for the "whys" behind an incident but of finding meaning and learning from each experience.

Our ego, or sense of self, is the most powerful drive leading us to commit errors. Identification with those errors and the inability to release them from our lives can act against us. We cling too dearly to our mistakes and allow them to define us, drive our thoughts, and dictate the things that we do. This clinging of attachment creates a circle of negative thinking, a vicious circle that, day by day, hampers growth and progress. We have to understand that it is in the nature of things to make mistakes, as though eliminating them entirely from our lives is not a realistic task. What is important is being able to overcome our mistakes without being possessed by them. We come out of this vicious circle only when we accept that our mistakes do not define us, and that from those mistakes, we learn and move forward in the direction of growth and advancement. It is then that one can shed the ego's need for perfection and accept mistakes along the way, which can indeed lead us to an authentic and fulfilling sense of self.

Letting go of the false belief that our mistakes define us is not easy, but it is a truly transformative experience. It takes humility and courage to recognize our mistakes and accept them as important lessons on our journey toward self-improvement, opening ourselves up to endless growth and learning. Letting go of our ego and embracing our flaws relieves us from the vicious cycle of attachment, enabling us to move in the direction of a more positive and fulfilling mindset.

We should not get bogged down by mistakes; instead, we should use them as stepping stones toward the path of personal and professional development. Thus, the shift in perspective allows us to let go of self-limiting beliefs and adopt a growth mindset, whereby one sees mistakes as opportunities for growth and improvement. In letting go of our mistakes defining us, we choose to create room for self-discovery and learning, ultimately making us the best versions of ourselves in the process.

It takes a great amount of courage, humility, and openness to accept our imperfections; but the reward is limitless, as we open ourselves to new possibilities and experiences. This shifts our approach to challenges instead of getting ourselves stuck in negativity and self-doubt and allows us to approach them with curiosity and openness. We stop our mistakes from defining us when we stop letting the limitations of a fixed mindset hold us back and instead grow and evolve. That is when the possibility for continuous improvement and personal growth is unleashed.

Challenges become opportunities for learning and development, not roadblocks or failures.

This will lead our lives to be governed by curiosity, openness, and the resilience to go through life rather than being caught up in a vortex of negativity and self-doubt. In this way, one leads a more satisfactory and content life, wherein one keeps on growing and learning, developing, and being constantly at one's best. It is this attitude that makes any person look forward to going through obstacles and coming out stronger and wiser on the other side. This is so we learn from our experiences, grow, and build up in life. And as I sit here today, I call upon the infinite intelligence of consciousness to guide you to a new paradigm of limitless potential. This course aims to free you from the chains of the conventionally created mindset that causes suffering and feelings of powerlessness and guide you into your true nature—unlimited potential.

To make this transformation possible, self-concept has to be redefined, and the ways of perceiving oneself have to be changed. By realizing that we are not limited beings but infinite ones with unlimited potential, we are able to unlock that true power within us and live a life full of abundance, love, and joy. This resource is your guide to tapping your inner wisdom and realizing your natural heritage of limitless potential.

Let's go past mere wants to a life filled with endless opportunities for growth and self-discovery. Through the infinite intelligence of consciousness guiding us, we can shatter the chains of our old patterns and beliefs that keep us contained and step into our true identity as powerful creators of our own reality. Without this key shift, all striving for a more fulfilling life and empowered self is blocked. It is critical that one becomes aware of and modifies the limiting beliefs standing in the way of realizing this potential.

They are usually deeply ingrained and, as such, cannot easily be overcome without proper guidance and support. May this literature be a lighthouse to direct you toward living anew. These insights offer a transformative journey through the wisdom and guidance of infinite intelligence in consciousness toward an empowered life of fulfillment. These pages are my hope for you to find your way out of restrictive perceptions and into an open door of possibilities. It means learning the right way to nourish your inner spirit and awaken, expressing your full potential for the creation of a life of purpose, joy, and abundance.

Let this be your guide on your journey toward a more fulfilling and empowered life. Our identity is embedded in the concept of the self; self-concept gives us the grounds to fit in the world mentally, emotionally, and behaviorally. If self-concept changes, then our daily experience and interaction will also undergo immense change. A positive self-concept may enable a person to face challenges with a growth mindset and come out resilient, whereas a negative self-concept prevents action since one will continuously doubt one's capabilities and miss opportunities.

Our self-concept influences our well-being, our relationships, how we communicate, and generally the way we treat others. This is a strong force in life, which really shows just how important our self-concept is. Without this self-concept, our experiences and relationships would differ greatly from what they would have been with it. Therefore, it is good for one to build a healthy and positive self-concept in order to live a prosperous life.

If our self-concept changes, then our entire view of life shifts, and we will make different choices than we did before and take roads we have not taken. It is something like changing an operating system on a computer: Options and opportunities that weren't available become workable. With a different self-concept, we access new possibilities and avenues in our lives that, up to then, were not available. That basically means that self-concept is very powerful and may affect our relationships, choice of professions, and personal development. Self-concept, therefore, has to be continuously evolved and worked on so that life experience can be positive and enriching.

In other words, the consciousness and perceived self of a person are therefore thought of as a sort of operating system for their life. Our thoughts, beliefs, and actions are often unconsciously dictated by our surroundings, like an armed intrusion into our coding system, often leading us away from our goals and desires. However, by understanding and changing our self-concept, we are able to change this cosmos-consciousness operating system and create a new reality for ourselves.

This, in one line, means the reprogramming of our minds, thoughts, and beliefs to align with our innermost desires and goals. It is really an empowering concept when we realize that all our power lies in shaping our reality, first by changing how we perceive ourselves. This is the journey into unlocking our unlimited potential by entering into this "operating system" and making conscious changes in the creation of a truly fulfilling life, one that is in alignment with the expression of our truest and highest self. At the end of this read, you will have obtained all the tools and knowledge that you need to enter this operating system and take charge of your life by engineering a future that aligns with your authentic self. It is a very exciting and transformative feeling when one understands that there is nothing "out there" that could be in our way, and that we can mold our reality from an inner dimension.

When our self-concept is differentiated, our whole life experience dramatically changes. It is from this developed sense of self and the way we perceive the world that our thoughts, beliefs, and actions emanate.

If our awareness of ourselves had been different, then so would our attitudes and interactions with others have been. Just like updating a computer's operating system, imagine if we could do the same for our self-concept and understanding of the world. In this reading, you will discover how to enter the cosmic operating system and change its code, allowing you to program a new reality for yourself. This new reality will be shaped by your own beliefs and perceptions, giving you the power to create your own unique experience. By tapping into this ability, we can shape our lives in unimaginable ways. The potential for personal growth and transformation is immense when we realize the power of our self-concept and its impact on our lives.

Detaching from material possessions is essential for connecting with our spiritual selves. Material goods often dominate our lives, pushing us to prioritize wealth and acquisitions. However, by detaching from these distractions and focusing inward, we can create a meaningful relationship between our spiritual and material worlds. This connection allows us to access higher consciousness and manifest our intentions with purpose and clarity. Shifting from survival mode to intentional living leads to a more fulfilling life, where we cultivate our inner beings and gain a deeper understanding of ourselves and our surroundings.

Detachment from material things can be frightening, but this is the only way one can bring balance between the spiritual and material self. True and lasting transformation comes from within and not from external changes that are happening. Material possessions may offer temporary satisfaction, but they cannot bring about true and abiding change. It is this realization of inner power that aligns us in the right direction to bring deep transformation. It is the journey of self-discovery and growth, emancipation from outer dependencies, thus nourishing the inner self to realize its full potential. True satisfaction and happiness flow from this inner alignment.

It is only by letting go of worldly attachments and embracing the spiritual self that our inner spirit is ignited. By attaching oneself to material possessions, one loses one's spirit. The realization that everything material will come to an end helps cultivate a deeper realization of oneself and the world surrounding us. This alignment brings about peace and satisfaction by shifting the focus of one's life from material things and social status toward values and beliefs within.

Our spirit is the real identity, rather than all that is hyped by society. Living a spiritual life brings one closer to an existence of meaning and purpose, full of love, joy, and inner peace.

We have been brought up, right from childhood, through the influence of parents, school, church, community, and society at large, with a fixed mindset that the powers and successes we have are from outside ourselves. We learn to equate material possessions and social status with a good life and are bombarded with images of wealth and fame. Such conditioning persuades us to believe that more wealth, more fame, or more influence holds the secret key to feeling powerful and successful.

We often overlook our inner power, instead relying on external factors for happiness and fulfillment. Breaking free from this conditioning allows us to reclaim power according to our values and beliefs.

Life is what you make it, but we often forget the innate mysticism within us. This mysticism is a powerful force waiting to be tapped into, yet many feel helpless, attributing their circumstances to bad luck, fate, chance, and karma. Disconnected from our inner power, we forget our potential. By recognizing and harnessing this mysticism, we shape our own lives. We are not victims of circumstance but rather creators of our reality. Embracing our inner magic empowers us to transform our lives and bring positive changes to ourselves and the world around us. This is a great time to let go of those restrictive beliefs and tap into the power that dwells within us to create our own destiny.

We will continue struggling with unnecessary hardships until we let go of the belief that our power lies in the hands of external forces. The real power resides within; how to use it for the benefit of all is our duty. Freedom from mass societal programming allows us to remember that we carry the key toward the greater good. This realization empowers us to inspire change, foster equality, and uplift the marginalized. This is the time to step into our true power and create a world with less suffering and more thriving. Let us wake up to realize our true potential and exercise that power in service of the good.

We must learn to let go of the victim mentality if we want to regain personal power and take responsibility for our own lives. The victim role gives our power away to circumstances and reinforces a cycle of negativity and helplessness. Disengaging ourselves from the victim mindset will enable us to take responsibility for our actions and bring positive change. This shift in perspective toward values allows the recognition of choice, taking responsibility for our lives, and hence fosters growth, resilience, and empowerment. It is only through releasing this victim mentality that we can regain control and create a better future.

When everything does not go right, it is easy to point our fingers at external factors or others. This, however, results in a victim mentality and stunts growth. We can learn from our failures and fully take control to make positive changes only if we acknowledge what we have done and accept responsibility. It is this feeling of urgency and control that allows us to move forward and achieve personal growth and success. By assuming responsibility, we're able to learn from mistakes, develop as individuals, and control our own happiness and well-being. Consequently, responsibility empowers us and gives us more control over our lives.

Guilt is an ego construction of self-blame that impedes our progress. Knowing that guilt does not exist within the universe, we can take responsibility for our actions without the weight of guilt. We can feel self-forgiveness and constructively accept our wrongdoings by changing our point of view. Knowing that guilt is a construction of the ego frees us to take a far more positive approach toward mistakes for personal growth and inner peace.

Living responsibly and without guilt leads to an empowered and fulfilling life.

It is through the movement from victimhood to taking responsibility that the true power to shape one's life is realized. The self-victimization attitude means giving away one's power; hence, one limits one's potential. Taking responsibility empowers us to take action and make necessary changes; hence, living becomes more fulfilling. This shift in mindset opens a person to inner strength and resilience, making one a happier, more empowered being. Eventually, taking responsibility allows us to create the life we want; this can be an incredibly empowering realization.

In the world as it is, where everything may easily point outward toward blaming circumstances beyond our control, taking responsibility for one's actions is paramount. The blame game only keeps one in a victim mentality and stunts growth.

On the other hand, this principle of agency is not a negation of our power to effect positive changes in our lives. This kind of mindset thus generates a lot of awareness, personal growth, as well as personal empowerment. It is through the recognition of our power to make something happen for ourselves that we are able to take responsibility and create a life worth living.

Accepting responsibility is how we grow as people. It means knowing our actions are within the control of our life responses. This instills in us a very proactive attitude toward challenges, hence improving greater awareness and empowerment within ourselves. Taking responsibility means learning from mistakes, changing when necessary, and taking responsibility for our happiness and well-being. It surely leads to a more empowered and fulfilling life.

It is a very powerful thing when one can realize that the power, the ability, or the capability to make positive changes lies in one's hands. We can choose not to blame anyone else, our circumstances, or even fate for creating our reality, but take responsibility and create the life we want. This new mindset enables us to focus on what we can change and work toward making positive changes. Knowing that happiness is ours to control empowers us to live a full and meaningful life that has benefits for ourselves and those around us. This, in turn, allows others to be inspired and motivated by positive energy, which can have a ripple effect in empowering others and changing situations. Taking ownership of ourselves allows us to live an intentional life with purpose.

By taking full responsibility for our lives and making conscious choices, we create an avenue to reclaim our lives and build a more meaningful and powerful way of living. Every time we allow external circumstances to determine our actions and decisions, we are renouncing the possibility of taking responsibility for our lives. Owning up to our choices and actions helps remove the limits imposed by others and allows us to create a life according to our values and objectives. It is all about self-knowledge and stepping out of our comfort zone to take risks. Consequently, overcoming one's fears and hurdles opens up new opportunities in life that the person may experience and carry forward. Taking responsibility for one's life means living authentically and confidently, based on choices that are made out of real desire and aspiration. In this respect, it is indeed an empowering process of creating a truly self-owned life.

This helps alter everything in our lives. It makes us more positive and resilient, more aware of ourselves, and shows us as stronger and capable individuals in every aspect. Taking on a growth mindset lets us view challenges as chances for further growth, not obstacles. It empowers the relationships surrounding us because we become more understanding and empathetic, which raises the effectiveness of communication, thereby developing stronger relationships. A growth mindset applied to our careers enables us to accept new challenges we may face, learn constantly, and upgrade our professional skills and knowledge. It enables us to pick up the pieces and move forward when failures occur. We can be at our best and realize our full potential by embracing change and learning from experiences. It further helps us as individuals and trickles down to others, forming a positive environment that is much more empowering toward growth and success.

Playing out the victim mentality may grant temporary reprieve by abdicating our responsibilities for what happened to us, but this is ultimately constricting in achieving the best in us. It will continue to limit us if we live our lives as victims. It is only when we let go of that kind of mindset and take responsibility for our choices and circumstances that we can realize our full potential and build a truly rewarding and powerful life. Owning our happiness and success gives us control, and that enables positive changes in our lives, leading us toward growth and fulfillment. It takes a lot of courage and self-awareness to leave behind a victim mentality. The payoff, however, is huge: Taking responsibility opens us up to new experiences that will help us achieve our goals and live a fulfilling life on our own terms.

Consciousness—the state of being aware and perceiving one's surroundings—is often considered to be the only reality. Without consciousness, the world loses its meaning. Our consciousness allows us to perceive and interact with the world, shaping it according to our thoughts and intentions. It gives us our sense of self and allows us to experience emotions, thoughts, and sensations. It is the driving force behind our decisions and actions, making it the ultimate reality governing our existence. Our consciousness evolves, shaping our reality in ways we may not fully understand. It connects us to the world and gives us a sense of purpose and meaning in life.

The ego, with its desire for control and survival, often leads us to deny our inner truth. It creates a life filled with struggle and limitations, causing people to live within the boundaries of their conditioning and miss out on the magic within consciousness. Clinging to the ego's need for control prevents us from experiencing the freedom and possibilities that come with embracing our true selves. Only by letting go of the ego can we tap into our inner power and live a life filled with wonder and fulfillment. Recognizing the limitations of the ego and breaking free from its grasp is essential to unlocking the beauty and magic within ourselves.

The image of a magician on a tarot card, forgetting his own magic and living a mundane existence, symbolizes the limitations we place on ourselves by restricting our awareness. Like the magician, many of us ignore our potential and settle for an ordinary life, missing out on our true power. We all possess unique abilities and talents, but fear and self-doubt often prevent us from embracing them. By breaking free from this limited mindset and embracing our inner magic, we can unlock our full potential and live a truly fulfilling life. The tarot card reminds us not to forget or neglect our true potential.

The ego, linked to our sense of self and identity, may resist accepting the truth of consciousness. This resistance often arises from fear of losing control or individuality. However, embracing the truth of consciousness allows for deeper awareness and connection with the world. It relaxes the ego's need to be constantly validated, allows a deeper understanding of the self, and of the interconnectivity between entities. In this way, acceptance brings unity and purpose, providing an existence that is more enriching. It brings peace and contentment without the compulsion to defend the ego. Embracing the reality of consciousness heightens our awareness, further allowing us to connect with ourselves, others, and the world on a different level.

Consciously living and living out our life's purpose require us to have a deep insight into the self and our environment. A good awareness of our thoughts, emotions, and actions is crucial; it grants us the ability to make conscious choices about what we do to be purposeful. This level of awareness can break down societal expectations and external influences and enable us to live authentically, as our actions are grounded in values and beliefs personally held. It helps us connect more deeply with other people, empathize with what they are experiencing, and contribute positively to our communities. We can only ensure that we make a relevant impact in this world through our journey toward awareness, which in turn helps us leave a meaningful legacy. It helps us strive to live purposefully in this world.

At the beginning of time, it is believed that our perfection was established, and it has no end. This concept suggests that from the moment of our existence, we were created in a state of pure perfection, and this state of consciousness is inherent in our nature. It is a fundamental part of who we are and cannot be changed or diminished. This idea challenges the traditional belief that perfection is something that needs to be achieved or earned through hard work and effort. Instead, it suggests that perfection is already within us, waiting to be recognized and embraced. This notion can bring comfort to those struggling with feelings of inadequacy, highlighting that our true essence is flawless and eternal, unaffected by external factors. Believing in our inherent perfection can guide us to live with more self-love and confidence, knowing that we are as complete and whole as we were at the beginning.

So in this journey of life, many people seek outer confidence and make efforts to enhance their outer appearance and possessions, thinking that these will create happiness and fulfillment. However, perfection and fulfillment can only be sought within us. No outer changes can ever truly meet inner needs or bring lasting satisfaction. We are all born with unique talents, strengths, and qualities and, therefore, are inherently perfect in our own way.

The inner self is what needs to be embraced and appreciated for our true happiness and fulfillment. Instead of striving continuously for perfection outside, we need to foster our inner self and understand the beauty and perfection that lie within us. In this way, we can live a more fulfilling life since a person learns to appreciate and love oneself.

People are chasing an illusion called perfection in order to be the best version of themselves, but they are often thought of as never good enough. Humans compare themselves with others and set unrealistically high standards for themselves, always striving toward a goal that is unreachable. What they fail to realize is that they are already perfect the way they are. Each person differs in strengths and weaknesses. By following this unreachable mirage of perfection continuously, time and energy are drained, eroding one's sense of self-worth. The imperfections within ourselves should be loved because they are what make us who we are. Instead of aspiring to reach impossible standards, self-acceptance and self-love are what need to be pursued. Only then will we learn how to cherish our worth and lead a fulfilling life without the additional burden of trying to be perfect.

In today's society, there is huge pressure to attain perfection. The images of "perfect" people distributed everywhere may often lead to feelings of inadequacy and a lack of belief in oneself. Nevertheless, people ought to understand that perfection is relative and can never be achieved. What is perfect for one may not be perfect for another. Instead of chasing this unreachable image, people should understand that they are already perfect the way they are. Everyone has their good points and flaws; it is these strengths and weaknesses that make them unique and distinct from others. It is in accepting imperfection that personal growth and happiness occur. If we can make ourselves understand that perfection is relative, then we will be able to drop these unrealistic expectations and love ourselves for who we actually are. It's time to take the focus off perfection and place it on our uniqueness and the perfection within.

Society is always telling us that we should be getting better and striving toward perfection. We are literally bombarded with messages of self-improvement, images of flawless individuals, so our minds are socially conditioned into believing that we are not good enough. In reality, this pursuit of perfection is futile in nature since we are already perfect in our unique ways. This societal conditioning has blinded us to seeing the beauty in our imperfections. Comparing our lives to others and striving to live up to impossible standards inevitably makes us feel incomplete. It's time to rise above the strict expectations of what defines perfection in this world and accept that it is in our quirks and flaws that we find our character. Instead of striving for an unattainable perfection, what we should aim for is self-acceptance and self-love, appreciation for ourselves, and our contributions to the world.

Our perfection is right inside us, just wanting to be embraced and loved. Too often, we work at perfecting our exteriors, looking for perfection in so many other external things. The world touts and screams it in unrealistic forms, so we believe it is something outside ourselves. True perfection can't be measured; it is within our unique qualities, flaws, and imperfections. It is the embracing and celebration of these aspects of our selves that unleash beauty from within and show us our worth. We need not strive for perfection in somebody else's eyes; we need to learn to love and celebrate ourselves as we are. That is where our perfection stands, which shall lead us toward a lively and genuine existence.

Manifestation is one of the powerful tools that allow us to create the reality we desire. This is all about converting our thoughts and beliefs into physical manifestations through focusing our energy and intention on the fulfillment of a particular goal or outcome. We must see a vision and align our thoughts, emotions, and actions with what we want; and it will surely be attracted into our lives. Manifestation taps into the vast potential that exists within the mind. The process is that one can manifest through a series of positive affirmations, visualization, and persistent action toward our goals, just like planting a seed in the soil of the subconscious mind that grows and manifests in the physical world. This, however, requires belief, trust, and patience in its full power since it is not an overnight process. It is a gradual process of life that empowers one to take control of one's life and create one's own reality rather than being dependent on destiny. Embracing the power of manifestation makes it easier for us to unlock our full potential and live an abundant life filled with joy and satisfaction.

The constant pursuit of self-improvement is many times driven by our ego, which seeks validation and recognition. The ego pushes us to compare ourselves with others and seeks perfection, where perfection is never reached. Our true self, the spirit, already is perfect and doesn't need any improvement; it is our center that guides us through our lives. Contentment and acceptance come from letting go of our egoistic wish to improve and instead connect with our spirit. That does not mean we will stop growing; it means the growth will consist of aligning ourselves with who we truly are, thus leading us to fulfillment and inner peace. Being able to make a distinction between improvement for ego purposes and real growth helps us find our balance and live authentically fulfilling lives.

Man's search for the truth epitomizes one big mistake that humans make on the path to understanding the world. As man reaches new milestones in technology and knowledge, the truth he seeks is projected outside his very being rather than inside. This misplaced pursuit has brought man into a futile journey of searching for validation and fulfillment from others, depriving us of the most important source of truth, ourselves. We have looked to religion, science, and philosophy, hoping the truth about our existence would be unraveled. However, what this paradox really suggests is that the key to the world's mysteries lies within a person and their consciousness.

Thus, turning inward and looking at thoughts, beliefs, and emotions, one can find many truths that provide better understanding of the self and everything around us. Only within oneself is it really possible to find the truth one has been searching for. The words "I am" may be simple, but they hold powerful keys to the unlocking of our true identity. In those two words is captured an aspect of self-realization and acceptance of oneself beyond any name or dictate from society. And with the words "I am," we acknowledge existence and declare being. This is an affirmation that gives us the right to remove all imposed, incorrect, and disabling self-concepts and simply be acquainted with our true self. It affirms the value within us, the potential within us, and declares that our life circumstances and experiences do not define us.

Embracing the power of "I am" will give us the key to unlock who we really are. Our true self, through this simple yet profound phrase, connects within us to find out who we are and what our unique purpose and identity are. It is in claiming our "I am" that we break loose from the expectations of society and move into realizing ourselves, which allows a greater sense of acceptance of what we truly are and what we are capable of attaining. These two words should be continually reflected upon, for they may be the key to unlocking our real identity and living a fruitful life.

Once we learn to accept and embrace our true selves, we allow ourselves to receive everything we need and want. In our true selves, we connect with our inner power; we align ourselves with the universe, having a higher awareness of our desires and intentions and, thus, a more focused way of manifesting. Self-acceptance means that we let go of all negative thoughts and ideas that block our way from what we want. Once we accept ourselves, we also tend to attract positive people and energy into our space, including positive energies and abundance. The confidence and love inside you will resonate within you and attract similar energies into your being. This, therefore, brings a very strong circle of manifestation, as your thoughts and beliefs shape your reality.

This is the power of manifestation innately held in this simple phrase, "I am." If one says, "I am abundant" or "I am successful," then a potent message is sent to the universe, aligning one with these ways of being. This harnesses our thoughts and beliefs and channels them into bringing into existence a life we authentically want. Only by truly believing in "I am" and correlating it with positivity and abundance do we open ourselves to many possibilities and opportunities.

To put it simply, we become owners of the ability to shape our own reality, and through the magic of manifestation with "I am," one can have a life full of joy, success, and abundance. It is so easy to get lost in this world full of distractions and external influences. We do not need to look toward others for validation and guidance; instead, let us look into ourselves to tap that great volume of wisdom and truth that is hidden within us. And turning the attention inward really brings out our hidden desires, fears, and abilities. The painful process, though it may be, which is confronting our personal demons and coming to terms with a number of generally uncomfortable truths, is so very rewarding. We find clarity, peace, and a sense of purpose through introspection and self-reflection. So let this shift in focus be upon us now, and let us find the truth that has awaited us deep inside ourselves; for it is only by deeply knowing ourselves that authentic living can take place and our potential in this world can be met.

Your world is a reflection of your conscience—this saying holds much truth. Anything that happens in our lives, everything we encounter, own, or experience, is a direct reflection of what we hold inside our mind and heart. The reality of our life comes into being and is shaped by our conscience or, so to say, level of consciousness. If we have a pessimistic mindset, we will attract negativity and challenges into our lives. Conversely, if our attitude is positive, we attract positivity and abundance. This involves not only material but also the spiritual aspects of life too. The state of our mind and soul is a determinant factor in the quality of our relationships, choices we are making, and the path we take in life. Developing a positive and conscious mindset is very much relevant for the construction of a full and harmonious life. We can create a far better reality by raising our levels of consciousness.

Another way to think about the interconnectedness of our internal and external realities is that whatever is within you will be in the outside world. In other words, our thoughts, feelings, and beliefs color the world we see, yet on another level, our experiences and actions shape the world in which we find ourselves. This is also reflected in that quote: As it is in heaven, so is it on Earth. It is this: What takes place in our inner world projects itself in the external world. Now, a more harmonious and peaceful outer world calls for awakening the positive thoughts, emotions, and beliefs inside us. By taking responsibility for what lies within us and how that might impact the outer, we try to bring more love, compassion, and positivity into our lives and others. Finally, by aligning our inner and outer worlds, we create a much more fulfilling existence worth living for ourselves and those around us. The meaning here is that the state of your conscience is the state of your world.

To put it simply, we become owners of the ability to shape our own reality, and through the magic of manifestation with "I am," one can have a life full of joy, success, and abundance. It is so easy to get lost in this world full of distractions and external influences. We do not need to look toward others for validation and guidance; instead, let us look into ourselves to tap that great volume of wisdom and truth that is hidden within us. And turning the attention inward really brings out our hidden desires, fears, and abilities. The painful process, though it may be, which is confronting our personal demons and coming to terms with a number of generally uncomfortable truths, is so very rewarding. We find clarity, peace, and a sense of purpose through introspection and self-reflection. So let this shift in focus be upon us now, and let us find the truth that has awaited us deep inside ourselves; for it is only by deeply knowing ourselves that authentic living can take place and our potential in this world can be met.

Your world is a reflection of your conscience—this saying holds much truth. Anything that happens in our lives, everything we encounter, own, or experience, is a direct reflection of what we hold inside our mind and heart. The reality of our life comes into being and is shaped by our conscience or, so to say, level of consciousness. If we have a pessimistic mindset, we will attract negativity and challenges into our lives. Conversely, if our attitude is positive, we attract positivity and abundance. This involves not only material but also the spiritual aspects of life too. The state of our mind and soul is a determinant factor in the quality of our relationships, choices we are making, and the path we take in life. Developing a positive and conscious mindset is very much relevant for the construction of a full and harmonious life. We can create a far better reality by raising our levels of consciousness.

Another way to think about the interconnectedness of our internal and external realities is that whatever is within you will be in the outside world. In other words, our thoughts, feelings, and beliefs color the world we see, yet on another level, our experiences and actions shape the world in which we find ourselves. This is also reflected in that quote: As it is in heaven, so is it on Earth. It is this: What takes place in our inner world projects itself in the external world. Now, a more harmonious and peaceful outer world calls for awakening the positive thoughts, emotions, and beliefs inside us. By taking responsibility for what lies within us and how that might impact the outer, we try to bring more love, compassion, and positivity into our lives and others. Finally, by aligning our inner and outer worlds, we create a much more fulfilling existence worth living for ourselves and those around us. The meaning here is that the state of your conscience is the state of your world.

Our conscience plays a great role in the way we understand and perceive the world. The conscience is that inner voice that beckons us toward conduct in conformity with our values and moral principles. If our conscience is clear, then it will be in harmony with our values, and most likely, we can look at the world in an optimistic light. Whereas, if our conscience is always burdened with guilt and negativity, we may see the world as bleak and unforgiving. Thus, states of mind and thoughts can completely change how we look at and conduct ourselves in the world around us. That means that our inner state can shape our outer reality. It shows how awareness of the self and responsibility for one's thoughts are essential features because they shape our experiences in this world. In this direction, the development of a good and clear conscience creates a more positive and secure reality—first of all for ourselves and also for the people around us.

The concept of the conscience has been debated and speculated upon for centuries, with many theories and beliefs tossed about as to the origin and influence of our consciences. One belief, however, is that all in our outside world is a reflection of ourselves inside. If this belief is held as truth, it simply means that everything outside our being is first created or tainted by our conscience. This infers that our every thought, deed, and experience are mere manifestations of what our inner self thinks and believes about us. The conscience shapes our realities and thereafter dictates the choices and behavior that we subsequently enact. Thus, the conscience will always be there to guide us toward what one perceives as right or wrong and, in the end, shapes who we are. Although this may be hard to fully realize, it just goes on to show how strong and deep self-realization and introspection are in mentally grasping the outside world. We know ourselves more by looking inward and understanding our conscience. In short, whatever is outside ourselves is an extension of our conscience. Your conscience is important—that is what keeps you present on this earth. What rings so true for me is that my life, with all it contains, is a direct expression of my level of consciousness.

I believe that the consciousness of our minds shapes our reality, and it's very much reflected in all aspects of our lives. Our thinking, beliefs, and perception set the filter through which we view the world. Whatever struggles, conflicts, or difficulties there are in our lives, they exist because of the more limited or negative level of consciousness we have been on. Conversely, if our level of consciousness is high, we will attract everything positive, abundant, and fulfilling. The relationships we engage in, the careers we choose to pursue, our health and well-being—everything to do with life, in general—are interconnected with our level of consciousness.

As one becomes more aware, notices what they are thinking and believing, and works at expanding one's consciousness, life can become more harmonious and fulfilling. I've had it happen; I have witnessed how it has really positively changed every other aspect of my life, and I've enjoyed the journey. It's one worth undertaking if anyone wants to make their existence more meaningful and significant. As a matter of fact, our life is truly a reflection of our level of consciousness, and with its elevation, we build a better world around ourselves and others. The only way to ensure that there are substantial changes not only in our being but also in the surroundings outside is by first focusing on the elevation and improvement of our consciousness.

Our outer world is just a reflection of our inner state of mind, thoughts, and beliefs. Therefore, the only option to make any positive changes in our outer world is to find the roots of these things in ourselves and change them first. This means taking responsibility for one's thoughts and working at shifting them to more positive and empowering ones. It's by raising our consciousness that we access inner wisdom and intuition, which enable us to make better decisions and take action in the direction of our goals and desires. Changing the internal landscape is the only way we will be able to manifest tangible changes in the external circumstances of our lives. Elevating our consciousness helps us learn to view life from a more positive angle. In the process, positivity flows more into our lives with regard to experiences and opportunities. All this is possible by working on improving our consciousness continuously to bring a positive change in ourselves that helps others also. Ultimately, giving top priority to inner growth and elevating our consciousness will help us create a more rewarding and fulfilling life.

Our reality is an elaborate construction that undergoes constant changes based on our thinking, belief systems, and actions. Our thoughts are important in molding perceptions of the world and the formation of our reality. If a person strongly believes in something, then there is a high likelihood of attracting experiences and situations that are conducive to those beliefs. When we believe we can succeed and deserve success, we take action to move ourselves in the right direction, making choices accordingly. In contrast, the more negative our beliefs about ourselves or our abilities become, the more likely we are to undermine our efforts unconsciously and create a reality that reflects those limiting beliefs.

It is important to realize the power of our thoughts and beliefs, taking ownership of them. Through conscious choice, we are also able to choose only positive and empowering thoughts that shape a reality that nurtures growth and happiness. Our reality is not, however, entirely a product of our thoughts, for certain factors emanating from the environment make their contribution. But our inner minds and thoughts dictate how we let those around us shape us and ultimately define reality. Our reality is simply a reflection of the internal state of our mind; hence, by creating a positive and empowering mindset within ourselves, we become capable of building a life that is truly fulfilling and purposeful.

As I reflect on my life, I am aware of the fact that my life really portrays my level of consciousness. My thoughts, beliefs, and perceptions create my reality and, therefore, determine the kind of experiences that I attract into my life. For example, while in a positive frame of mind, I may let opportunities pass my way, and things often go well. The more negative and limiting thoughts and beliefs I hold, the greater adversity I seem to come across. This realization has led me to cultivate personal growth and self-awareness to improve my consciousness and, hence, my life.

With this in mind, I can intentionally choose positive thoughts and beliefs, change my attitude, and invite more abundance and joy into my life. Equally, I appreciate being surrounded by positive influences and continuing the search for knowledge and wisdom to expand my consciousness. It is a journey, but one that has brought me greater clarity, peace, and fulfillment. I really do believe that through focusing our inner state of mind and consciously raising our level of awareness, we can create a reality in which we manifest our highest potential and life purpose.

Manifestation has recently become very popular, and this is one sure method by which people can make their dreams come true.

However, despite the great amount of effort that we try to put in, sometimes our manifestations don't seem to work as expected. This article explores six possible reasons behind these failed attempts. First, we need to establish the fact that manifestation works on the principle of cause and effect: Our invisible reality is the cause, and the world we live in is the effect. This approach also appears in the Bible when God called into existence those things that did not exist. Once this is understood, it can be a game-changer in how we go about manifesting. To truly unlock the full potential of manifestation, we must thoroughly understand and embrace this principle.

A quantum physicist might explain the difference between the implicate order, the unseen reality, and the explicate order, the physical world we perceive. The explicate order is what we can see, touch, and feel in our daily lives while the implicate order is the underlying force creating this reality. Everything in this present moment, including your intentions and desires, is brewing in the implicate order. As was already said, if one intends to use manifestation for their good, then one must have clarity about what they intend to achieve, being very specific and unambiguous.

The universe cannot determine what exactly we want, and manifestation slows down or halts when we are not certain of what we want. Therefore, when reflecting on our desires, we should be specific about what we want and envision the feelings we will have once the wish manifests. The clearer and more specific our intentions, the easier it becomes for the universe to assist us in bringing them into reality.

The concept of unique reality states that the consciousness of "I am" is the substantial factor in our lives. That which appears as a projection of our consciousness is no more than the visible tip of an iceberg while all the rest is hidden but no less crucial for its existence. This concept has been developed and investigated by many philosophers and spiritual traditions throughout history. In this connection, Western philosophy draws on idealism, the notion that reality is fundamentally of a mental nature and that the physical world is a product of our minds. Eastern philosophy presents this idea as nonduality, where there is no basic division between the mind and the world, but instead all reality is one in substance and essence.

This potent and profoundly changing idea could take us to yet another new depth regarding the understanding of ourselves, our place in the world, and even the nature of reality itself.

Other reflections on the relation between our minds and the world are as follows: Thoughts and beliefs bring our reality into being. The way we think about the world shapes our experiences of the world. We always have the tendency to see the world as if it were a hostile place when we believe the world is such. Yet thinking that it is a beautiful world allows us to see the world as a beautiful place.

We are all woven into a tapestry of humanity, and through our actions, and even our thoughts and beliefs, the ripples seamlessly pour right into the lives of other human beings. When we act in compassion and kindness, it's ultimately building a world filled with more compassion and kindness. This is also true in reverse; when we are consumed by hate and divisiveness, then we create a world that's just as full of hate and division.

We are not an island to ourselves, but part of a greater whole. We each fit into a large and interconnected web of life. Once we all realize this, we can try living our lives more meaningfully and in a more sustainable manner. The connection of our minds with the world that surrounds us is intriguingly complex. There is still so much that is not known, but the more we learn, the more we truly realize how all of us are interconnected.

It is easy to get caught up in the physical world and forget about the vast unseen potential that holds everything in existence. However, our thoughts and beliefs shape the world we see, making it a projection of our state of mind. Therefore, to manifest our goals and desires, we must have consistent focus and belief in ourselves. Doubts and lack of faith create resistance, hindering our ability to achieve our desires.

Additionally, a scattered or directionless mind can weaken our intentions and energy toward our goals. Ultimately, through awareness and focus, we can tap into the unseen potential and create our unique reality. It is a powerful reminder that inherently, so much power is wrapped up in each of us, extending into the shaping of our own and collective states of consciousness, hence, the reality we are wanting to manifest.

We must remember to stay centered in our "I am" consciousness and use it to intentionally create a fulfilling and purposeful life that resonates with our deepest desires. By embracing and mastering the idea of one's unique reality, we will have truly unleashed our capabilities for a life full of purpose, joy, and abundance. This work teaches about the power of your conscience and its role in manifesting new realities. The conscience is a unique reality, and through our connection to divinity, we can tap into this powerful force to create the life we desire.

However, strong attachment to certain outcomes and reluctance to embrace change can hinder this process. Clinging tightly to specific expectations and fearing the unknown creates obstacles in our energy flow, preventing the universe from aligning with what is truly best for us. This resource explains how consciousness uses the conscience as a creative tool to manifest new realities, emphasizing the cause-and-effect mechanism behind this process and how our self-concept shapes our world.

Ultimately, the physical universe is a manifestation of our conscious being, and we can mold the character of our reality by sculpting our thoughts and beliefs. We can let the flow take us as we release attachment to outcomes and trust divine timing, rather than coming from a place of needing to control anything. We continue to open ourselves up to an abundance mentality, knowing that the universe has our highest interests in mind. Just as life is creation and transformation, like the heartbeat from real to unreal, so is the spirit to matter. We may allow ourselves, by surrendering to this flow, to be touched by the beauty in life and trust that everything happens at the perfect time as given by the universe.

We let go of attachment to results, and that is the only way we can actually be present and enjoy the journey rather than focus on the destination. Allowing trust in the universe and timing opens us up to infinite possibilities and abundance in all areas of life. By staying centered within our "I am" consciousness and using it intentionally, we are able to create a fulfilling, purposeful life that reflects our deepest desires. It is the understanding and harnessing of this particular reality that gives us the fullness of our potential, whereby we get to live a life full of purpose, joy, and abundance. The concept of a real or unreal world and consciousness is complex. Many believe that what we perceive as the world is just an illusion, created by our own separate consciousness.

This separation leads to fear and ultimately creates the illusion of an external world.

However, this world serves a purpose, to act as a mirror and guide us back to our true selves. This realization can only be achieved through aligned action, actively engaging in the manifestation process and aligning our actions with our intentions. Simply waiting for things to happen without taking inspired action will not lead to progress. In the future, true security will come from maintaining creativity and constantly adding value and meaning to our lives, rather than relying on external sources such as income. By relearning how to truly live, we can break free from the illusion of separation and find true fulfillment in life.

I hold a somewhat radical opinion about keeping a job as the sole source of income, and I do not expect everyone to agree. In my view, relying on just one source of revenue is risky. Depending solely on employment is a gamble we should protect ourselves against. We should always try to have multiple sources of income for the purpose of financial stability and security. Having only a job restricts your capacity and slows down your growth. That is why having a backup plan and finding other opportunities becomes so crucial, whether it is starting a side business or investing in different ventures. You've heard the saying "Better to have it and not need it than to need it and not have it." We can't afford to place all our eggs into one single basket. We must seek out opportunities and take action toward our objectives proactively. Abundance mentality means ever-seeking growth and expansion in life.

With today's economy, it has never been more important to have multiple streams of income. Such an approach helps deter unexpected financial storms that may arise from losing a job or a reduction of income. There are several ways one can develop multiple streams of income: starting a side business, investing in either real estate or stocks, creating an online course or product, engaging in affiliate marketing, and freelancing, just to mention a few. The key is to find something you are passionate about and willing to apply a work ethic to. It's about having a diversified portfolio of income streams to create more security for your future and that of your family, which ultimately equates to more financial security, greater time control, and expanded opportunities for growth. Though it may require some initial investment in terms of effort and resources, it is really worth the investment because of its long-term benefits.

There are so many resources to get someone going: books, articles, online courses, and financial advisors who can provide personal advice. These days, with the economy being so unstable, creating several streams of income isn't just a prudent move; it's a sure way to increase your chances of financial stability and success.

## Breaking Free from Limiting Thoughts and Hidden Obstacles

The concept of infinite intelligence, the spirit of consciousness, God, or a higher power creating the world is fundamental for many. However, certain spiritual philosophies suggest a different perspective. They propose that the world is an illusion created by our individual consciousness, rather than by a divine being. This view challenges the traditional belief in an external creator, suggesting instead that our perception of reality is shaped by our thoughts and beliefs.

These philosophies tackle the appearance that the world is a dream of separation, an illusion in our minds. Realizing this, we can begin to understand how all beings are connected and realize our real nature within a larger consciousness. As difficult as it may be for many to digest, it sheds new light on our existence by calling for a sense of responsibility in our thinking and acting in the creation of our reality.

The change in perspective dares us to think outside the box about higher powers and places the power in our hands, inviting us to create our reality through our individual consciousness. It emphasizes the power of one's mind and that a person should learn to control their thoughts in order to create their reality. This concept invites us to go beyond the physical and to connect with the spiritual aspect of our being in order to understand more about the mysteries of our being and our purpose.

Then the function of this illusory world becomes clear, to act as a mirror that guides us in the direction of our true selves. If the world is not real, then what is? It is an innocent misunderstanding within our conscience, a fleeting idea that has already been cleared up. However, deep-seated, limiting beliefs and internal barriers often interfere with this process of creation. Most of those stem from past experiences or even childhood, which may also have led to self-sabotage, acting as a block to attaining what is being set up as an aim.

These need to be recognized and let go of in order for the universe to align. Some of these limiting beliefs could sound like "I do not deserve to be happy" or "I will never have success," which block our complete belief in manifestation. Negative past experiences can create a fear of failure or a lack of trust in the manifestation process. Overcoming these barriers involves much inner reflection and effort, but once released, we can then open ourselves to the limitless possibilities of manifestation.

Upon letting go of these limiting beliefs, we can then align with the universe's energy, facilitating the easier manifestation of our desires. Basically, it develops in a person an attitude of abundance through growth and expansion in all walks of life. By truly realizing the actual nature of our existence and the potential of our consciousness, we can apply our infinite potential to create a full and meaningful life.

Limiting beliefs and internal barriers shape our lives in ways often beyond our recognition. Formed during childhood, these deep-seated thoughts are influenced by our upbringing and the norms around us, eventually evolving into doubts, fears, and insecurities that keep us from reaching our goals. Because these beliefs work at the level of our unconscious mind, sometimes it is hard to recognize them. It is only through developing an increasing awareness of such beliefs and working directly to challenge them actively that we can break ourselves free from their grip and develop a more empowering mindset. This takes a great amount of effort and deep self-awareness, but the reward is well worth it, a more enriching, successful life. Raising one's consciousness and a change in perspective have the power to shape realities and unlock the ultimate human potential.

In fact, there is an urgent need to cross over these barriers if anyone intends to live a life sincerely desired.

Impatience will, more often than not, disrupt the process of manifestation, as manifestation calls for patience and faith. Doubts, frustrations, and lack of confidence in the process can inadvertently push against the flow of manifestation. We have to search for new ideas and paradigms that will challenge the status quo and change our perceptions about the world and ourselves to enable us to manifest what we want. This involves constantly seeking essential knowledge through reliable sources on consciousness and personal development, looking beyond the surface to find deeper meaning and spiritual experiences in everyday situations, and maintaining patience and faith in the manifestation process.

Changing our concept of self and abandoning our ego-based identities can give us a far better realization of who we really are. That can generate in us an environment of peace and satisfaction. That is going to involve introspection and meditation with mental silencing to let go of our false stories and cultural conditioning that have defined and shaped our identity. It's a tough journey, but the reward for those who take it with an open heart and mind is immeasurable. By giving up the ego, we are able to find ourselves, the soul, and finally live a more authentic life.

The saying "Until you make the unconscious conscious, it will direct your life and you will call it fate," speaks to the power of self-awareness and inner change. It tells us that our lives are driven by unconscious beliefs, which are part of a personality we may be unaware of. By bringing these hidden aspects and motivations into our conscious awareness, we take responsibility for our lives and create our destinies. This requires a deeper understanding and acceptance of our inner selves, rather than relying solely on external factors.

The belief in scarcity can limit our potential and hold us back from living our best lives. However, adopting a mindset of abundance can lead to a whole new level of existence. Many people remain trapped in the trance of scarcity, never realizing their full potential. By committing to spiritual principles and shedding our false identities, we can tap into our inner power and find true fulfillment. This journey requires introspection and a willingness to break free from societal conditioning.

Change is an inherent part of our human experience, but it often begins within. The world we see is a projection of our consciousness, and true changes come from transforming our own thoughts and beliefs. Transformational coaching provides a powerful tool for anyone wishing to make significant and impactful changes in life. This coaching fosters personal growth and a shift in one's perspective to bring about change that endures. Through this process, a different reality is created, whereby one achieves set goals and creates lasting change in one's life.

We must understand that actual transformation occurs at the levels of our minds and perceptions. Usually, people feel that changes in the world around us will give them happiness and fulfillment; however, real change comes through inner transformation. This is because what we see is a projection coming from our consciousness, and even when changes occur in the physical world, the true transforming reality is caused by shifts in our thoughts and beliefs.

But again, sometimes these outer changes are temporary. Perhaps we should change our thoughts and beliefs instead of the external world. That is not easy; it could even be a total realignment of one's thinking and living. Seeking help from a transformational coach, mentor, or therapist can provide much-needed support and encouragement. As we change ourselves, our lives can become more rewarding and purposeful. Real change comes only from within and is a continuous process of growth and development.

This self-transformation is not easy; rather, it entails significant changes in attitudes and lifestyle. There is a need to break free from old patterns and adopt new beliefs and behaviors. Of course, this change will not be easy, and at times it may seem like a mountain too difficult to climb. It is here that a transformational coach helps the individual bring about lasting changes from within by guiding them, motivating them, and keeping them accountable.

The type of coaching that goes beyond goal setting and action plans is one in which the root causes of our behaviors and patterns are examined. In this process, individuals can create a new reality for themselves by pursuing a new career or relocating. After all, true change does indeed come from within. Yes, perhaps a coach may be able to take you through the steps, but it is truly up to you to make the change.

Everyone has wants and desires, some of which may seem unrealistic or out of reach. But if true evolution is to take place and a higher plane of vibration is reached, one must shed ideas and concepts that keep us bound to limited thinking and paradigms. Sometimes that is very hard to do because people hang onto their mental baggage. Self-discovery is the process of peeling off false self-concepts to reveal your true self. The process may be hard on the ego, as this marks the beginning of the ego's dissolution. Transformational coaching thus provides a venue to look at one's true desires free from the pressures and burdens of the outside world and tap into one's talents. With this awakened state of self, one can henceforth set goals and begin to work toward them with determination.

It is within us that real change happens, which then manifests in the world around us. Changing ourselves truly brings about lasting change in our outer circumstances. Transformational coaching supports people in connecting with their own inner power and potential to make extraordinary changes. It helps people live a more fulfilled and authentic life.

Our self-concept plays a big part in setting the pace for the world we see. To arrive at a higher level of consciousness, changing or altering this level requires a more positive and empowering self-concept. In order to ascend to a higher level of consciousness, it becomes indispensable to accept a more positive and empowering self-concept. When we suffer from a lack of self-esteem, we become alienated from our essential selves and identified with an incomplete reproduction of the self. But what would happen if we could get into contact with our unlimited, eternal, omnipotent selves? What if inside every one of us lies such a force capable of creating entire universes? What if thoughts and imagination could become reality? It sounds fanciful, yet it is true. We tend to limit ourselves in life by eliminating options that appear unreachable, but through the process of transformational coaching, we may discover strengths in ourselves and plot a realistic course toward a new reality. A coach can be invaluable in motivating and reminding us that we have the power to shift our perspective and create a better life. Release the limitations and begin to play with the unlimited possibilities within.

Traditional coaching works on setting up a goal and generating an action plan.

On the other hand, transformational coaching takes into consideration the balance of three different pillars: awareness, alignment, and thoughts. Awareness allows clients to envision a more satisfying life and determine if the desired outcome is in congruence with the client's values. Alignment links self-awareness with the desired outcomes, ensuring the goals are not in conflict with one another. Thoughts focus on changing a person's state of consciousness through challenging old beliefs and creating new paradigms. It is holistic in approach, inviting clients to explore a lifestyle that brings them satisfaction and, hence, personal growth toward living a life in alignment with their true desires.

Changing your life begins with changing your self-concept and your beliefs. It is this reinvention, the process of abandoning one's habit of being the same person, that brings about positive change, hence transformational coaching. Whereas in traditional coaching a preset goal serves as the guide for the process, in transformational coaching the focus is directed toward awareness, alignment, and thoughts. Once awareness is aligned and perspective has shifted, one can identify what real action can be taken.

A journey such as this requires the setting of goals in relation to a deeper knowing of the self, including questioning desires and motives. It is within us that the power of change actually rests, and transformational coaching empowers us to connect with this deeper power in order to live a more fulfilling and authentic life.

## Let's Finish What We Started!

Knowing the next chapter, we understand more deeply why our goals are what they are and why we must continue listening, both to our inner conversations and to those around us. Though many focus on surface-level strategies, they often miss the importance of aligning our goals with our true desires and fostering meaningful connections. By breaking free from egocentric thinking, engaging in self-examination, and mastering both internal and external actions, we can unlock our full potential.

Let's stay motivated and remember our "why" as you dive into this book. Make sure to take note of the activities in the first chapter and see if you can keep up with them!

Here are some questions for you:

How do you feel after doing the daily affirmation? Did it boost your confidence?

How do you see yourself now, and how has it impacted your daily goals and ultimate wish?

How far are you from completing your journal? Feel free to share your thoughts!

# CHAPTER 4

## COMMITMENT TO DELVE DEEPER INTO CONSCIOUSNESS

The primary cause of unhappiness is never the situation,
but your thoughts about it.

—Eckhart Tolle

Our consciousness, shaped by beliefs and experiences, often reflects the ego and lower self rather than our authentic nature. To access a higher level of awareness, we must move beyond surface perception and embrace spiritual consciousness, acknowledging the profound influence of the subconscious mind. Our consciousness is structurally capable of embodying and bringing into being. According to Earl Nightingale and Napoleon Hill, the mind's ability to conceive and believe determines what can be accomplished. Unlocking true potential and manifesting abundance depend upon recognizing and directing this inner power. By recognizing the limitations imposed by ego and past experiences, we expand awareness, align our beliefs with truth, and release restrictive thinking, opening ourselves to deeper insight, personal prosperity, and meaningful transformation.

In *Power vs. Force*, Dr. David Hawkins explains how different levels of consciousness carry varying degrees of manifestation power. Higher levels are more stable and progressive, guiding personal development. According to Hawkins, internal discipline in thought, speech, belief, and feeling must align with external discipline in behavior and action. True discipline emerges not from force, but from embodiment of the desired behavior and state of mind.

This journey toward reprogramming the inner mind goes beyond simply changing thoughts and beliefs. It involves delving into the spiritual aspects of manifestation and distinguishing between the consciousness of being and the conscience of the mind. Figures like Napoleon Hill, Earl Nightingale, Neville Goddard, and Nikola Tesla have significantly contributed to our understanding of consciousness manifesting desires. Napoleon Hill's concept that "whatever the mind can conceive and believe, it can achieve" underscores the power of belief in shaping our reality.

These mental processes influence our perception and outcomes.

Living in selfishness, below the consciousness level of 200 out of 1,000, people focus solely on their own needs, driven by primitive instincts and lacking awareness of their inner power. They exhibit aggressive behavior and cling to materialism, rejecting new ideas. In contrast, those at higher levels of consciousness transcend selfish desires and focus on altruism and collaboration. At the level of Courage, above 200 out of 1,000, individuals pursue truth and are guided by higher values like love and inner trust.

Wealthy individuals internalize their goals and believe in their ability to achieve them, understanding that believing is seeing. At high consciousness levels between 400 and 500 out of 1,000, achievements are seen as extensions of being and consciousness. Societies, individuals, companies, and institutions that succumb to pride after achieving success often decline when they forget the source of their achievements.

According to Hawkins, different levels of consciousness determine beliefs, emotions, behaviors, and ultimately, the varying experiences and results we produce in life. Thus, while some struggle with economic success, others seem to move toward it with relative ease. To understand consciousness is to understand manifestation. Higher levels of consciousness align individuals with their true being, enabling them to manifest desires with ease. Hawkins's map of emotions and levels of consciousness illustrate this, demonstrating that higher consciousness levels correspond to greater achievement potential.

Looked at through the perspective of being aware of the Source and infinite intelligence these levels represent more than just personal growth; they signify remembering our spiritual identity. Moving above 200 is not just about self-improvement; it's about waking up to being an expression of the Abundant Creator. In this understanding entitlement changes from an ego-driven demand to a divine right. Abundance is not something we force through effort; it flows naturally when we align with the Source Awareness. Privilege becomes a position rather than a social advantage: the awareness that we are part of, rather than competing for, universal intelligence. Discipline is no longer forced control; it becomes natural once we embody a new identity. Thoughts, emotions, and actions are in harmony and our nervous system becomes regulated and not dysregulated because they come from our identity not from effort. Manifesting abundance shifts from striving to allowing; from chasing results to expressing our nature. In this state, abundance is not pursued as though it were missing—it is lived as a natural expression of ourselves. We reclaim our power not by dominating but by consciously aligning with the infinite intelligence that is, in everything. Napoleon Hill emphasizes the importance of dreaming, hoping, wishing, desiring, and planning before acquiring wealth.[37] The world reflects our inner selves, and our level of consciousness shapes our self-definition. Neville Goddard's teachings highlight that outer circumstances reflect our inner state of mind.[38] Our environment mirrors what we believe and hold in our conscience.[39] This understanding helps in achieving lasting change by focusing on changing oneself rather than external circumstances.

Manifestation is bringing our thoughts and ideas into physical reality by bringing an intention from the unseen into the scene. In this way, by focusing the mind on our innermost desires and tapping into the infinite intelligence of consciousness, we create a reality that reflects our dreams. Ultimately, understanding and harnessing the power of manifestation highlights the extraordinary capabilities of our spiritual consciousness and its ability to shape our physical experiences as human beings connected to a higher spirit. Everything that exists in the universe is an offspring of consciousness, and everything which the consciousness beholds as its product is the result of imagination. Each idea, each thought, each act is born from that endless power, which is the mind. Behind every behavior lies a specific intention, serving as the inner measure of router willpower. Success is too often obstructed by this very perception. Our attention must be based upon spiritual intent rather than upon physical and mental effort. By concentrating only on these aspects, a lack of real power and manifestation will be our result. So says the law of manifestation: Where our attention is directed is precisely what manifests into our lives. The more we center our thoughts on positive ones and have a clear vision of what we want to manifest in our lives, the more likely we are to attract opportunities and experiences that will support us. It is a principle that reminds us how influential our thoughts and beliefs

---

37  Hill, *Think and Grow Rich.*

38  Goddard, *Feeling is the Secret.*

39  Nightingale, *The Strangest Secret.*

are in creating the reality we exist in and that they play a big part in shaping it. This law shows us that it is largely within our mindset and attitudes that we find true happiness and success in life. It, therefore, goes without saying that our thoughts and beliefs are vital to shaping our reality. Focusing our attention on goals and intentions time and again will create a channel through which the mind may allow our intention to actualize in real life. The field of all possibilities never forgets or loses the effects of our thoughts and intentions; thus, it becomes an urgent matter for us to consciously choose what we put our attention toward. The mystical teachings of Helena Blavatsky, Napoleon Hill, and Earl Nightingale similarly emphasize the primacy of the mind in manifestation. These individuals understood that the great architect of manifestation recognized the real power of manifestation as consciousness and, in fact, the essence of creation. If one observes their lives, one can see exactly what level of consciousness they engage with. They believed in molding a new reality within their imagination until it materialized in the physical world around them. Infinite intelligence, spiritual energy, resides within each person and empowers us to be the master architects of our own lives. In much the same way that architects and engineers use their imagination to design and construct three-dimensional structures, our subconscious is the medium through which we manifest into the physical realm. Through my studies, I came across an experiment by HeartMath that really drives this point home and gives me another key regarding alignment. That study demonstrated that if we want to bring what we want into physical manifestation, our intentions need to be aligned with our emotions. Conversely, it is when we are in a state of disarray that our misaligned thoughts and emotions disrupt the power of manifestation.

Alignment is about being logical and consistent; it is one of the most powerful concepts in our lives. It has helped many individuals, including myself, to maintain focus and control in various situations without succumbing to panic. This ability to understand and comprehend a situation rather than being overwhelmed by it has enabled me to take a proactive approach to solving problems. Now, with the full year of 2023 behind me, I can be grateful for the strength provided by alignment to keep me steady during the highs and help me through the lows. I am sure that, with the consideration of 2025, this principle will make my mind more resilient, less anxious, and will generally improve my mental and physical well-being. Indeed, alignment really endows me with the capability to view any situation with resilience and optimism; it is a tool in my life that I will always treasure. The three stages of consciousness play a crucial role in different aspects and types of human agency. Motivation, which is the driving force behind an action, is primarily linked to the unconscious mind and is therefore far removed from the actor's reflective awareness. However, this does not mean that the unconscious should be seen as a source of negative or dark forces. Instead, motives are often seen as needs or desires. These desires reflect different states of consciousness, with the ability to manifest them becoming faster as one becomes more conscious. True happiness is found in being conscious from our core, independent of external factors. While desires may sometimes be viewed negatively, it is not the desire itself that is problematic but rather our attachment to it. It is important to maintain control over our desires and not let them control us. The model being discussed acknowledges that individuals have a level of knowledge about their actions that may not always be easily articulated, known as practical consciousness. This concept emphasizes the ever-evolving nature of consciousness and its integral role in human agency. Practical consciousness and the rationalization of actions are interconnected, as both are essential in our daily lives. Many of our actions are automated and do not require further explanation or justification.

Sociologist Anthony Giddens argues that individuals are always "knowing," possessing practical consciousness that guides action even when it cannot be directly articulated. This practical consciousness is based on unquestioned and rationally undoubted knowledge, allowing for routines and traditions to be consistently reproduced. However, this knowledge can also be raised to the level of discursive consciousness if people reflect on their actions and can verbally account for them. In his theory of discursive consciousness, Anthony Giddens underlined the central role of self-reflection and discourse in better understanding one's actions and inadequate adjustment to the complexities of modern society. A heightened level of self-awareness allows individuals to navigate changing situations effectively. However, this consciousness is not always present and can vary in different contexts. As individuals delve deeper into consciousness, they may realize that their true desire is not for a specific goal, but for a sense of satisfaction and happiness. Ultimately, the highest level of consciousness involves surrendering one's plans and desires to the "I am" presence, trusting in its guidance and receiving everything one truly needs. Giddens's theory places immense emphasis on self-awareness and intentional action as essential to successfully guiding our way through modern society. He notes that our mental activity, in the form of attention, memory, problem-solving, and persistence, is determinately important in obtaining what we want and comprehensive understanding of our wants. He further suggests that desires originate in the pursuit of happiness, yet their behavioral expression depends upon one's level of consciousness.

While Giddens's theory stresses that a well-lived life arises from self-awareness and conscious action, we must also remember—at the depth of our being—that surrender to the higher self is essential. The self-help dimension lies in cultivating self-awareness that moves us toward a more conscious and fulfilling existence, realizing that our desires originate from within our inner dimension and lead us to a life of completeness. This realization frees us, for we understand that our desires are states of consciousness and that they stem from the ultimate reality within our being. In this light, his theory encourages us to embrace our inner divinity and live consciously in pursuit of true happiness and fulfillment. The levels of comfort and interest significantly impact our ability to process information and engage with our surroundings. When stimuli are interesting or comfortable, our attention is readily available, and we can engage in conscious information processing.

However, overly intense, challenging, or stressful stimuli narrow our attention as our stress-buffering and coping mechanisms activate to restore balance. To blame others or the circumstances around them reflects spiritual immaturity. Ultimately, everything in our world is a projection of ourselves, and it is up to us to regulate our attention, level of consciousness, and stress-coping mechanisms to navigate life's challenges.

Our desires reflect our level of consciousness and often reveal our mental well-being and spiritual condition, whether they stem from positive or negative emotions. While pure desires reflect goodness and alignment with our true selves, harmful desires may reveal inner struggles and the ego. It is crucial to treat those struggling with negative desires with compassion rather than judgment or aggression. Understanding these processes and their development strengthens perseverance. However, individual differences among people, stimuli, and situations determine a person's ability to maintain focus and avoid distractions. Teachings for children about their desires and goals should focus more on self-regulation—that is, aligning desire in accordance with love and compassion toward others for higher states of consciousness and a better life. What matters is not merely the desire itself but the level of consciousness from which it arises. Behavioral states of arousal serve as observable indicators of the necessary bio-behavioral activity for varying functions, considering physiological, psychological, and motor engagement levels. The human body is a masterpiece, designed intricately to adapt and respond to various internal and external demands. It constantly shifts arousal levels as we move through different sleep stages, working to restore and prepare for a more alert state.

While a certain degree of arousal facilitates sustained attention and information processing, self-control, or the return to a relaxed state, is equally important once the arousal level increases since higher cognitive functions depend on it. As great authors and motivational speakers like Wallace D. Wattles, Napoleon Hill, Earl Nightingale, and Neville Goddard emphasized, change in the world begins with a transformation of self-concept. It serves no useful purpose to just try to effect change without first changing the internal beliefs and mindset within ourselves. Our concept of self is that from which we build. By changing our concept of self, we connect with our inner power and our capacity for manifestation of our desires and for making a difference in the world. True change unfolds from the inside out, and we must focus on our personal growth first before trying to change the world outside us. In doing so, we align with the natural developmental process of life itself and what human beings go through, finding ourselves in a vantage position where we can make positive, lasting changes in the world. It, therefore, places great emphasis on our self-concept being in tandem with our authentic selves and the bringing of our wishes into form through the understanding of ourselves and positive intentions toward others in our manifestation journey. Our arousal levels also play a significant role in our motor activity, affecting factors such as muscle tone, coordination, strength, and planning. Therefore, maintaining balanced arousal is essential for achieving our desires and living a fulfilled life.

In conclusion, prioritizing self-care and striving for calmness and relaxation in both sleep and awake periods is crucial for overall well-being, as agitated movements with tight muscle tone and restricted motion indicates elevated arousal levels that require relaxation to regain regulated state transitions, activity levels, movement, and cognitive processing. Trying to change others is impossible, but when we learn to change ourselves, it becomes unnecessary. The idea of changing the world can seem overwhelming, irksome, and impractical; most importantly, it is an encompassing endeavor that could even include changes in the political and social systems ingrained in our lives. Some of these systems and beliefs have been in existence for quite a long period, to the point where they become hard to change. Most people consider world change to be an unreachable task because of how they approach it. It, however, isn't necessary to take it head-on. Instead, transformation begins with small, intentional acts that may eventually start an avalanche. By diffusing love, compassion, and positivity in our daily interactions, we actually trigger a chain reaction that motivates others to continue this vortex of change. One other thing that is very important to note: No single person can change the world; it needs effort from everyone. While we can only hope for a better world, it's through sharing and inspiring others that true change takes place. Even the smallest yet significant actions by each and every individual can cause change. The challenge may seem impossible, but we shouldn't be discouraged since change begins with each one of us. And with more of our small changes, we can change the world. Together, we can build a brighter future for generations to come. In today's society, children are constantly being exposed to external distractions and live in a fast-moving world. It's important that they get time and space for reflection within themselves, get closer to nature, and develop their inner being. This serves not only their personal development but also provides foundational building blocks for their journey toward an empathetic and mindful society. As adults, it is our responsibility to guide children toward this understanding, especially in the face of technology. Prioritizing self-reflection and inner growth opens us up to miracles and creates a more harmonious society. This state of grace allows us to tap into our unlimited supply of abundance and receive blessings without end. However, to fully manifest this abundance, we must raise our level of consciousness and belief.

To ascend to a level of awareness of abundant manifestation, we must change our thoughts, perspectives, and actions, dying on one level to be born on another.

Each state of consciousness is transcended by the seceding states through an awareness of its own limitation. Inseparable from this is the concept of different levels of consciousness corresponding to different states of manifestation. It is not an accident that at this exact moment, this message has come into your hands, but part of universal functioning: You are perfection, and perfection can never falter. However, at a superficial level, there is much to correct, and each person you encounter is a spiritual being on their journey toward remembering this truth. Therefore, it is essential to be compassionate toward others, even if they may seem difficult to us, as we too have been, or may currently be, difficult for someone else.

The key is to remember that we are all climbing an evolutionary ladder toward remembering who and what we truly are. It is important not to envy those who seem ahead of us nor label those who appear to be behind us as impossible. We are all on the same path of transcending duality and awakening to our true selves.

What I found most compelling is the concept of infinite intelligence and consciousness, the idea that we emanate from it. It is indeed humbling to realize that, ultimately, each one of us is connected through a higher, divine source. According to this concept, infinite intelligence contains the purest form of consciousness, unmarred by limitations and restrictions. It's said to be the source of all creation, the essence of our being.

I remain deeply grateful for this understanding, as it fills my heart with overwhelming love and deep gratitude toward the beauty and mystery of life.

As written in Ecclesiastes, apart from God, life remains incomplete and unsatisfying, no matter how it may look to others. This strongly shows that mere human strength and ego alone are insufficient to make the lives of individuals successful; it is about being aligned with the presence of God for fulfillment to take place.

This concept applies not only on a personal level but also on a universal and spiritual level. The teaching says that material possessions will not bring us true happiness and that we have to search for something more meaningful with the help of a supernatural connection. Such realization can provide meaning and fulfillment in life, motivating one to live a virtuous and compassionate life.

The concept of knowledge covers data or information gathering, introspection, self-reflection, and the power of imagination leading to the highest consciousness and infinite intelligence. Knowledge isn't simply knowing; it's a state of absolute certainty, devoid of doubt, belief, interpretation, discussion, or speculation. It's a state of consciousness that needs no further evolution, recognized when one stops questioning. This state of being isn't a personal achievement but a manifestation of the internal presence.

Though the ego may resist these principles, being permissive toward them and following the guidelines allows us to evolve and reach higher levels of consciousness.

This journey requires open minds and hearts as we move to the next step toward true knowledge.

It's essential to remember that change starts from within, as Wallace D. Wattles,[40] Napoleon Hill,[41] Earl Nightingale,[42] and Neville Goddard[43] emphasized.

## The Road to Success: Essential Ingredients and Strategies

Success doesn't happen overnight. It requires hard work, dedication, and the resilience to endure when circumstances are difficult. Although some assume that success comes easily, it demands sustained effort and unwavering willpower to forge on in the face of adversity. Those who achieve substantial success invest countless hours of practice and remain focused despite unforeseen setbacks.

Having realistic and achievable goals, along with the determination to see them realized, is essential in the process of success. Well-defined, realistic goals provide clear direction, allowing larger aspirations to be broken into smaller, manageable steps. This approach not only sustains focus but also builds momentum through incremental achievement.

While hard work is important, the right mindset and attitude are equally vital. This means maintaining a positive and determined outlook toward achieving your goals. It involves not viewing mistakes and setbacks as deterrents to progress, but rather recognizing challenges as opportunities for growth that lead to greater success. Resilience and a growth mindset work together, allowing failures to

---

40    Wallace D. Wattles, *The Science of Getting Rich* (Elizabeth Towne, 1910).

41    Hill, *Think and Grow Rich*, 65.

42    Nightingale, *The Strangest Secret*.

43    Goddard, *Feeling is the Secret*.

be transformed into valuable learning experiences. Success cannot be sustained through hard work alone without the proper mindset.

Two pillars of success are clarity of vision and sustained focus. You must understand your objectives and align your actions accordingly. This requires effective prioritization, efficient use of time, and minimizing distractions. Prioritizing helps organize goals into a clear structure, allowing you to manage time more effectively and focus on what matters most. Sustained discipline and focus are required to maintain progress, and avoiding distractions help conserve time and energy for long-term goals.

Successful individuals commit to continuous learning and self-improvement. In a constantly-evolving world, growth requires continuously expanding one's knowledge and skills. They actively seek growth deliberately and treat challenges as learning experiences.

Another very important ingredient for success is maintaining a positive mindset. Positivity plays a critical role, as it helps individuals navigate challenges and setbacks with resilience, keeping them motivated even during difficult seasons. Success is reinforced by surrounding oneself with supportive, like-minded individuals who encourage growth and perseverance.

Success is essentially the result of determination, hard work, and adaptability. While luck and external factors may influence outcomes, a combination of these traits truly drives lasting success. Determination prevents discouragement and the abandonment of goals, hard work provides the consistent effort required, and adaptability helps individuals overcome obstacles and seize opportunities. Together, these traits enable people to push beyond limits and continually improve themselves. While luck may contribute, it is ultimately determination, hard work, and adaptability that create lasting success.

External factors such as socioeconomic status and available opportunities can influence success, but true fulfillment comes from discovering one's passion and purpose. Fulfillment arises from pursuing what brings joy, meaning, and personal significance. Discovering and aligning with that purpose—through vocation, service, or creative pursuit—leads to a more satisfying and meaningful life.

When goals are clearly defined, actions become more focused and intentional. This clarity provides direction and motivation, enabling you to prioritize actions and make decisions aligned with your goals. Achieving goals brings fulfillment, builds self-confidence, and inspires the desire to pursue even greater aspirations. A clear understanding of your goals is essential for personal growth, success, and overall well-being, as it directs effort toward meaningful pursuits.

Success is not a destination but an ongoing journey—one that requires a positive attitude, resilience, and adaptability. Determination sustains forward momentum in the face of challenges, while a growth mindset transforms setbacks into opportunities for learning and improvement.

True success requires balance: self-awareness, willpower, flexibility, and supportive relationships. Self-awareness allows you to understand your strengths, weaknesses, and values, helping you set realistic goals and make informed decisions. Determination keeps you moving forward through obstacles, flexibility allows you to adjust when circumstances change, and a strong support network provides encouragement and guidance along the path toward realizing your full potential.

First comes the definition of success because it is subjective and may be different for every individual. Once success is clearly defined, specific and achievable goals should be set in harmony with one's values and passions. This clarity creates a meaningful path forward.

It is equally important to maintain a positive attitude and believe in yourself, as self-belief fuels perseverance and helps overcome inevitable obstacles. Continuous learning and growth, whether through formal education or self-development, equip individuals with the skills and knowledge needed to adapt to changing circumstances. Success is often built through setbacks, and continuous learning develops the ability to navigate challenges as opportunities for personal growth.

Surrounding yourself with a motivated and encouraging group creates an environment that supports persistence and resilience. These individuals offer insight, encouragement, and guidance, which are essential for overcoming obstacles and maximizing your potential. Growth and success require leaving your comfort zone. Taking risks and trying new things will push your limits and expose you to new experiences and skills.

It begins by defining success personally and setting achievable goals. This process requires planning and taking consistent action toward those goals. Rather than becoming discouraged by failures or setbacks, it is essential to remain open, adapt, and continue improving. Surrounding yourself with positive and supportive people reinforces motivation, guidance, and clarity, helping you stay focused and resilient on the path to success.

## Being Unapologetically Authentic

Being unapologetically authentic is one of the most powerful ways to manifest the life you desire. Simply, it's about being yourself—not caring what others think or about the expectations of society. It is a harmonious flow of thought, feeling, and action where one connects with the core of their desires and transforms them into reality. Being true to yourself attracts positive energy and opportunities that resonate with your authentic self. This authenticity allows you to clearly set intentions and take inspired actions toward your goals, unblocking fear or doubt. It also helps you release limiting beliefs and negative thoughts that stand in your way of manifesting your ideal life. Only when people embrace their authenticity can inner peace, confidence, and self-empowerment can they develop the core components needed to find satisfaction.

People-pleasing often suppresses personal desires by placing greater value on external approval than on inner fulfillment. While the need for acceptance is natural, it can lead individuals to neglect their own needs and sacrifice happiness. Releasing the urge to please everyone restores personal freedom and allows authenticity to emerge. Letting go of external validation strengthens self-worth, builds confidence, and creates space for genuine growth and satisfaction.

Learning about manifestation initially sparked excitement and determination within me. As I immersed myself in books and motivational material, positive changes began to take shape. I felt happier and more at peace—no longer burdened by circumstances beyond my control. Most importantly, I realized that living for others leads away from fulfillment because our time is limited and is meant to be spent cultivating joy, love, and meaning for ourselves and those we care about. This shift redirected my focus from external validation to inner peace, revealing that true mastery of manifestation lies in self-discovery and personal growth rather than material gain. When concern over external judgment fades, resilience grows, and decisive action toward personal desires becomes possible.

Living by our own rules, as opposed to those imposed by society and the opinions of others, frees us to nourish what we consider important. That freedom gives life authenticity, where our lives reflect who we are, not a duplicate of what others want. Remaining unique in ourselves, like-minded people enter our lives and join us on our journey, helping to lift one another up. This self-discovery journey builds relationships based on acceptance and mutual understanding that truly enrich our lives with fulfillment and purpose. Living by your own values rather than those imposed by society or the opinions of others allows life to reflect who you truly are.

Empathy emerges as a powerful tool for understanding both personal and collective challenges. By cultivating empathy, we create meaningful connections that foster compassion, inclusion, and support. This awareness ensures that individuals feel seen and valued, strengthening communities and encouraging positive shared growth. Practicing empathy deepens relationships and contributes to lasting change and collective well-being.

In hindsight, with Percy's paradigm for being likable, we realize how authenticity applies to the building of real connections. The fact that he was transparent with himself, not concerning himself with what anyone else thought of him, reinforced the importance of not compromising our values and beliefs. His example serves as a reminder to be ourselves and define who we are, remaining resilient against societal pressure.

By cultivating authenticity, prioritizing personal growth, and practicing empathy, we give ourselves a strong foundation for fulfillment and purpose. Every step into self-discovery and acceptance is another move toward a life rooted in peace and genuine connection, affirming that we have the right to create a life that truly feels like our own.

## Time to Take It to the Next Level!

The idea here is to put it all together with what we have learned from our visualizations, affirmations, and journaling so far. Now, we're really going to focus on the visualization of our future selves, starting with setting an ideal future in our mind's eye. Here are few short instructions that I want you to follow, which you may find beneficial after you have finished reading this guide:

Find a quiet space and sit comfortably where you won't be disturbed for the next ten to fifteen minutes. Relax and breathe. Close your eyes and begin taking some deep breaths. Breathe slowly in through the nose, hold for a few seconds, and slowly exhale through the mouth. Continue this until you feel calm and centered.

Visualize your ideal future: Build a life where all your needs and desires have manifested. Picture yourself in your future living this most ideal life.

Pay attention to the details: What does your day look like? Where are you living? What kind of work do you do? Who is with you?

Engage all your senses: What do you see, hear, smell, taste, and touch in this most ideal future?

Feel the emotions: Allow yourself to feel the emotions as though this reality has already manifested. Feel the delight, serenity, satisfaction, and thrill as if it is already happening.

Set the vision: Identify a simple phrase or affirmation that describes this vision for you, similar to little commentaries such as "I am living my dream life" or "I am abundant and fulfilled." Repeat this phrase a few times, anchoring the vision in your mind.

Come back to the present: Gradually come back to the present moment. Open your eyes and take a few deep breaths, feeling refreshed and inspired.

Now, let me name our journal for this book: "The Daily Gratitude and Affirmation Journal."

Continue to write in your journal. Take some time each morning or evening for this process. Write down three things you're grateful for, such as a nice cup of coffee, a supportive friend, or an achievement that recently occurred. Then write down three affirmations describing your future self and the life you are creating—for instance, "I am confident and successful" or "I attract abundance with ease."

After that comes reflection and visualization. Take a minute or two and reflect on your daily gratitude and affirmations. Visualize how these contribute to your overall goals and dreams. Close your eyes and envision yourself living those affirmations, feeling the emotions that come with them.

# CHAPTER 5

## THE PATH TO PERSONAL GROWTH AND SELF-DISCOVERY

The only journey is the one within.

—Rainer Maria Rilke

My growth and self-discovery have been shaped by the insights of philosophers and artists whose work illuminates the extraordinary power of the mind and the significance of manifestation. As one philosopher observed, even the smallest details of our lives reflect a higher, unseen order. This perspective suggests that everything we experience is connected to a deeper, underlying intelligence, often understood as infinite wisdom. Much of this understanding emerges through engagement with the subconscious mind, offering a richer view of ourselves and the world around us.

The concept of God has both divided and inspired thinkers for centuries. While cultures and religions describe the divine in different ways, some view God not as a tangible being but as a state of consciousness attainable through awareness and inner development.

From this perspective, reaching infinite intelligence represents unity with the divine. Such an understanding transcends traditional boundaries, inviting deeper self-reflection and spiritual practice as pathways to expanded consciousness and personal growth.

Napoleon Hill famously asserted that our beliefs and self-faith are potent tools for manifesting our desires. By elevating our consciousness and harnessing our mental potential, we can create a life of abundance and satisfaction. The law of attraction underscores the power of our thoughts, but it is crucial to complement this belief with proactive effort and resilience. Through this realization, I have discovered that combining faith, determination, and action is key to achieving our goals.

During periods of crisis, recognizing that global systems endure while crises remain temporary has given me clarity and resolve. This perspective allowed me to move through uncertainty with greater confidence and remain committed to personal growth. Releasing rigid mental control and trusting the unfolding process encourages alignment, making manifestation more fluid and less resistant.

By reducing mental interference and aligning with inner truth, fulfillment becomes attainable beyond perceived limitations.

The teachings of philosophers and artists have imparted that personal growth and self-discovery demand a willingness to embrace change, challenge existing beliefs, and flow with life's natural rhythm. The principles of manifestation and the law of order profoundly influence our ability to attract and achieve our deepest desires. By minimizing mental interference and understanding these principles, we can attain genuine fulfillment and surpass even our greatest aspirations. This capability is inherent within each of us, regardless of our current level of understanding.

The law of manifestation—intimately linked to the law of conscience cause and subconscious effect—reveals that our external reality mirrors our internal state. True manifestation occurs when we cultivate mental prosperity. Many seek wealth and abundance, mistakenly believing they must acquire external possessions before becoming their true selves. Instead, focusing on our essence, followed by action, ultimately leads to achieving our desires. Scientific research supports that our expectations and past experiences significantly influence our brains, underscoring the necessity of shifting our internal state to realize our goals.

In *Get Rich Like Instant Coffee: Unlocking Your Purpose for Financial Freedom*, I emphasize the importance of connecting with our spirit, the boundless aspect of ourselves. By transcending mental limitations and allowing our spirit to guide us, we can live more fulfilling and empowered lives. This approach becomes even more effective when we collaborate with like-minded individuals, as it elevates collective consciousness. It is essential to concentrate on our internal world and reduce external distractions to fully harness this technique.

Embracing a belief in our capabilities and harnessing this belief can transform our lives into realms of purpose and abundance. This belief allows us to break through the shackles of self-imposed constraints and realize our full potential. Our thoughts and ideas need fertile ground to bloom, much like a seed requires fertile soil to grow. By internalizing the teachings of "I am," we can craft a reality that reflects our inherent abundance. The Bible attests to unified will and understanding as the means powerful enough to align people's consciences and desires and bring them into reality.

Cultivating resilience and flexibility forms a foundation for financial freedom. A person's steadfastness and openness to change support the building of a successful journey. When a growth mindset perceives an obstacle as an opportunity for learning rather than defeat, adaptability helps move individuals in the right direction toward achieving their goals. With resilience in mind, clarity and strategic action allow us to navigate the complex dynamics of financial undertakings more effectively.

Perhaps the most important foundation is developing a strong sense of purpose and aligning our actions with it. A clear and compelling vision of what success means to us helps guide direction and motivation. Regularly refining that vision and acting in alignment with it allows us to make constant, incremental progress toward our goals. This focus on purpose-driven action helps us remain committed and resilient in the face of challenges.

Furthermore, nurturing a network of supportive people is equally important. Surrounding ourselves with mentors, peers, and friends who share our values and ideals can provide meaningful insight and encouragement. This network not only keeps us motivated but also offers practical advice and accountability, further strengthening our journey toward financial freedom and personal fulfillment.

## Pilgrimage of Self-exploration to Insights: Reflective Exercise

I vividly remember a project I created during my college years while pursuing my bachelor's degree in digital arts and film production. At that time, while on campus, there was a counselor who also served as a life coach. She was one of my instructors, and she inspired me to pursue a path as a transformational personal development mentor. Although I had already attended workshops and seminars across various cities and states, the first meaningful project I created was for myself, titled "Halfling Travels: Who Am I."

This interactive exercise was intended to help me look at myself and refine my identity. It asked me to make a list of one hundred words that describe my character, personality, and traits, both positive and negative. At first, I thought it would be an extremely difficult assignment, but as I started looking around for different words and writing them down, it became an incredibly enlightening process of discovering various aspects of my life and who I am. It turned into a disconcerting yet gratifying journey of discovery that helped me realize my strengths and weaknesses.

By the end of the exercise, I had gained a clearer understanding of myself and a deeper appreciation for the qualities that make me unique. The project supported my personal development and revealed insights that continue to influence both my personal and professional life. I recognized that integrity and responsibility guide my actions and decisions, and that many of my core traits have been shaped through lived experience.

I realized that determination and perseverance have gotten me through tough situations and helped me realize my ambitions, and at the core of everything, there is kindness. Being self-aware helps me continue to improve myself. These qualities not only benefit me but also positively serve others, reminding me to live life with purpose and stay true to myself. Spirituality has played an important role in my life because it has helped me stay grounded in higher purpose. Overall, I believe integrity, responsibility, values, leadership, honesty, determination, kindness, enthusiasm, self-awareness, and spirituality are essential parts of my life.

During my time with Percy Ford, who often emphasized the importance of good friends, I met Kenneth L. Funderburk. Kenneth taught me about finding success by satisfying personal needs and recognizing one's purpose in life. He stressed achieving financial freedom by believing in the gifts God gave us. Kenneth comes from an exceptional academic background, having graduated from Samford University, attended graduate school at Mississippi State, and earned his Juris Doctor degree from the University of Alabama. He has practiced law for over fifty years, and his interests are twofold, the art and music community; he also serves as a senior partner in a law firm.

Kenneth values sharing his experiences with others, believing they can be incorporated into fiction writing. His mother's words about the value of accumulated life experience have stayed with him, and he enjoys sharing his stories. Despite his busy career, through conversations with Kenneth, I gained valuable insight into success, fulfillment, and answering a personal calling.

He urges the importance of stepping outside your comfort zone, doing activities you would not normally pursue, and attending events or conferences related to areas of interest. Through my conversations with Kenneth, I was able to gain valuable insight into success, fulfillment, and following one's calling in life. His words and achievements continually remind me never to settle for mediocrity but, instead, to follow my passion and embrace the unknown.

## Complete Guide to Manifest Your Best Life

John Dewey observed that when individuals cannot anticipate the consequences of their actions or understand guidance from those with experience, they struggle to act with intention and intelligence. Without reflection or foresight, actions lose direction and meaning. This insight underscores the importance of awareness and conscious decision-making in shaping a purposeful life.

The questions in this book are designed to help you discover your purpose, which can lead to success and allow you to profit from it. Using a journal as a workbook, you will be able to record your thoughts and ideas. These questions will help you build a life that reflects your soul's deepest desires. It is a transformative road to the best life, inner wisdom, and full potential. You will be guided through thought-provoking exercises, journaling activities, and reflection tasks designed to bring more clarity, awareness, and understanding of yourself and what you want. This newfound awareness will empower you to take inspired action and turn whatever you want into reality.

Great practical tools and strategies are on the way that will help you face challenges head-on, shift those beliefs, and open up to a more positive mindset. With dedication and commitment, you will feel empowered to create the life you truly deserve and live it to the fullest.

These are life principles—presented in question form—that will serve as guidelines for discovering one's true purpose and living one's full potential. Answering these questions will reveal your purpose, talents, weaknesses, strengths, and fears. By tearing out each page and placing it where you have the most conversations, whether about yourself, your services, or your business life, you'll discover your true calling.

If your conversations tend to center on personal experiences, consider writing about your life. If your focus is business, explore starting a venture aligned with your strengths. If your passion lies in helping others, becoming a social entrepreneur may be your calling. The subjects that consistently energize and inspire you often point directly to your purpose and the work that will bring lasting fulfillment.

Your purpose is where you feel the most at home. Science tells us that our brains are composed of thousands of cells that store images. When we think, we activate these cells and the images within them. This workbook aims to help you think of yourself and money in a new way by building cells of recognition for prosperity. It guides you to envision wealth, prosperity, good health, and a happy, fulfilled life.

Lasting fulfillment comes from recognizing a deeper reality beyond appearances and aligning awareness with inner truth.

Many people won't believe in these ideas until they discover them for themselves. This workbook aims to lead you to a new awareness of prosperity ideals. Self-help books, audio tapes, seminars, and workshops often promise answers; but the key to success lies in correctly applying the information. To do so, you must first find yourself and get into a quiet, stress-free space to calm your mind. This is where you will find life's purpose, happiness, and self-worth.

We are by nature creators of ideas. Your purpose becomes an idea, which, once picked up by the imagination, taps into the immense power of the subconscious. Through repetition and emotion, this idea develops into a definite aim and positive plan. This workbook helps you apply these principles to your life, leading you to your most inner desire for success.

An adventure is waiting to guide you to the life you were meant to live. This resource is packed with brainstorming ideas to help you discover your purpose, achieve success, and reach financial freedom. You'll find guidance to tap into ideas that can shape your fortune and future.

By blending the "I am" spirit consciousness and cosmic awareness with your conscious mind and emotions, you can make a real impact on your hidden inner mind, connecting with the source of all creative knowledge. Let's dive into this journey together to transform your life and achieve the financial freedom you deserve.

Thomas Edison (inventor) said, "I know Infinite Intelligence rules this world. It requires Infinite Intelligence to organize it and expects Infinite Intelligence to keep it on its path. It's mathematical by precision."

The creative imagination will send you ideas in the form of hunches or flashes of inspiration, which may seem unrealistic at first. Trust me, I understand the skepticism. I've used these ideas myself, overcoming my own limitations, learning disabilities, economic hardships, past failures, and even a background that included prison. These experiences shaped my limiting beliefs and self-perception, holding me back from success. The key to overcoming these obstacles was changing how I saw myself and believing in my potential.

Successful people often don't share how they achieved their success, but it's not about the books, seminars, or motivational speeches alone. It's about seeing yourself as already successful and believing in that vision. I had faith in my creative ideas and the infinite intelligence within me. This faith, combined with persistence and determination, helped me achieve my goals. As you read *Get Rich Like Instant Coffee: Unlocking Your Purpose for Financial Freedom*, remember that my passion and hunches from infinite intelligence guide me.

Infinite intelligence, to me, is the source of creative knowledge within everything. It reveals what you need to know at every moment. This creative power can bring new thoughts, ideas, inventions, and opportunities. For instance, it inspired me to write books, attend workshops, and network with successful entrepreneurs. These experiences and the questions in this workbook helped me find my life purpose and set me on the path to becoming a self-made millionaire.

Achieving your dreams requires absolute belief, total applied faith, unwavering persistence, and a willingness to make sacrifices. Sometimes this means finding a cheaper living arrangement or cutting liabilities to save money and grow your capital. By doing so, you can eliminate overhead expenses and generate resources to fulfill your vision. Once you have a burning desire and a definite plan, you can achieve anything you want. Remember, the universe provides: What you're looking for is also looking for you.

Reality is far more than what we perceive with our senses. The world we see around us is only a minute part of a vast invisible reality from which everything arises. Within this invisible reality, spiritual truth lies at the heart of every being that exists. It gives life to mystical understanding and is the source of all wants, feelings, and thoughts. Through this connection to the spiritual world, valuable understanding of oneself and the world can be attained.

The spirit within us acts as the driving force behind everything. It links us with divinity, and our outer world reflects the spirit's thoughts, feelings, and beliefs. Recognizing this inner spirit and nurturing it helps lead a purposeful and successful life. The manifestation of matter-energy is an expression of something far more fundamental and invisible, a reality studied by quantum physics. In this invisible realm, explanations emerge that challenge conventional perceptions of the cosmos.

This involves the infinite intelligence of spiritual consciousness and its vast capabilities. This boundless realm holds all knowledge and wisdom. Accessing spiritual consciousness empowers a person with deeper awareness of self and the universe. Bridging the physical and spiritual realms leads toward spiritual enlightenment, a concept echoed across spiritual traditions throughout history.

Awareness is the means through which infinite intelligence is expressed. It operates on many levels: self-awareness, awareness of others, and awareness of the world. Through awareness, we give meaning to experience and take conscious action. Expanding awareness allows access to inner wisdom and higher consciousness, laying the foundation for personal growth and enlightenment.

It is the instrument through which infinite intelligence expresses itself, yet it is often clouded by the ego. The ego seeks control over thoughts and behavior, obscuring higher awareness. True awareness lies beyond the ego, reaching a higher plane of perception. By recognizing this, we elevate consciousness and connect with others more deeply, leading to a more fulfilling life.

Consciousness and conscience differ in important ways. Consciousness refers to awareness of one's environment and experiences while conscience guides ethical and moral action. Inspiration through the spirit of infinite intelligence finds expression through the mind, helping balance awareness and moral guidance in a harmonious life.

The notion of the world as a dream where desires manifest and a higher reality exists may seem far-fetched, but it reflects a deeper longing for truth. This guide helps readers explore this concept and discover their true selves. It challenges beliefs and opens the mind to higher understanding. The journey of self-discovery is not easy, but knowing one's true self is its own reward.

What happens in this apparent world can be chaotic, but true satisfaction lies in realizing a higher reality beyond it. This work guides readers to question beliefs and open themselves to deeper understanding. The journey may be difficult, but it is worth the effort. Finding one's true self is the ultimate reward, and embracing this journey is a necessary step toward true enlightenment.

## The Power of Resourcefulness for Success Realization

Being resourceful is a fundamental characteristic that helps one attain success; it involves the ability to adapt to new challenges, think creatively, and foster a strong network of valuable relationships. These relationships with clients, employees, or business associates can pay off in many ways, such as through referrals and financial opportunities. Embracing the practice of doing favors without expecting immediate returns can fortify these connections and create pathways to new opportunities. Acts of kindness often leave lasting impressions, and support from your network can materialize in unexpected ways, propelling you toward your goals.

From early childhood, we are taught that life is more than just play; it reflects a deeper, more profound intelligence. Despite the obstacles and conditionally molded thinking we encounter, each of us has the potential to be successful and live a life of affluence. To tap into this potential, one must take responsibility for one's life, set realistic goals, and overcome beliefs that limit progress toward those goals.

A shift in focus from blaming the outside world to taking action toward growth and fulfillment is required to achieve wealth and happiness. In family dynamics, financial disparities can sometimes lead to tension. For example, the contrast between a wealthy friend and a less affluent stepfather can highlight economic differences. However, by prioritizing shared love, support, and understanding, families can navigate these disparities and build stronger bonds. This approach fosters unity and imparts valuable lessons in gratitude and humility, demonstrating that true wealth is found in relationships and emotional connections rather than material possessions.

Resourcefulness not only reflects individual capability but also the wise use of collective strength. Collaboration with others and utilizing their strengths can drive innovation and create new possibilities. Effective teamwork allows resources, knowledge, and skills to be pooled together, increasing the likelihood of success and making it easier to achieve goals.

Resourcefulness also requires a visionary mindset. Anticipating potential challenges and planning ahead enables you to navigate uncertainty while capitalizing on opportunities as they arise along the path to success.

Another core element of resourcefulness is adaptability. In a fast-paced world, the ability to change course or adjust strategies based on new information or shifting circumstances is invaluable. Embracing change with flexibility and an open mind allows you to stay ahead of trends and remain competitive.

Resourcefulness also involves nurturing a strong professional network. Valuable advice, insights, opportunities, and mentorship can come from peers and industry leaders that might otherwise be inaccessible. A healthy network requires regular engagement, offering help when possible and seeking guidance when needed.

Equally important, resourcefulness requires the right attitude. An optimistic and resilient mindset not only helps you endure challenges but also encourages others to collaborate with you. Positivity can transform obstacles into opportunities and foster a culture of success.

Resourcefulness is also a continuous process of learning. Staying current with industry trends, developing new skills, and expanding knowledge enhance adaptability and innovation. Lifelong learning remains one of the most powerful tools for maintaining relevance and competitiveness.

Problem-solving skills are another essential aspect of resourcefulness. When confronted with obstacles, a resourceful individual approaches problems with a solution-oriented mindset, considering multiple alternatives and applying creative strategies to overcome difficulties.

Resourcefulness can be described as making the most of available resources. Using time, money, and energy wisely often yields significant benefits. It involves optimizing processes, maximizing efficiency, and avoiding waste.

Networking should always be approached with sincerity and authenticity. Meaningful relationships are built on trust and mutual respect, not transactional intent. By nurturing genuine connections, you create a reliable support system that enriches your journey.

Additionally, resourcefulness grows through accepting feedback and learning from failure. Criticism and setbacks provide valuable insight into how future efforts can be improved. Viewing failure as a learning opportunity rather than a defeat opens the door to continued growth and success.

Finally, resourcefulness must be paired with patience and persistence. Success often requires sustained effort over time. Being resourceful means seizing opportunities while maintaining a long-term perspective and continuing to work toward goals despite obstacles along the way.

The power of resourcefulness for success lies in the art of adaptation, innovation, and important relationship building. People will better be able to negotiate the complexities of their personal and professional lives toward the realization of their goals and full potential by leveraging collective strengths, keeping a positive attitude, and committing to continuous learning.[44] "The infinite intelligence of my subconscious mind reveals to me my true purpose" (Joseph Murphy).[45]

The true power of resourcefulness lies in adaptability, innovation, and the ability to build meaningful relationships.

---

44    Hill, *Think and Grow Rich*, 73.

45    Murphy, *The Power of Your Subconscious Mind*, 44.

# Key Goals for Self-fulfillment and Societal Progress

Achieving a life marked by both success and fulfillment is underpinned by two central goals: success and happiness. Success is rarely a solo endeavor; it hinges on cultivating supportive relationships and capitalizing on opportunities through strategic connections. Investing your time and energy into building relationships with key individuals who can advance your objectives is essential. On the other hand, it is equally important to bypass those people who are not building you up. This narrow approach helps you utilize your resources effectively to move you faster toward your significant milestones.

From the perspective of personal and professional growth, two goals are imperative. First, one should pursue constant improvement through realistic target achievements, new skill acquisition, and expanded knowledge. It is this continuous process of self-evolution that pushes an individual out of their comfort zone, thereby leading to resilience and growth. The second goal is career success, which may include earning a master's degree in your field, starting your own ventures, or making meaningful contributions within your profession. Reaching these objectives provides financial stability and a sense of direction and fulfillment, helping individuals move toward a more meaningful and purposeful life.

From a broader perspective, two major goals crucial to overall human development include economic prosperity and stability, as these foster improvements in living standards, job opportunities, and infrastructure. Secondly, social equity and justice ensure that all individuals are given equal opportunities regardless of background or status. Achieving these goals requires collaborative efforts among governments, businesses, and communities to develop systems that are sustainable and supportive of all, creating a just and prosperous society for present and future generations.

Personal fulfillment also requires clarity of goals and a clear plan of action. Goals should be clearly defined, measurable, achievable, relevant, and time-bound, commonly known as SMART goals. This structured approach allows individuals to track progress and remain motivated. Regularly revisiting these goals ensures continued personal growth and alignment with broader aspirations.

Another important aspect of self-fulfillment is developing a well-rounded lifestyle. This involves creating harmony between work, relationships, activities, and health. Maintaining balance across these areas helps prevent burnout and encourages happiness in all aspects of life. By embracing balance, individuals can pursue their goals with energy while living a fulfilling and healthy life.

Lifelong learning is also essential for continuous growth, both personally and professionally. Staying curious, open to new experiences, and willing to learn new skills maintains adaptability in an ever-changing world. Lifelong learning expands personal capacity and professional potential, leading to sustained success and fulfillment.

Building a strong personal brand is another important goal for professional success. A well-defined personal brand clearly communicates your unique value, strengths, and expertise, distinguishing you within your field. Nurturing a positive reputation and highlighting achievements can open doors to new opportunities and accelerate career advancement.

Strong relationships form the backbone of professional success. Relationships cultivated with mentors, colleagues, and industry leaders provide valuable support, guidance, and opportunities. Effective networking is not about the number of connections but about building meaningful, mutually beneficial relationships that foster growth.

Through challenging experiences, resilience and adaptability have been essential for me. The ability to overcome adversity and adjust strategies in response to changing circumstances supports long-term success. Embracing a growth mindset and viewing challenges as opportunities for learning strengthens resilience and motivation.

Self-awareness is another crucial element of personal fulfillment. Understanding your strengths, weaknesses, values, and passions enables intentional decision-making and goal setting. Continuous self-reflection, supported by feedback from others, offers insight into areas where growth is needed.

Contributing to the community through acts of service adds another layer of fulfillment. Giving back fosters purpose and connection while making a positive difference. Volunteering, mentoring, and supporting charitable causes are meaningful ways to enrich both individual lives and society.

Developing emotional intelligence is equally important for personal and professional growth. Awareness and regulation of one's emotions, combined with empathy for others, enhance communication and relationships. A high emotional quotient supports leadership, collaboration, and overall well-being.

Setting healthy boundaries is also essential for maintaining balance between work and personal life. Clear boundaries prevent overcommitment and ensure time for rest, relaxation, and personal interests. This practice promotes productivity, reduces stress, and increases satisfaction.

Gratitude and celebration, both large and small, play a vital role in personal fulfillment. Acknowledging progress and honoring achievements fosters a positive mindset and reinforces motivation. Regular reflection on accomplishments strengthens commitment to goals and makes the journey more rewarding.

In summary, fulfillment is built through clear goal setting, balanced living, continuous learning, and meaningful relationships. When personal development, career success, and societal contribution come together, individuals are able to build well-rounded lives while contributing to a fair and prosperous society.

Let's check in and see how you're doing up to this point.

## Visualization Exercise

Imagine your perfect day five years into the future. What do you do, feel, and experience? Describe this day in vivid detail, focusing on all aspects of your life, including career, relationships, health, and personal fulfillment.

## Journaling Prompt

Reflect on a recent challenge you experienced and successfully overcame. How did you navigate it? What strengths or resources did you draw upon? How does this experience shape your belief in your ability to overcome future obstacles?

## Manifestation Reflection

Consider a goal you are currently working toward. What steps have you taken so far? Which beliefs or attitudes have supported or hindered your progress? In what ways do you need to shift your thinking to better support the realization of this goal?

# CHAPTER 6

## MASTERING THE LAWS OF ATTRACTION, ASSUMPTION, AND THE POWER OF THE WORD

What you are thinking about is activating a
vibration within you.

—Abraham Hicks

The law of attraction, often understood alongside the law of assumption, has gained attention as a framework for understanding how beliefs shape reality. Rather than functioning as a single key to success, it offers insight into the dynamic relationship between thought, belief, and experience. By aligning our thoughts, emotions, and actions with what we seek to manifest, we engage the creative process and begin attracting outcomes that reflect our inner state and intention.

Einstein's theory of relativity, which revolutionized physics, suggests that energy and matter are interchangeable, a concept extended metaphorically in the law of attraction to posit that our thoughts and emotions have vibrational energy that attracts corresponding experiences into our lives.[46] This is a realization that places our power in our own hands: a means to carve our realities by controlling our states of mind and emotion.

These teachings urge us to look beyond superficial desires into the deep connection with our deepest aspirations, which allow for holistic personal growth and transformation. This, I will discuss further in a later chapter. They remind one that this is not a matter of passive acceptance of fate but, rather, of being an active agent in co-creating a life. This perspective invites us to understand and evolve our knowledge about consciousness and its role in manifesting our highest potential.

The law of attraction focuses on visualization and desire while the law of assumption emphasizes living from the identity of fulfillment.

The law of attraction underlines that our thoughts and beliefs have the power to shape reality; thus, when we visualize and feel what we want, we attract it. It reminds us that what we are seeking already exists and, with intention, can be manifested in real life. In contrast, the law of assumption delves into living from the emotion of already having achieved our desires, resonating with the concept of the "I am" and our true identity beyond ego-driven needs. It encourages us to align with our divine selves and embody the state of fulfillment rather than perpetually seeking external validation.

Both laws encourage us to look beyond surface desires and connect more profoundly with ourselves and the power of manifestation. Together, these principles weave into an integrated approach to personal development that goes well beyond simply fulfilling superficial wishes. We develop a deeper connection with ourselves and the unfolding manifestation of our highest selves.

---

46    Rhonda Byrne, *The Secret* (Atria Books/Beyond Words, 2006).

Mastering manifestation involves understanding three key elements. Firstly, our thoughts and emotions play a crucial role in attracting what we desire. Being mindful of these inner states directly influences our ability to manifest. Secondly, it is equally important to maintain positivity and joy about our desires, even when doubt sets in, as this helps maintain a high vibrational frequency that brings more positivity into our lives. Finally, being grateful for what we have creates a sense of abundance that puts our desires in tune with the universe for manifestation.

The power of manifestation is better understood when the realization comes that both the law of attraction and the law of assumption play a major role in it. These principles teach us to embody the feeling of already having our desires fulfilled, aligning with our true selves beyond mere material wants. Strengthening our self-concept and confidence is also crucial, as it fuels our ability to manifest effectively.

Though debated, the law of attraction postulates that our thoughts create our reality. In saying this, if we focus our thoughts on what we want, emitting positive vibrations, we attract certain experiences into our lives. Although this might not have any scientific proof, the idea essentially aligns with the belief that inner thoughts and beliefs manifest in outward reality. Understanding the law of assumption goes deeper, urging us to focus on assuming the reality we desire internally, regardless of external appearances.

This practice runs in complete contrast to the feeling of being determined by the interaction of sensory perception while tuning us to create our reality by means of our inner state and belief systems. Embracing these principles allows one to tap into the mind to manifest a desired reality and a life of fulfillment.

In the case of manifestation, inner dimensions carry more weight than outer perceptions. Our five senses can limit us, making it crucial to quiet them to access our inner power for successful manifestation. By focusing on feelings over material possessions and cultivating positive emotions, we align our vibrations with the universe, attracting abundance and fulfillment. These principles from the law of attraction and the law of vibration guide us to manifest our truest intentions, leading to a purposeful and satisfying life.

Understanding and applying these principles involves trusting in our thoughts and emotions to shape our reality. Despite debates, the law of attraction suggests that by aligning our thoughts with what we desire and emitting positive vibrations, we attract corresponding experiences. Similarly, the law of assumption challenges us to assume the reality we desire internally, regardless of external appearances, thereby influencing our external reality through our inner beliefs.

To harness manifestation effectively, it's vital to practice daily gratitude, visualization, and positivity. These techniques, grounded in psychological strategies like cognitive reframing, empower us to evoke our best selves and attract positive outcomes. Sharing goals with others fosters accountability and opens doors for collaboration and support, enhancing our journey toward success.

In manifesting desires, it's essential to trust in a nonvisible reality beyond sensory perception. This shift allows us to break free from limitations imposed by the physical world and create a different future aligned with our aspirations. By focusing on the end results we desire, such as abundance and happiness, we can use the law of attraction to manifest our dreams, including financial stability and overall well-being.

Through deliberate communication and collaboration, involving others in our journey strengthens our resolve and amplifies manifestation efforts. It's about acknowledging present circumstances while believing in a reality beyond what our senses reveal, ultimately shaping a fulfilling and abundant life.

Understanding the connection between our thoughts and physical well-being empowers us to manifest vibrant health. Utilizing the law of attraction and the law of assumption, we can manifest our dream careers and attract success and abundance. Defining goals and motivations while shifting perspectives and exploring new possibilities is crucial. Visualizing future success and taking action aligns our vibrations with desired outcomes, drawing opportunities into our lives.

Real-life successes like Kabir, inspired by David Copperfield, illustrate how these laws can transform careers. By acting as if our goals have already been achieved, we influence the universe's response to our desires. Many deny their desires due to disbelief in their achievability, entranced by the material world and its illusions. However, affirmations, visualization, and consistent action can break this spell, empowering us to achieve our aspirations.

The law of attraction teaches that our own energy and frequency attract our life experiences, beyond what our senses perceive. Embracing this understanding shifts our perspective from scarcity to abundance, harnessing our creative power to manifest dreams. By behaving as if our desires are already reality and reinforcing positive beliefs, we attract corresponding vibrations. This mindset allows us to tap into our potential and create a life aligned with our deepest desires.

The visualization technique offers a practical approach to attracting desires. Clarity in defining goals, coupled with relaxed visualization and heartfelt gratitude, channels energy toward manifestation. By trusting the universe and letting go of doubt, we open ourselves to receive our dreams. This technique is a proven method for achieving goals and realizing aspirations through dedicated practice and belief in the power of manifestation.

In summary, understanding our ability to shape reality through thought and action empowers us to manifest health, success, and abundance. By embracing these principles and techniques, anyone can unlock their potential to create a fulfilling life aligned with their deepest desires.

The power of manifestation and tapping into our inner selves is a transformative tool that has been utilized by successful individuals throughout history. In today's materialistic society, however, many are hypnotized by external circumstances, limiting their potential for growth. By relying solely on our senses, we become enslaved to the material world, missing out on internal opportunities for change. Techniques like visualization allow us to access our inner selves and manifest our desires, shaping a brighter future.

Personally, I've experienced the profound impact of visualization in my own life, particularly when overcoming challenges like a debilitating back injury diagnosed as a slipped disc and sciatica. My journey with a learning disability further reinforced my belief in visualization's power. It taught me that our thoughts and beliefs profoundly influence our reality. This understanding deepened through experiences where visualization not only improved my health but also attracted opportunities for growth and abundance. It's a practice that requires consistency and belief in its efficacy, transforming lives when embraced wholeheartedly.

The law of attraction and the law of assumption underscore how our thoughts and beliefs shape our reality. Focusing on desires while maintaining positive beliefs can break cycles of negativity and attract positive outcomes. This contrasts sharply with fixating on obstacles, which often leads to disappointment. Real-life examples, such as that of a determined cashier manifesting a directorship through unwavering belief, highlight how attitudes and assumptions can transcend circumstances and manifest dreams.

By harnessing the law of attraction and the law of assumption, we unlock our potential to create the lives we desire. Understanding their principles empowers us to navigate life with positivity, visualizing and attracting what we truly want. Our thoughts have immense power to influence our reality, making it crucial to foster positivity and visualize desired outcomes to manifest them into our lives.

## Divine Communication and Universal Connection

God, the infinite intelligence consciousness, communicates with us through our subconscious mind in various ways. Intuition serves as a form of guidance, offering sudden realizations or gut feelings that direct us without conscious awareness. Dreams are another avenue through which God uses symbols and imagery to convey messages, providing insights and warnings. Through prayer and meditation, we silence the conscious mind, fostering a deeper connection with God and allowing direct communication with our inner mind.

This connection to God and the universe offers unique, personalized communication, guiding us toward understanding our purpose and life's path. It emphasizes our profound interconnectedness with the cosmos and our role in its ongoing evolution. Our thoughts, emotions, and consciousness resonate within this vast web of energy, shaping our reality and influencing our interactions with the universe.

Our existence is intricately tied to the universe, not only from a biological standpoint, but also mentally and spiritually. We depend on Earth's resources for survival, underlining our attachment to the natural rhythms of the universe. Our relationship with the universe is further illuminated through technology, making it easier for anyone to appreciate its mysteries and their place within it.

In embracing our integral part of the universe and greeting it, we open ourselves to infinite possibilities and understand more about our existence. The brain is complex yet powerful, processing information and thoughts that continuously change and interconnect. It serves as a channel through which the universe interacts with us, our means of manifesting desires and fulfilling purpose.

This awareness empowers us to live purposefully, using the brain and spiritual connection to create a fulfilling and influential life. This course underlines the importance of taking care of one's mental and spiritual health and aligning thought and action further with the universal energies molding our reality.

Open discussions within the family about goals and responsibilities bring closeness and harmony, uniting each family member's aspirations toward one purpose. We can support each other in successfully and happily reaching our aspirations together by communicating openly with each other about our dreams and duties. When these conversations are guided by the principles of infinite intelligence, we make decisions in keeping with universal values, leading to a more fulfilling and meaningful life. This helps strengthen family bonds through mutual understanding, which in turn provides an opportunity to grow in a positive way and helps us lead a harmonious and prosperous life.

## Cosmic Consciousness and Parallel Realities Understanding

Cosmic consciousness is an elevated state of awareness where individuals feel a profound sense of interconnectedness with the universe. This state dissolves the boundaries between the self and the external world, leading to a life-changing understanding of one's place in the cosmos. Practices like meditation, self-inquiry, and spiritual awakening can help us access this consciousness, fostering gratitude and humility. For example, a young woman who experienced cosmic consciousness through meditation gained a deeper understanding of her purpose and interconnectedness with all things.

Connecting with cosmic consciousness encourages a greater sense of peace, clarity, and unity. This begins by quieting the mind through meditation and letting go of distractions. By being present and mindful, individuals can tap into universal wisdom. Gratitude and humility play crucial roles in this journey, reminding us of our place in the vast universe. As seen in John's story, his profound meditation experience led to a deeper connection with cosmic consciousness, bringing peace, clarity, and a sense of purpose to his life.

Richard Bucke's work, *Cosmic Consciousness*, underscores the idea that everyone has the potential to transcend their ego and connect with universal consciousness. This state, seen as the pinnacle of human evolution, promotes a heightened awareness of the interconnectedness of all things. Bucke's ideas inspire many to explore beyond their limited perspectives, aiming for unity and a deeper understanding of the universe.

Whether one believes in cosmic consciousness or not, it highlights our interconnectedness and the impact of our actions on the world. It encourages us to think beyond individual experiences and see the broader, interconnected web of existence. This concept challenges us to be more mindful and compassionate, understanding that our thoughts and actions resonate beyond ourselves. Ultimately, cosmic consciousness invites us to explore our inner selves, fostering a deeper understanding of our place in the universe.

## There Are Two Worlds

We live in two worlds: the physical and the spiritual. The physical world, experienced through our senses, is governed by scientific laws and is constantly changing. The spiritual world, on the other hand, is intangible and encompasses our beliefs, values, emotions, and innermost thoughts. These two realms coexist and influence each other, shaping our understanding of ourselves and the world. Embracing both can lead to a more fulfilling and holistic life.

In our everyday lives, we navigate multiple worlds, including the physical and digital realms. The physical world is tangible and experienced through our senses while the digital world, a creation of our minds, is constantly evolving with technological advancements. The digital world has transformed communication, learning, and entertainment, yet it also brings challenges like cyber threats. Balancing these worlds is crucial for a harmonious existence, ensuring we do not neglect one for the other.

## The Interconnectedness of Inner and Outer Actions in Personal Development

This section explores how our thoughts, actions, and well-being interact through the interplay between internal and external activities. Internal activities are those that occur inside one's mind, such as thoughts, feelings, and beliefs, which play a major role in influencing our behaviors and actions. For instance, positive thinking builds resilience in the face of adversity; hence, positive thinking promotes constructive behaviors such as problem-solving. Negative inner dialogue can promote frustration and avoidance, which may be revealed as counterproductive behaviors. Cultivating positive inner actions is therefore essential for enhancing our external actions, fostering healthier interactions, and advancing personal growth.

The important interplay between inner and outer actions arises from the fact that inner self-awareness and premeditated decision-making underpin action. Inner actions include practices such as self-reflection and goal setting that drive outer behaviors because they teach us to establish healthy habits and routines. In turn, outer experiences and interactions ultimately shape inner thoughts and emotions, creating a continuous feedback loop. It is through balancing these dynamics that one can grow as a person and forge strong relationships, which significantly impact our well-being and how others perceive us.

Motivational speaker Richard Hardner explains how inner and outer actions create a profound impact on our consciousness and manifestation. He explains that maintaining higher states of consciousness is necessary for achieving goals effectively. This requires mindfulness and self-awareness to align intentions and aspirations. Hardner offers insight into the inner strength that can turn dreams into reality through improving consciousness and making deliberate choices in thoughts and beliefs.

He also suggests listening to one's muse as a means of realizing creativity. This is achieved by quieting the mind, observing thoughts and feelings without judgment, and considering mistakes as part of the creative process. We reach our creative potential by immersing ourselves in sources of inspiration and activities that challenge the intellect. Hardner's teachings encourage accepting unconventional ideas and embracing a supportive community in which creativity can be expressed authentically.

The relationship between our inner and outer actions and our ability to maintain a higher state of consciousness is key to personal fulfillment and manifestation. As we work toward developing awareness and aligning internal thoughts with external actions, we find it easier to influence our external reality and move toward our goals.

Inner understanding, or self-awareness, refers to a deep awareness of our emotions, thoughts, and beliefs. This knowledge helps us navigate the inner world more effectively and act with intention in the outer world. For example, identifying and working through limiting beliefs can change one's approach to challenges and open new pathways toward goals.

Outer knowledge, or situational awareness, concerns how we perceive and respond to external conditions and interactions. This awareness enables us to act appropriately within our environment and in personal or professional relationships to achieve constructive outcomes. For instance, awareness of others' needs and expectations allows us to build stronger relationships and improve collaboration.

Holistic awareness integrates inner and outer dimensions into a unified experience. This expanded awareness connects internal dynamics with external events, making life more coherent and meaningful. When we understand how internal states affect external environments and vice versa, we can align inner desires with outer achievements.

Inner awareness is a foundational principle in manifesting a fulfilling life. It involves regular self-reflection to recognize core values and aspirations. This clarity supports better decision-making and helps align goals with one's authentic self. Inner awareness lays the foundation for sustained, purposeful action.

Equally important is developing outer awareness, which involves sensitivity to the dynamics of our surroundings and the needs of others. Through empathy and adaptability, we improve our ability to navigate social and professional environments, build meaningful relationships, and recognize opportunities aligned with our goals.

Holistic awareness unifies inner and outer perspectives, allowing for balanced goal achievement. Aligning internal motivation with external opportunity creates cohesive direction toward success. Integrated understanding also helps individuals respond to challenges and utilize available resources effectively.

One of the most important practices for gaining inner understanding is self-reflection. Examining thoughts, emotions, motivations, and actions provides valuable insight into personal growth and development. Self-reflection highlights areas for improvement, supports meaningful goal setting, and aligns actions with core values.

Mindful observation strengthens outer understanding. By attentively observing interactions and external influences, individuals gain insight into effective responses. Mindful observation fosters presence and supports better decision-making for improved personal and professional outcomes.

The integration of inner and outer insights promotes holistic understanding. Combining self-awareness with situational awareness enables strategies that are both personally meaningful and contextually appropriate. This approach supports balanced decision-making and effective goal attainment.

Empathy is another critical component of outer knowledge. Empathy deepens understanding of others' perspectives and needs, fostering supportive and collaborative relationships. Effective communication and cooperation contribute to shared success and satisfaction.

Holistic understanding precedes purposeful action. When internal motivation aligns with external reality, actions become intentional and effective. Purposeful action focuses effort on meaningful fulfillment and success.

Resilience supports the interaction between inner and outer action. It allows individuals to adapt to challenges and setbacks with strength and positivity. This balance enables inner stability and outer flexibility, supporting continued progress toward objectives.

Setting strategic goals integrates inner values with external opportunities. Goals rooted in personal values and aligned with real-world conditions increase motivation, commitment, and attainability.

Continuous learning supports both inner and outer growth. Curiosity, openness to experience, and skill development enhance adaptability and innovation. Lifelong learning strengthens both personal and professional development.

Ultimately, integrating inner and outer awareness is central to personal growth and a fulfilling life. By cultivating self-awareness, situational understanding, and holistic perspective, individuals align internal motivations with external realities, resulting in meaningful and satisfying accomplishment.

## Reprogramming the Subconscious Mind

Reprogramming the subconscious mind can profoundly change one's life. It means the deliberate implantation of empowering beliefs into our inner mind through effective techniques such as affirmations, prayer, visualization, and hypnosis. We have to resolve and conquer the limiting habits that were developed in our childhood years, and we have to rebuild a new self for a better future. This will be highly rewarding, though quite demanding. The commitment to such a change enables us to rise to our fullness and experience a happier and more successful life.

One of the most powerful methods for reprogramming the inner mind involves the emotional freedom technique (EFT). EFT combines aspects of acupressure with cognitive therapy to treat emotional blockages. It entails the identification of the issue at hand, formulating a setup statement that recognizes the problem yet affirms self-love, and then tapping certain designated meridian points with positive affirmations. This process may bring about emotional healing and positive life changes.

Reprogramming the inner mind is also about reflecting on oneself to weed out and work through deeply ingrained negative beliefs and thoughts. These can be replaced by visualizing positive affirmations and reinforcing them through repetition. Other ways of rewiring the inner mind include hypnosis, meditation, mindfulness, and journaling. Although this is a time-consuming process and requires one to be patient and not give up too easily, it can create profound personal transformation and increase fulfillment.

This reprogramming may also be supported by surrounding oneself with positive influences and being more mindful of one's thoughts. Other effective techniques may involve neurolinguistic programming. One can break these negative patterns and build a more positive, empowering mindset with consistency and determination.

The reprogramming of one's inner mind is done in such a way that still pays respect to the infinite intelligence, for example, infinite intelligent consciousness, Jehovah, God, or the Holy Spirit. Recognizing that the spirit of God resides within us, we can use this process to live a fulfilling life guided by divine power. This requires self-awareness, determination, and faith, allowing us to let go of illusions of control and trust in the greater plan. Embracing this divine power within helps us tap into our highest potential and fulfill our purpose, leading to a life filled with love, growth, and purpose.

# The Power of Our Subconscious Mind

Neville Goddard posits that Jesus Christ symbolizes our subconscious mind, decoded through ancient symbols.[47] He teaches that understanding these symbols—JOD for creation, HE for life, VAU for man, and HE for divine feminine—empowers us to manifest desires through practices like visualization and positive thinking.[48] This view aligns with Earl Nightingale[49] and Napoleon Hill,[50] who advocate harnessing the subconscious mind's power for personal success. They emphasize replacing limiting beliefs with positive affirmations and aligning thoughts with goals to shape a fulfilling reality.

The subconscious mind, influencing our thoughts and actions, is likened to a garden where beliefs grow into reality.[51] Techniques like affirmations and visualization reprogram it, enabling us to overcome fears and achieve our potential. These concepts resonate with biblical teachings emphasizing the role of thoughts in shaping our lives.[52] Verses like Proverbs 23:7[53] and Romans 12:2[54] highlight the importance of renewing our minds with positive beliefs, aligning them with spiritual growth.[55]

Our internal mind's power extends beyond personal growth, shaping our reality through thoughts and beliefs. Harnessing this

---

47    Goddard, *Feeling is the Secret.*

48    Ibid.

49    Nightingale, *The Strangest Secret.*

50    Hill, *Think and Grow Rich.*

51    Murphy, *The Power of Your Subconscious Mind.*

52    Walpola Rahula, *What the Buddha Taught* (Grove Press, 1959).

53    Proverbs 23:7, *The Holy Bible* (KJV).

54    Romans 12:2, *The Holy Bible* (KJV).

55    Mitch Horowitz, *The Miracle Club: How Thoughts Become Reality* (Inner Traditions, 2018).

power, the late Neville Goddard,[56] Earl Nightingale,[57] and Napoleon Hill[58] were of the opinion that this enables one to rise above challenges, building success in one's personal and professional life. This inborn enabler to shape one's destiny, rooted in the field of one's thoughts and beliefs, underlines the capacity to create a meaningful life aligned with purpose and potential. Harnessing the power of our minds through creation manifestation allows us to shape our reality and fulfill our innate desires for existence and purpose in the universe.[59] This concept projects that through visualization and belief in our goals, combined with inspired action, anything desired can be manifested into reality. However, it is of high importance to take responsibility for our thoughts and our actions because negative thinking does manifest outcomes undesired.[60] By focusing on positivity and intentional action, we can make deep changes in our lives and offer positive construction to the universe.

Jeremiah 29:11 reminds us that God's plans are for peace and a bright future[61]; hence, we must make sure that our goals in life articulate with the call to serve a higher purpose. This binds well in the way we pursue financial success and personal fulfillment. The guidance emphasizes unlocking our full potential and steering clear of complacency, which is like letting ourselves become stagnant and unhappy. It pushes us to continue reaching for more and keep

---

56   Goddard, *Feeling is the Secret*.

57   Nightingale, *The Strangest Secret*.

58   Hill, *Think and Grow Rich*.

59   Murphy, *The Power of Your Subconscious Mind*.

60   David R. Hawkins, *Power vs. Force: The Hidden Determinants of Human Behavior* (Hay House, 1995).

61   Jeremiah 29:11, The Holy Bible, English Standard Version (ESV).

on growing, embracing our natural ability to achieve and find true happiness.[62]

Understanding the principles of abundant prosperity and financial freedom is one of the main keys to designing a well-rounded life. It not only requires breaking free from chains of negativity but also proactive approaches toward wealth and success. By teaching ourselves and our future generations about the importance of financial stability and self-sufficiency, we are providing them with a shield of armor to face challenges and establish a sound future. This being proactive will ensure personal stability and will show positivity in our contribution to community life and further to the world in general.

Basically, it means that by embracing our inner power and learning how the creation and manifestation process works, we not only create a better life but also contribute to making the world a better place for all people. It's about realizing our potential, taking intentional steps toward what we want, and encouraging others to do the same. All these processes of personal and collective fulfillment underscore the great power of every thought and action in shaping an existence that answers the best hopes of our souls.

## Prosperity-Conscious Mindset

Understanding the power of thoughts and beliefs is crucial in harnessing the conscious mind to create wealth. Setting clear financial goals and developing a strategic plan are essential steps guided by the conscious mind's decision-making capabilities.

Rich individuals build lasting wealth by adhering to fundamental money principles often overlooked by others. Paying oneself first, living

---

62   Mitch Horowitz, *The Miracle Club: How Thoughts Become Reality* (Inner Traditions, 2018).

below one's means, and prioritizing investments over unnecessary spending are key strategies. This disciplined approach ensures financial stability and paves the way for building assets rather than liabilities. It's about making money work for you through high-yielding, secure investments and creating passive income streams.

Emotional discipline plays a significant role. Avoiding debt and unnecessary expenditures allows individuals to maintain financial independence. Living frugally and debt-free, rather than impressing others with material possessions, is critical in achieving long-term wealth. By implementing these principles consistently, individuals can secure their financial future and live abundantly.

The mindset of prosperity involves envisioning oneself already in possession of desired wealth and success. By visualizing and believing in this reality, individuals imprint these goals deep into their subconscious. Wealthy individuals don't harbor negative associations with money; instead, they cultivate a mindset of abundance and opportunity. Developing a prosperity consciousness involves aligning thoughts, emotions, and beliefs to attract wealth effortlessly.

In essence, mastering the conscious mind's role in wealth creation involves adopting positive beliefs, disciplined financial habits, and a clear vision for prosperity. By integrating these practices into daily life, individuals can manifest their financial goals and live a life of abundance and fulfillment.

"If you do not see great riches in your imagination, you will never see them in your bank account" (Napoleon Hill, *Think and Grow Rich*).

The influence that the inner mind plays in the manifestation of wealth comes from the fact that it cannot differentiate between real experiences and what it envisions. Through constant visions of yourself as a person of success, you can train your inner mind to embrace the positivity such beliefs bring. First, it starts by convincing yourself that you can be successful, and through this, the inner mind will seek and pursue opportunities that fall in line with this philosophy. Although this may sound a little unorthodox, many scientific studies support the fact that our inner mind can produce physical results through our thoughts and emotions.

Throughout history, remarkable inventions have stemmed from individuals harnessing the power of their imagination. John Ericsson's ironclad warship, Philo Farnsworth's electronic television system, Henry Ford and William Durant's gasoline automobile, and Willis Carrier's air conditioner are testaments to human creativity and innovation. These inventors tapped into their God-given talents and imaginative abilities to create what seemed impossible to many. They serve as examples of how the mind, when focused and inspired, can conceive and materialize groundbreaking ideas that benefit society.

The essence of creation lies within each of us, rooted in the same source that brought everything into existence. By quieting the mind and tapping into this creative potential, individuals can envision solutions and innovations that not only generate personal profit but also serve the greater good. Oprah Winfrey's words, "God, use me for a purpose greater than myself," resonate deeply with this concept of using one's talents to benefit humanity. Our true calling and purpose, therefore, lie in using our inner mind to create solutions that uplift and empower others, thereby contributing to collective prosperity and fulfillment.

"Nothing is impossible. The word itself says, 'I'm possible'" (Audrey Hepburn).

# The Power of Imagination in Innovation and Manifestation

The history of human innovation, such as William Bourne's early submarine plans and Cornelius Drebbel's first working prototype, underscores the power of imagination in creating what was once considered impossible. This creative force is rooted in the idea that everything, as stated in biblical and scientific perspectives, originates from energy and internal mind. The biblical notion of creation speaks of the void being filled with God's spirit, emphasizing that all physical existence evolves from nonphysical energy into tangible matter. This understanding posits that our ability to visualize and believe in the unseen is pivotal in manifesting our desires.

Throughout history, engineers and inventors, including African Americans during times of adversity like slavery, have demonstrated remarkable creativity and perseverance. They utilized their passion to innovate despite challenging circumstances, affirming the human potential to create solutions that benefit society. This creative drive is inherent in humanity, bestowed upon us by a divine source, empowering us to shape our reality through ingenuity and belief in the limitless possibilities of existence.

Key to this process is the fostering of a mindset of faith and belief in self and one's ideas. As Napoleon Hill said with reckless abandon, "Thoughts become things," and here, focused intention intertwined with positive thinking has created numerous successes. This connects again to biblical teaching about love, commanding to love God and to love one's neighbor, and spiritual principles intertwine with personal and societal prosperity.

Practical steps include mindfulness, where individuals observe and redirect negative thoughts toward positive outcomes, fostering a mindset of abundance rather than scarcity. This is the basic shift in consciousness necessary for a person to transcend restrictive thought patterns and allow them to realize their truest and fullest potential. By focusing one's thoughts and actions in a manner inspired by love, gratitude, and compassion, anyone can raise their consciousness to manifest their highest ideals and, in that process, serve their own fulfillment and the higher good of humankind.

## Proven Strategies to Multimillionaire Status

Achieving wealth without a substantial starting sum involves focusing on skill development, leveraging opportunities, and prudent financial management. Continuous learning and networking can also enable people to create streams of income through side hustles or small businesses. Frugal living, coupled with disciplined saving, enables investment in assets that generate passive income, thus fostering long-term financial growth. This path demands persistence and dedication but offers a viable route to wealth creation for those committed to personal and financial development.

Success in financial goals necessitates clear objectives and unwavering dedication. Building marketable skills and expanding knowledge are crucial steps toward financial empowerment. Cultivating relationships with influential figures and managing finances wisely are equally important. Embracing a positive mindset, taking calculated risks, and maintaining discipline in spending and investment strategies are fundamental. Aligning personal actions with aspirations and visualizing success are keys to manifesting financial dreams. It is a journey that requires commitment, resilience, and focused pursuit of prosperity.

Success within this journey requires strategic planning, disciplined execution, and continuous education on personal finance and market dynamics. It requires persistence through setbacks and flexibility amid economic changes. Stephen King's road to success, especially with his novel *Carrie*, depicts the transformational power of creative perseverance and strategic risk-taking. These experiences have taught him to inspire others with lessons that challenge conventional wisdom and pursue strategies leading to financial stability and personal satisfaction on a sustainable basis. King's advance of $2,500 for *Carrie*, which later earned him $400,000 from paperback rights, shows how significant rewards can come from perseverance in creative efforts.

Napoleon Hill, author of *Think and Grow Rich*; J. K. Rowling, one of the most celebrated authors of the *Harry Potter* series; and Amanda Hocking, a self-publishing success story, are figures from history to the present day whose legacies demonstrate persistence, foresight, and resilience in creating extraordinary success. Hocking's story, in which her initial goal of $300 for a *Muppets* trip turned into $2.5 million from self-publishing, inspires others to forge their own paths to financial success and personal fulfillment.

This is what my story looks like—how I became a billionaire.

Clemer Leggett's journey toward financial success is truly filled with determination, hard work, and a clear vision for the future. Growing up poor, Leggett learned the value of a dollar early in life. Instead of allowing that circumstance to define him, he used it as motivation to make a better life for himself. Starting from humble beginnings and working several jobs, every penny he saved later became an initial investment in personal development and education. Throughout the years, through continuous learning and strategic networking, Leggett rose up the corporate ladder before striking out on his own.

# The Power of "I AM"

The power of "I am" is huge in our lives; it's a reminder that whatever we put out into the world, we become. Our thoughts and words shape our entire existence. We need to pay great attention to our inner dialogue. Positive affirmations such as "I am strong," "I am capable," and "I am worthy" enhance self-confidence and self-esteem while negative thoughts make one feel limited. When we decide to believe in ourselves and finally speak positively, we are able to intentionally create a life filled with joy, success, and fulfillment.

This again reminds us that our thoughts and words are not just passing thoughts, but they build reality. This quote about the power of "I am" is a counsel of great importance in our lives, and one that will continue to be. This is the belief that whatever we put out into the world, we become. Our thoughts and words have great power, and as we think of ourselves, so we are in our whole being. We should be reminded that our thoughts and words are not transitory but that we may not always know the heights to which they can lift us and the depths to which they can lower us.

It's a reminder that we must remain aware of our inner dialogue, as well as the words we speak because they literally frame our reality. The power of "I am," however, inspires us to be responsible for our actions and to promote a very strong sense of self-worth and confidence. Consciously choosing to believe in oneself and positively speaking about oneself opens up the doorway to a life of success, fulfillment, and joy. It reminds us that we have the power to create our reality through our thoughts and words, and it's up to us to use that power for our highest good.

With positive affirmations, we make use of the power of "I am" to create a completely different mindset. On the other hand, negative self-talk is degrading and makes us feel diminished in self-esteem. The power of "I am" also has an effect on how others view us, thus enabling us to be an inspiration to others and to influence their lives. In the end, this phrase shapes our thoughts, beliefs, and actions, leading us toward a life of fulfillment and authenticity.

The creative and innovative thinker in me develops these ideas into tangible reality competently, with proper planning, effective communication, and diligent execution. I break down concepts into smaller tasks and collaborate with my team, using all available resources to enhance our ideas. Being organized, adaptable, and collaborative is how I believe our ideas will exceed expectations and leave a mark on the target audience.

The phrase "I am" holds immense significance in both religious and historical contexts. Moses used "I am" as an identification statement and purpose, proclaiming a belief in his own self-evaluation and connectedness to God. It was a powerful statement from God, whereby He introduced Himself to Moses at the burning bush, establishing and sealing Moses's authority and determination to lead the Israelites out of slavery.

Most successful celebrities mention the phrase "I am" in their speeches, which reveals confidence, determination, and a strong drive to achieve their goals. Because they keep telling themselves who they are becoming, they stay focused and motivated in their careers. This also depicts humility and appreciation for their success and keeps reminding them that they are in control. By embedding "I am" into their conversations, these celebrities have inspired others and continue to inspire themselves toward greater heights.

## Setting Goals: The Magic

Long-term and short-term goal setting were taught in college, followed by prioritization in order to understand which goals needed attention first. It also requires the discipline of revisiting and adjusting them as new aspirations emerge. Discovering one's purpose is exciting, as it leads to a joyful life where you appreciate the natural flow of achievements manifesting from your written goals. Witnessing my goals materialize was both gratifying and surprising.

By converting goals into specific, measurable, and objective desires with certainty, I found that the internal hidden mind actively seeks solutions and pathways to achieve these aims.

Studies support this, showing that setting clear targets activates the subconscious to find the necessary means to reach them. Here are some powerful Bible verses that can help you find your identity and purpose. The Lord says, "Before I formed you in the womb I knew you, before you were born, I set you apart; I appointed you as a prophet to the nations." This means that even before you were born, God already had a purpose and plan for you. The infinite intelligence endowed you with versatility and ordained a path for your life. By writing down your goals and setting timelines, you align with this divine blueprint and manifest plans ordained by God.

Ephesians 1:9 reads, "God made known to us the mystery of his will according to his good pleasure, which he proposed in Christ." This means that God's works are accomplished through our inner mind, interlinked with the infinite intelligence of the universe, God Himself. Philippians 2:5–7 says, "In your relationships with one another, have the same mindset as Christ Jesus, who, being in very nature God, did not consider equality with God something to be used to his own advantage; rather, he made himself nothing by taking the very nature of a servant, being made in human likeness." It explains the mindset that should be considered when striving to live in a Christlike way.

Goal setting is necessary in order to be successful; goals should vary between short-term and long-term ones. Starting small can be a practical approach to achieving financial independence. Consider acquiring skills in various fields such as YouTube channel creation, business marketing, graphic design, real estate, and more. These can be started with relatively small capital investments and, in turn, create wealth that allows you to chase bigger dreams, such as publishing books or creating something of value for society. With strategic planning and building on a solid foundation, you can become independent and successful.

## The Power of an Idea

The power of an idea is simply incredible; it may shape our beliefs, influence our actions, and even alter the course of history. Ideas might inspire revolutions, great inventions, or social change. Whether simple or complex, abstract or concrete, an idea stirs and compels us toward the realization of goals. An idea is an igniter. Starting as a thought inside the mind, it can be nurtured into something much greater, believed in, and take on dimensions of its own, cutting across boundaries and binding people from all walks of life, across diverse backgrounds and cultures.

The power of an idea lies in inspiring people and giving them the drive to act. From the invention of the wheel to landing on the moon, everything significant that has happened in the history of mankind started with an idea. An idea is powerful, and how we choose to use it for the betterment of humanity depends upon us.

Ideals are very often considered unattainable standards or goals that one strives to reach. The influences on ideals come from personal experiences, cultural influences, and societal norms. Personal experiences, such as upbringing, education, and engagement with other people, are major influences from which an individual's ideals take shape. Equally important in building ideals are those stemming from cultural influences, including religion, traditions, and values.

These factors help individuals develop beliefs and principles that guide their actions and decisions. Societal norms and expectations further shape ideals, as people often conform to standards to be accepted and respected by others. Over time, these personal, cultural, and societal factors come together to shape an individual's ideals, which can vary greatly from person to person. Ideals can also evolve and change as individuals experience new things and are exposed to different perspectives. The creation of ideals is a complex process unique to each individual and continues to evolve throughout their lifetime.

How has it been going so far?

Let's keep up with the daily journaling, affirmations, and visualizations, from exploring the power of ideas to manifesting our goals and opening up to limitless possibilities. Before moving on to the next chapter, though, let me ask you a few questions:

1. How have the personal experiences recorded in your daily journal, along with those influenced by culture, contributed to the ideals you visualize and manifest? Reflect upon a time when your visualization created a key achievement in your personal life.

2.  What are some of the most powerful ideas you have affirmed
    in your journal that have inspired or motivated you toward
    your goals? How does writing these affirmations nurture and
    develop those ideas?

3.  How do you actively engage the power of visualization and
    daily affirmations to channel your ideals into actual positive
    changes in your life and in the lives of those around you?
    Reflect on these visualizations in light of what you have
    written in your journal.

# CHAPTER 7

# Consciousness and the Symphony of Subconscious Manifestation

The only person you are destined to become is the person you decide to be.

—Ralph Waldo Emerson

Think of your consciousness as the conductor of an orchestra, where every thought, emotion, and belief functions as an instrument. Together, these elements create a rhythm that shapes the reality you experience. The subconscious mind, often overlooked, operates in the background as the foundation of this orchestra, determining whether the overall harmony is balanced or discordant.

In this chapter, we explore the essential roles that consciousness and the subconscious mind play as they work together to shape clarity, purpose, and fulfillment.

Often, these systems operate on autopilot, driven by ingrained mental programming that has developed over many years, if not decades. With increased awareness of these inner processes, you will start identifying specific limiting beliefs. These are deeply rooted and often affect your life almost subliminally.

You need to raise them into the conscious arena where they can be looked at, doubted, and replaced with more enabling beliefs that are in tune with what you really want. It is through such self-discovery that the foundation is laid securely, in balance with conscious intention and the inner mind.

The power of consciousness lies in its ability to illuminate these hidden layers, helping us to see beyond the surface level of everyday thoughts and reactions. Awareness is the first step in manifesting the life of your dreams. The first steps toward awakening to your true potential start with learning how to question the assumptions you have about yourself and about the world. Lasting change begins when subconscious beliefs are brought into conscious awareness, questioned, and deliberately replaced with more empowering perspectives.

Once these limiting beliefs have been recognized and addressed, the inner mind needs to be rewired in congruence with your conscious intentions. Effective methods such as visualization and affirmations go a long way in doing so. By practicing these regularly, you will be able to instill new, positive belief patterns into your inner mind. While changing thought patterns does help, it is also necessary that, for true transformation to take place, one must take consistent action in the physical world.

You create a feedback loop between your thoughts and your actions through purposeful steps toward your goals, reinforcing the new beliefs that you are cultivating. It is a continuous process, requiring ongoing reflection and readjustment so your inner and outer worlds may remain in harmony with the ongoing manifestation of a life of abundance, purpose, and fulfillment that you envision.

## Consciousness: The Conductor of Your Reality

Consciousness is the part of you that is aware, alert, and actively making choices. Consider it as the conductor in your metaphorical orchestra, directing which notes are playing, when, and how they should sound. It is the place where deliberate thought occurs, where your choices, your intentions are set, and where your attention is directed.

However, it is not consciousness alone that creates your reality. It is very important to set intentions and direct your attention with your consciousness, but it is your subconscious mind that truly conducts the symphony and manifests those thoughts into physical form. In short, the difference between the two levels of the mind, the conscious and the subconscious, is a very important one for a person to be aware of when manifesting.

You can think of consciousness as being multilayered, somewhat like an iceberg. The visible tip serves as a symbol of your surface consciousness, representing the things that you are immediately aware of within your thoughts and perceptions. Beneath that tip, however, lies a large, complex network composed of subconscious beliefs, memories, and patterns, driving nearly every decision you make, mostly without your even realizing it.

It is the journey of taking responsibility for one's internal orchestra, ensuring that all the instruments, each belief, thought, and feeling, are in harmony with creating the symphony of a life one truly desires to live. Through this awareness, one becomes more capable of manifesting dreams and living a life that resonates with one's true self.

# The Subconscious Mind: The Hidden Maestro

If your consciousness is the conductor, then your subconscious mind is the orchestra itself. It's the silent, unseen force that drives your habits, behaviors, and ultimately, the reality you experience. The subconscious mind is where the real magic happens, as it is responsible for about 95 percent of your mental activity, quietly controlling everything from your heartbeat to your deepest, most ingrained beliefs about life.

While your conscious mind can direct your attention and set intentions, the subconscious mind is where true transformation takes place. This hidden maestro is home to all your beliefs, habits, and emotions, which, in turn, shape the quality of your life. Every automatic action you take, every instinctive response you have, stems from this powerful part of your mind.

To manifest the life you desire, you must learn to work with, not against, your subconscious mind. It's not enough to consciously want change; you need to engage with the subconscious beliefs that drive your behavior. These beliefs have often been ingrained over years, sometimes without your awareness, and they are what determine whether you move forward or stay stuck in old patterns.

Think of your subconscious mind as a vast, fertile field. Your conscious thoughts are the seeds you plant, but it's the subconscious that determines how those seeds will grow.

My journey, as discussed in this book, illustrates this process vividly. I recognized that my subconscious mind was initially filled with limiting beliefs that held me back, despite my conscious efforts to succeed. It wasn't until I began to address these underlying issues, reprogramming my subconscious with new, empowering beliefs, that I experienced profound personal and financial transformation. My story serves as a powerful reminder that to create lasting change in your life, you must dig deep into your subconscious and cultivate the beliefs that align with the life you truly want.

By aligning your conscious desires with the deep-seated programming of your subconscious mind, you can unlock your full potential. This means regularly feeding your mind with positive affirmations, visualizations, and practices that reinforce the new, desired patterns. It's about creating a partnership between your conscious and subconscious minds, where both work together to produce the symphony of a fulfilled and abundant life.

## The Role of Beliefs and Programming

From the moment you are born, your subconscious mind begins to absorb information, creating the foundation of your beliefs and behaviors. Every experience, every word spoken to you, and every emotion you feel are recorded and stored within your subconscious. These recordings, over time, shape the beliefs that guide your actions and reactions. For example, if you grew up hearing that money is scarce and hard to come by, this belief likely became deeply embedded in your subconscious. As a result, it might influence how you perceive opportunities, manage your finances, and even how you view your potential for wealth.

These beliefs, formed during your formative years, often operate in the background, influencing your life without your conscious awareness. They can either propel you toward success or hold you back from achieving your full potential. The challenge is that many of these beliefs were not consciously chosen by you; they were inherited from your family, your culture, and your early experiences. They might have served a purpose at one time, but as you grow and your desires evolve, these old patterns can become obstacles.

The key to manifesting the life you desire lies in identifying and reprogramming the subconscious beliefs. This process of reprogramming involves more than just positive thinking; it is about deep, intentional work. This is not a simple task; it requires both awareness and a deep willingness to confront and change the patterns that no longer serve you. Reprogramming the subconscious requires intentional practices that replace limiting beliefs with empowering ones.

My journey, as illustrated in my personal development work, shows the transformative power of challenging and changing these deep-seated patterns. I recognized that much of my initial struggle stemmed from subconscious beliefs that I had absorbed from my environment; beliefs about money, success, and self-worth. By bringing these beliefs to the surface and consciously reprogramming them, I was able to create a new reality for myself, one that aligned with my true desires and potential.

As you begin this journey, remember that change doesn't happen overnight. Reprogramming your subconscious is a gradual process, but with persistence, you'll start to see shifts in how you think, feel, and ultimately, how you live. By challenging the beliefs that have held you back and choosing to create new ones, you open the door to a life that truly reflects your deepest desires and fullest potential.

## Techniques for Reprogramming the Subconscious

1. Affirmation and visualization: Through repetition, affirmations can help replace negative beliefs with positive ones; likewise, visualizing desired results can help override

a negative mindset. Since repetition works well with the subconscious mind, the more one practices these techniques, the more effective they become.

2.  Meditation and mindfulness: Through meditation, you can tap into deeper levels of the mind; it is where you are able to observe and change subconscious patterns of behavior. Mindfulness does much the same work, but in real time. While meditation is a reflection on what has already passed, mindfulness is being present and aware of your thoughts and reactions in the moment, allowing you to choose how to respond differently.

3.  Emotional healing: Emotions are the language of the subconscious mind. Through the healing of past emotional traumas, you can release trapped negative energy within the subconscious and replace it with empowering, positive emotions that serve your goals.

## The Symphony in Action: Manifesting Your Desires

Now, by understanding how one's consciousness interrelates with the deeper mind, the inner symphony can be harnessed to manifest the reality one desires. The entire process involves aligning your conscious intent with underlying mental programming so that both function in perfect harmony, creating the life you envision.

As you have learned, your consciousness functions as the conductor, guiding your intentions and focus toward your goals. However, it is in your deeper mind, the hidden inner maestro, that the significant work of shaping your habits, beliefs, and behaviors takes place. For the manifestation of your desires, it is crucial that these two elements are in alignment. If your conscious mind desires something, but your deeper mind holds conflicting beliefs, it's like attempting to perform a symphony with out-of-tune instruments. The result is dissonant, and life can feel misaligned with your true aspirations.

I want to underline here that success in manifestation lies exactly in such alignment. Quite often, I was really surprised by how my subconscious beliefs managed to defeat my conscious efforts for many years, that is, until I began the conscious work of reprogramming my subconscious mind by challenging and changing all those deep-seated patterns that were holding me back. It was then that the manifestation of the life I wanted really started.

Set crystal-clear, conscious intentions to activate your symphony: Know exactly what you want to create in your life. Be specific and deliberate about the goals you set because your subconscious mind will respond to clarity. Then, harmonize these intentions with your unconscious beliefs. This can be done through daily affirmations, visualizations, and meditation practices to further reinforce the new constructive beliefs you're cultivating. The more this is practiced, the more your mind will start to fall in line with your conscious wants.

Remember, this process requires patience and persistence. Much like perfecting a symphony, it also takes time for the mind to properly align. But with consistent effort, you will start to see results, first small shifts, then much larger, more profound changes as your inner and outer worlds begin to harmonize. As Leggett says, it's about much more than external success; it is about living a life in tune with oneself where all parts are playing their note.

Through these steps, you literally become the conductor of your life, orchestrating every thought, belief, and action into one symphony so that your desired reality can take form. This is manifestation, the creation of a life truly reflective of who you are and want to be. As you continue to hone your inner symphony, you find that the outer world naturally reflects the harmony within—thus, a purposeful, fulfilling, abundant life ensues.

## Setting Clear Intentions

Manifestation starts with clear intention. The clarity of your conscious mind regarding what you intend to bring into your life is the sheet music for your symphony, serving as a blueprint that your subconscious mind will follow. Setting an intention, clear and specific, is so important that it is considered the backbone of any desire.

As I always say, clarity is crucial. When you are clear about what you want, you provide your deeper mind with a precise target. This is not the moment for vague desires or incomplete concepts. You need to state exactly what you want to achieve, whether it be financial success, personal growth, or deeper relationships. The more detailed and vivid your intention, the easier it will be for your deeper mind to understand and work toward those goals.

But that is not all. Your intentions should also align with the deepest values and desires of your heart. Without deep, reflective consideration of whether your goals are a genuine expression of what you want or believe in, you will find it hard to cultivate the focus and energy necessary for manifestation. Through his journey, Leggett has found that once intentions are congruent with core values, they tend to grow in strength and momentum. This alignment creates a powerful synergy between your conscious desires and your subconscious programming, which results in more effective and sustainable manifestation.

First, to have clear intentions, ask yourself what you really want and why. Be thorough in examining your motives so that your desires are not shaped by external pressures or temporary fancies. Write them down in detail and place them somewhere where you can view them often. Allow these intentions to remain visible, as this practice places your goals at the forefront of your mind, helping to imprint them into the subconscious.

When your intentions are clear and aligned, your manifestation process becomes more effective. As you set your intentions, let the first note of your symphony guide the entire composition of your life. With this blueprint clear, the inner mind can take over, orchestrating the steps, thoughts, and opportunities necessary to bring into life that which is desired.

## Aligning Subconscious Beliefs with Conscious Goals

Once your intentions have been set, the second most important thing to do is to align your inner mind with those conscious decisions. While it is quite easy to proclaim what you want on a conscious level, plunging deep into the inner mind, the place where your core beliefs and habits lie, is where the real work begins. When this doesn't happen, and your subconscious beliefs are not in agreement with your intentions, resistance will most likely manifest through self-sabotage, procrastination, or even fear.

As I always say, this is where most people get stuck. You consciously may be determined to achieve a certain goal, but deep inside, your unconscious mind may be running on obsolete programming that conflicts with your efforts. Perhaps you were brought up to believe that one can only have success after sacrificing a lot, or that you do not deserve to have much. These perceptions, resulting from your upbringing and conditioning, can build significant inner resistance to the very things you try to manifest.

The first step in bridging this gap is to go back and reassess those subconscious patterns that you have identified, examining how they match up against your new intentions. Start with your feelings about your goals: Are you feeling excited and confident about them, or do you find yourself reopening the door to fear and doubt? These feelings can be indicative of where your inner mind might still be holding onto limiting beliefs.

My personal journey illustrates this process. I had to dig deep into my own inner mind to uncover beliefs that were sabotaging my success. Only by addressing those beliefs directly was I able to clear the path for my conscious goals to take shape.

Shifting these deep-seated beliefs requires consistent effort. Begin by using affirmations that directly counter your old beliefs.

For example, if your unconscious mind firmly believes that you do not deserve success, your affirmation should begin like this: "I deserve all the good things life has in store." Another critical concept here is visualization. Create in your mind a clear image of what your life looks like as if you are already living in the fulfillment of your goals. Through repetition and emotional engagement, these practices help rewire your subconscious mind, replacing limiting beliefs with ones that support your intentions.

This alignment process takes time and patience, but it's essential for removing the inner resistance that blocks manifestation. When your subconscious beliefs and conscious goals finally align, you'll notice that you can move with more ease and flow toward what you want. It's not like you'll be fighting yourself anymore. Everything will start to fall into place: Thoughts, actions, and opportunities will support the life that you want to create.

## The Power of Consistency and Persistence

Manifestation is not a point-in-time event; it is a process that takes a great deal of consistency and persistence. Of course, you cannot set an intention and get instant results. The magic behind manifestation lies in being consistent enough to renew your intentions time and again and in patiently programming and reprogramming your inner hidden mind. This is where, more often than not, the journey can get really arduous, and it's where far too many people give up if their hoped-for results do not materialize immediately.

I have learned through my own experience that the subconscious mind does not change overnight. It's just like planting a seed: You need to water it regularly even though, from the outside, it looks like nothing is happening. Your hidden mind has been programmed over years, probably decades, and so it takes its sweet time to absorb the new lessons and follow the new instructions. That's why consistency is so important.

The more frequent you are with affirmations, visualization, and meditation, the more solid the new programming you seek to install will be. Another important factor to consider is persistence. There will be times when doubt creeps in, when progress seems slow, and one may even feel tempted to abandon the process completely. But this is where you will need to dig in and persist. I always say the outcome that you want may be just around the corner, but if you quit too soon, you will never know it. It's in those times of challenge that your persistence pays off greatly.

Look at your efforts like running a marathon and not a sprint.

Manifestation is all about staying on course and committed, even though the finishing line isn't in view or even anywhere near in sight. Every time you utter affirmations, visualize your goals, and take action toward your dreams, you are closer to your goals, even if you cannot see this right away. The tiniest step serves as a notice to your mind that you really mean business about your intention, and little by little, such steady effort develops, and it pays off in real, concrete results.

Also, be patient. The subconscious mind takes time to change and believe in new goals. Be easy on yourself as you undergo this process; remember, not everything works according to plan, which is how life works. My story is a testament to the power of staying the course. I didn't achieve my success overnight but through years of persistent effort and unwavering commitment to my goals.

Eventually, these two elements of consistency and persistence build powerful momentum. Every time you practice consistency, you ensure that a strong base is built, which will support the materialization of your desires. Remember, it may be a long journey, but every day spent reinforcing intention brings you closer to living the life you want.

Don't underestimate the power of showing up, day in and day out, trusting the process. Your patience and persistence will then be reflected in the blossoming of your intentions.

## Overcoming Obstacles and Challenges

Even with the clearest intentions and the most diligent subconscious reprogramming, challenges are inevitable. These obstacles are not indicators of failure; rather, they are opportunities for growth and refinement. Every challenge you encounter is like a mirror reflecting an unconscious belief that still needs your attention. By confronting these challenges directly, you can continue to fine-tune your inner symphony, ensuring that it plays in perfect harmony with your deepest desires.

I would like to remind us that life's difficulties are not meant to derail us; they are meant to guide us. When you face a challenge, it is an invitation to look within and ask yourself what belief or pattern might be causing this resistance. Perhaps it is an old fear that you have not fully addressed, or maybe it is a doubt that is lingering just beneath the surface. These challenges are your unconscious mind's way of signaling that there is still work to be done.

Instead of seeing obstacles as roadblocks, begin to view them as valuable feedback. They are there to help you grow—to push you toward a deeper understanding of yourself and your desires. My experience was filled with setbacks and challenges, but each one offered me a chance to dig deeper into my inner awareness, to identify and release the beliefs that were holding me back. Through this process, I was able to strengthen my alignment with my goals and ultimately achieve success.

When you encounter a challenge, take a moment to pause and reflect. What is this situation trying to teach you? What belief might be at the root of this obstacle? By asking these questions, you shift your focus from frustration to curiosity, opening the door to personal growth and transformation. This mindset allows you to approach each challenge as an opportunity to refine your inner symphony, bringing you closer to the life you desire.

Remember, overcoming obstacles is not just about pushing through; it is about understanding the underlying causes and addressing them at their core. This is where true change happens. By embracing challenges as part of your journey, you not only overcome them but also strengthen your resolve and deepen your alignment with your goals.

As I have learned, the path to success is rarely a straight line. It is filled with twists and turns, and every challenge is a chance to adjust your course. Do not be discouraged by setbacks; they are an essential part of your growth. With each obstacle you overcome, you gain more confidence, clarity, and control over your life. You are not just playing your symphony; you are mastering it, ensuring that every note resonates with your true desires and intentions.

## Identifying Limiting Beliefs and Emotions

Personal development entails the capability of identifying and understanding one's limiting beliefs and negative emotions. Limiting beliefs are deeply ingrained beliefs that hamper us from realizing our full potential and shape the way we relate to the world. These beliefs normally stem from experiences, society, or even self-doubt; and they then manifest in behavior and thought patterns. To identify these, start by reflecting upon recurring challenges or setbacks in your life. Ask yourself questions like the following: What hidden beliefs might be contributing to these problems? Common limiting beliefs are those such as "I'm not capable" or "I don't deserve success." Once you find the source of the core belief, you can begin to free yourself.

Negative emotions often accompany limiting beliefs, thus creating a kind of vicious circle. For instance, if someone considers themselves unworthy of success, the emergence of certain opportunities could consequently trigger fear, anxiety, or even depression. These emotions mirror the limiting belief and, at the same time, reinforce this belief, which makes it even more difficult to change. This interaction between beliefs and feelings really shows just how interlaced they are and how significant it is to focus on one's beliefs and emotions.

Observe your responses to different situations. Limiting beliefs are reflected in strong negative feelings; they indicate which beliefs need to be changed. For example, if you begin to pursue a new goal and feel extreme unease or fear, then that could indicate a belief about being unworthy or incapable. Keeping a journal as a record of your emotional responses, and noting when they tend to occur, can help identify the beliefs behind them. By looking through your list, you can recognize patterns and understand which limiting beliefs are influencing your life.

Another priceless area that can be considered when analyzing limiting beliefs is self-talk. The language one uses while referring to oneself reveals the deepest beliefs. "I can't do this" or "I'm not good enough" reflect limiting beliefs, and these are often accompanied by emotions such as frustration or inadequacy. Gaining more cognitive awareness of such self-talk patterns will provide you with a platform to question them and change the way you frame them. For example, replacing "I can't" with "I'm learning how to" reframes the limitation and aids in shifting both the belief and the associated emotions.

Similar observations about limiting beliefs and emotions may also be gained from trusted friends or mentors who can provide feedback. Others may notice patterns in your behaviors that highlight underlying beliefs that you may not see. Open conversations with such people can often yield valuable perspectives and support for identifying and addressing limiting beliefs. Their observations can help you begin to see more clearly how your beliefs and emotions interact.

Since both are usually present, effective change needs to address both limiting beliefs and negative emotions. These negative emotions of fear, guilt, or shame support the limiting beliefs while the limiting beliefs, in turn, support these negative emotions; as a result, they form a reinforcing cycle that is hard to break. Both the beliefs and the emotions can be transformed through cognitive restructuring, emotional-release exercises, and mindfulness practices. Consciously challenging and reframing limiting beliefs decreases the intensity of the negative emotions associated with them.

On the other hand, empowering beliefs and joyful emotions complement each other. If you have an empowering belief, like "I am capable" or "I deserve success," then emotions such as happiness, excitement, and confidence arise. This positive emotional state then strengthens and reinforces the empowering belief even more, creating a virtuous cycle of growth and fulfillment. Positive beliefs allow a person to attract and sustain joyful emotions that promote well-being and success.

These limiting beliefs and their negative emotions can be identified and transformed through self-reflection, examining emotional responses, and analyzing self-talk. As you start to see how these two interact, you will be able to make changes in both areas, moving toward a more positive, empowered mindset. Becoming aware and putting forth the effort will help you break the cycle of limitation and negativity, enabling you to foster positive beliefs and joyful emotions that support personal and professional growth.

## The Final Movement:
## Living in Harmony with the Universe

As you continue to fine-tune your inner symphony, the changes you have been working toward will begin to manifest not only in your outer world but also within your being. This last movement of your journey is about living in harmony with the universe, where your thoughts, emotions, and actions flow with the natural rhythm of life.

When you finally get to that point, you'll notice that your whole outlook on everything has dramatically shifted. Yes, obstacles will still come along, but you will greet them with a sense of inner peace and assurance that whatever situation arises is one from which you can further grow and learn. Sometimes I refer to this state as a type of effortless alignment, wherein you are no longer swimming upstream but rather downstream, cocooned by the universe.

Living in harmony with the universe simply means that your thoughts are no longer in conflict with your emotions or your actions. In this respect, your conscious intentions align completely with your deep inner beliefs, creating a powerful synergy that naturally attracts experiences, people, and opportunities that resonate with the truth of your desires. This is not something that just happens; it is a product of constant inner work, self-reflection, and a commitment to authenticity.

The deeper this harmony becomes, the more life will begin to unfold with less friction. Synchronicities, those moments when everything seems to fall into place, will happen more and more often. You will be in tune not just with the world outside but also with the energies that shape your experiences. It's the universe answering your inner symphony, a reflection of the harmony you've created deep within yourself.

But living in harmony with the universe is not only about reaching your goals; it's also more about embracing the journey and finding that sense of joy and fulfillment in each moment. It's about trusting the process, even when the outcome isn't immediately apparent. In my teachings, as in life, aligning with the flow of existence opens infinite possibilities. One realizes that the universe becomes a partner in the journey to your highest potential.

All this comes into play in this final movement, creating a life that not only expresses your wishes but is also filled with serenity, purpose, and a deep sense of connection. You don't just take part in life anymore; you are a co-creator, shaping your reality alongside the universe as your partner in creation.

In this state of harmony, remember that this is not the end. This is a continuing dance with the universe, one in which you keep growing, refining, and continually fine-tuning your inner symphony. Move into this last movement in full harmony with the universe, knowing that your life is a brilliant manifestation of that alignment.

## Synchronicity and Flow

When your inner orchestra is in concert, you will begin to notice coincidental events, known as synchronicities, that are so meaningfully charged that they seem to guide you toward your desires. These events will be much more than mere coincidences; they will be definite signs that you are in sync with the universe and that your desires are manifesting in divine timing.

I have often referred to synchronicities as the universe's way of showing you that, yes, you are headed in the right direction. You get these nods from the universe, like, "Hey, all that cleaning up of your thoughts and beliefs has paid off." These meaningful coincidences may come in the form of an unplanned opportunity, a chance meeting with the right people at the right time, or even an unexpected insight that gives you the needed push. These are the moments when the outer world begins to reflect the alignment you have cultivated within.

The process is amazingly empowering when synchronicities start occurring because this strengthens your faith in the manifestation process. It's about recognizing them for what they are, not random flukes, but conscious alignments showing that your desires are unfolding in due course. Trust in this process, as this is how you keep positive energy flowing through your life. Through trust, you open up to these synchronicities, and life starts to unfold with ease and grace.

But for that, one has to be really open and receptive to the signs. Sometimes synchronicities are subtle, and unless one is in a frame of mind to notice them, such signs may be missed. I recommend you adopt an aware and grateful attitude; that way, you will know exactly when such moments occur and how to appreciate them. You will also acknowledge those moments, which, in turn, will foster your connection with the universe and evoke even more synchronicities.

It means living in a state of flow where you no longer push or force outcomes, but instead you allow whatever needs to happen, trusting that the universe is aligning events in your favor. That doesn't mean you sit back and wait; action is still required, but your actions are guided by intuition and a deep knowing that you're supported every step of the way.

Once these synchronicities start happening in your life, life becomes much more interrelated and meaningful. These moments remind you that you're never alone in your journey and that the universe is actively co-creating your reality. May these be signs for you that you are on your path of growth, and may they invite you to move further, knowing you are perfectly in sync with the flow of life.

## Gratitude as a Daily Practice

Gratitude is perhaps one of the most powerful tools that you can use to keep your life in balance and your inner orchestra playing in perfect harmony. By applying gratitude in your life, you do more than merely acknowledge life's positive aspects, you reprogram and fortify positive subconscious patterns that attract even more of what you desire into your reality. Gratitude can shift your focus from what you lack to what you already have, cultivating an abundant mindset that aligns with the energy of manifestation.

As I always say, gratitude is the secret to keeping the flow going. The mere acknowledgment of the little things in life, especially when done with thanks, is a strong confirmation signal to your mind that you appreciate the richness in your life. What you are doing is not only embedding it deep in your unconscious being but also priming yourself for attracting more of the same kind of energy, resulting in more abundance and fulfillment in your life.

Incorporating gratitude into your daily life doesn't have to be complicated. It can be as simple as taking a few minutes each morning or evening to reflect on what you're grateful for: the love of family and friends, the great opportunities that came your way, or how far you have come with your goals. By acknowledging these blessings, you help your mind stay focused on the positive side of the journey. You will find that, in due time, as gratitude becomes a habit, there is a shift in your general perspective; and life feels fuller, more vibrant, and more connected.

Lastly, be the conductor in the orchestra of your life. You have the power to conduct your thoughts, emotions, and actions in a specific direction toward creating the reality you want. Embody this role with confidence and clarity of purpose, for now you not only have the tool but the insight to bring into being a life full of abundance, fulfillment, and joy. Gratitude is what will keep you anchored in this process, ensuring that your inner symphony will continue ringing with the music of manifestation. Each of your words of gratitude aligns you with the universe more deeply, allowing your desires to unfold with grace and ease.

Gratitude is not merely a reaction to the blessings in your life; it is also the active creation of more. A simple yet deeply powerful practice, it will keep you in harmony with the flow of life and allow you to manifest your deepest desires with clarity and joy. And as you move forward on this journey, remember: The symphony of your life is yours to conduct, and gratitude is the melody that will take you to a life of purpose and abundance.

Let's do this…

## Practical Exercise: Orchestrating Your Inner Symphony

This exercise is targeted at aligning your conscious intentions with your unconscious mind, ensuring they act together to attract what you want. Based on the next steps, you will go through a process of introspection, reprogramming, and action and set in motion an effective pathway to manifestation.

### Step 1: Setting Your Conscious Intention

Objective:

Set clear, concrete intentions that reflect precisely what you want.

Instructions:

1.  Find a quiet, comfortable place where you won't be disturbed. Close your eyes, take a few deep breaths, and let your mind relax.

2.  Reflect on your desires: Focus your mind on what you truly want in your life. It may be related to a career, a relationship, health, personal growth, or some other area of life. You can lie to others, but at this juncture, you need

to be very honest with yourself. Shift your focus to what is important to you, not to what you feel you should want.

3. Setting intentions: In clear words, write down your top three intentions. Let those intentions be specific, measurable, and achievable. For example, instead of saying, "I want to be successful," quantify it: "I want to achieve a 20 percent increase in my income over the next six months by building new competencies and seizing new opportunities."

4. Confirm your intentions: Read your intentions out loud. As you do this, close your eyes and see them already manifest. Feel the emotions that come with achieving those desires, joy, satisfaction, and gratitude. This further confirms your intent and begins reprogramming the subconscious.

## Step 2: Subconscious Reprogramming

Goal: Align your subconscious mind with your conscious intentions by identifying and changing your limiting beliefs.

Directions:

1. Limiting beliefs and emotions: If any doubt, fear, or negativity arises when you think about your intentions, identify it. If one of your intentions is improving your income, then limiting beliefs may include thoughts such as "I don't deserve to make more money" or "Making money is too hard."

2. Identify your negative beliefs and feelings: Take another sheet of paper and write these thoughts down. Be as specific

and absolute as possible. Allow any thought that works against your intentions to surface.

3. Challenge and reframe: For each limiting belief, write a counterstatement in the form of a positive, empowering belief. Using the example above, a limiting belief such as "I don't deserve to earn more money" can be reframed as "I am worthy of financial abundance and welcome its influx."

4. Affirmation and visualization practice: Spend one to two minutes every morning and night focusing on your new, positive beliefs. Say to yourself, "Yes, this is true," and with your eyes closed, see your desired outcomes as already fulfilled. Fully engage the feelings associated with these beliefs being true.

## Step 3: Daily Practice of Awareness and Alignment

Objective:

Practice aligning your thoughts, feelings, and actions with your intentions on a daily basis.

How it works:

1. Mindful morning routine: Start your day with one act of mindfulness every day. Take five to ten minutes just to meditate and breathe, clearing your mind. When you feel settled, repeat your intentions to yourself and visualize those things coming into your reality for the day.

2. Midday check-in: Stop in the middle of your day and take some time to check in. Are your thoughts and actions

aligned with your intentions? If at any time you feel or sense negative thoughts or emotions, take a brief second to reframe them using your positive affirmations.

3.  Evening reflection: Take time to reflect on how your day has gone. In a journal, record any positive signs or synchronicities you experienced. If things weren't easy, reflect on what limiting beliefs may be at play and how you can reprogram them.

4.  Gratitude practice: Before going to bed, write down three things that happened throughout the day that you're grateful for. This shifts your focus toward abundance and strengthens positive programming in the unconscious mind.

## Step 4: Taking Inspired Action

Objective:

Turn your aligned thoughts and emotions into tangible, concrete action that advances you further toward your goals.

Directions:

Exercising the intention: Take each of those intentions and write down concrete actions you can take to bring those intentions into being. Then, break those actions down into smaller steps that you can easily take right away.

Prioritize and schedule: Figure out which of these actions will make the biggest difference, and put a timeline on them. Then, schedule them accordingly into your routine.

1. Act as if: Make every action as though your desire has already manifested. When doubts enter your mind, refer back to your affirmations and visualizations to fortify positive beliefs.

2. Check and readjust: Take time occasionally to reflect on your progress. If something doesn't feel right, make adjustments as needed. Manifestation is fluid, and being open to change will keep you more in tune with your vision.

## Step 5: Writing the Symphony of Your Life

Objective:

Through this step, you will learn how to align your inner and outer worlds in such a way that you will be able to manifest your life as a true reflection of the person you desire to become.

Directions:

1. Checking in: Check in once a week or once a month. Reflect on how aligned you feel with your intentions, and whether your subconscious mind is reflecting your conscious purpose.

2. Champagne moments: Recognize and celebrate each step taken toward your goals. This positive reinforcement strengthens your belief in your ability to manifest your desires.

3. Love the synchronicities: Welcome the synchronicities and opportunities that arise as your conscious and subconscious minds align. These are the signs that your inner symphony

is finally playing harmoniously, and your manifestations are unfolding.

4.  Constant evolution: Realize that this is a process that never truly ends. The moment you achieve your goals, you set new intentions and keep refining that inner symphony. Remember, personal growth and manifestation both take a lifetime, and the longer you work with either, the better you will get.

By consistently following this exercise, you will, in a short time, start to witness astonishing changes in your life. First, your inner world begins to fall into alignment with your desires, and then your outer reality reflects this harmony. This is the power of orchestrating your inner symphony by using the alignment of consciousness and the subconscious to manifest the life you truly want.

# CHAPTER 8

## FAITH AND ALCHEMY OF THOUGHT

*Consciousness is the infinite within us, and everything we see, and experience is an expression of that infinite essence.*

—Ernest Holmes

The power of decision, guided by the spirit of faith, is a transformative force in the lives it shapes. Faith is not merely belief; it is also the force that directs decisions, sustains momentum, and turns thought into action. When faith is grounded in clarity rather than emotion, it becomes a stabilizing influence capable of reshaping both inner perception and external results. This chapter explores how thought, when refined through faith, becomes a catalyst for meaningful change.

Throughout history, individuals who achieved lasting success understood that faith was never separate from strategy. It informed their decisions, strengthened resilience, and allowed them to move forward without hesitation. When thought aligns with belief and belief aligns with purpose, action follows naturally, and progress becomes inevitable.

This chapter invites you to consider faith not as an abstract concept, but as an active element in shaping outcomes. By understanding how thought, belief, and intention interact, you gain greater command over the process of creation itself.

Napoleon Hill, in his bestselling book *Think and Grow Rich*, asserted, "Whatever the mind of man can conceive and believe, it can achieve." This timeless axiom underscores the importance of faith as a mental catalyst. In the context of personal mastery, faith is more than belief, it is the unyielding conviction that what one seeks already exists in potential form, waiting to be claimed through conscious alignment.

Stephen Afterburner emphasized this truth when he said, "Faith is the bridge between the invisible and the visible. It is the invisible hand that draws substance from the realm of thought into the world of form." With time, the fruits of this strategy were both personal success and inspiring others to use faith to make wonders happen.

Donna Hunt has proven to be a highly successful entrepreneur and philanthropist who embodies faith in all personal and professional matters. This proactive woman understands that one can intuitively look to a higher power for guidance when making key decisions that strengthen resilience and positivity in times of adversity strikes. Through her philanthropy, Donna demonstrates how faith-driven decisions can create meaningful impacts, encouraging others to mirror these actions throughout their own journeys.

Capital creation is indispensable to the growth and sustainability of any business. There are various ways to achieve this, suited to different business scales and needs. Traditional bank loans and venture capital require a solid business plan and track record. Crowdfunding enables startups and innovators to raise funds from the general public. Bootstrapping, using personal resources, suits those with limited access to traditional funding. Reinvesting profits allows for organic growth over time. Effective capital creation demands strategic planning tailored to specific business requirements.

Understanding one's current financial standing and setting realistic goals are foundational steps. This means increasing income through investments or additional sources of revenue and managing expenses by economizing on costs and maximizing savings. Investing in appreciating assets, such as stocks or real estate, also enhances the long-term stability of one's finances. Moreover, entrepreneurship, creating a business or investing in one, can give an active opportunity to generate income or build growth passively.

Strategic decision-making and careful financial planning are key to sustainable capital creation. Brian Maune exemplifies capital creation by identifying market needs and leveraging his expertise. Recognizing a gap in affordable transportation options, he established a car-sharing service, partnering strategically and employing technology for streamlined operations. His initiative not only met community needs but also generated revenue and capital. In another venture, Brian Maune utilized his financial acumen to thrive in real estate investments, expanding into diverse sectors through smart management and investor relations. His entrepreneurial spirit and strategic insights have not only propelled personal success but also created opportunities for others in profitable ventures.

In conclusion, effective capital creation requires foresight, strategic investment, and proactive financial management. Brian Maune's ventures illustrate how identifying market gaps and leveraging expertise can lead to successful businesses and sustained capital growth. His achievements underscore the importance of entrepreneurial vision and strategic planning in achieving financial success and community impact.

# Challenges and Strategies for Achieving Financial Success Through Self-help Books

Creativity is a multidimensional powerhouse of human experience that includes speaking, cognition, emotions, action, and internal creative power. The ideal self greases the wheels because it is made of our deep desires and wishes. By harnessing these components and making them resonate with our ideal self, we create our dreams and bring into reality the things we envision for our lives. With all these resources, not everyone has reached their aspired success. This may be due to a host of reasons such as inconsistencies, negative thinking, unresolved emotional issues, or lack of sufficient action in pursuit of set goals.

A fulfilling and successful life is one that is deeply self-aware, nurtured, and built upon continuously. Merely reading self-help books or conducting various techniques of manifestation is not enough if someone is not working toward their goals. Progress cannot be meaningful if the inner blocks are not eradicated, and manifestation only acts as a catalyst. It is likewise very important that success is clear in oneself, and that alignment exists with one's deep desires, rather than trying to simply manifest external symbols of wealth. Manifestation can indeed create incredible transformations in people and help them build the life of their dreams, through hard work, consistency, and a deep understanding of themselves.

The deeper we go with our thinking, emotions, actions, beliefs, internal creative power, and self-talk while connecting to our Ideal Self, the more we will be able to find the key to an enjoyable lifestyle with excellent health and successful relationships. It is a journey of self-searching, willpower, and letting go of acquired beliefs to fully tap into our creative potential and manifest the life we truly want.

Manifestation enables a person to create a well-rounded life, one that is in alignment with their innermost desires, bringing immense joy and completeness. However, not everyone who has read self-help books on manifestation, including those on manifesting money, has achieved the goal of becoming a millionaire.

Nevertheless, the manifestation of money depends greatly on one's mindset. Negative beliefs or self-limiting thoughts may hinder a person's ability to attract wealth, even with guidance from self-help books. A lack of financial literacy can likewise be a barrier, as practical knowledge is essential for managing finances effectively. External factors such as economic conditions and personal circumstances can also affect financial outcomes, regardless of manifestation efforts.

Some self-help books encourage quick fixes or overnight wealth, which can lead to unsustainable spending patterns that hurt long-term success. This may also stem from a lack of support or mentoring since such structures provide guidance, accountability, and encouragement. Additionally, individuals may procrastinate or engage in self-sabotaging behaviors that undermine the manifestation process.

The pursuit of millions may also conflict with perceived core values or priorities, leading to reduced motivation. Furthermore, limited opportunities related to income level, social class, or geography may restrict financial outcomes.

Fortunately, difficult financial situations can be addressed through deliberate steps. First, expectations must be reconsidered, recognizing that financial success includes obstacles and setbacks. Achievable goals should be set according to individual circumstances and market conditions. Second, consistent action is required through a structured action plan with dedicated time for financial planning and implementation.

Equally important is challenging limiting beliefs, often with the support of a therapist or coach. Financial literacy can be enhanced through courses and professional consultation. External risk can be softened by creating resilient financial plans and emergency funds. Discipline in investing means avoiding short-term gains in favor of sustainability.

Support and mentorship from groups, communities, or individuals can provide guidance and resources. To overcome procrastination and self-sabotage, individuals must identify personal triggers and develop motivation strategies. Finally, realigning values and goals ensures financial pursuits remain fulfilling and aligned with core priorities.

Through continuous personal growth, education, networking, and manifestation used responsibly, individuals can create realistic and sustainable financial plans that move them closer to their goals.

**Now, here are reasons why most individuals may not have become millionaires after reading self-help books:**

1.  Unattainable expectations: These self-help books often paint an overly rosy picture—one that may be unrealistic about the problems and complexities that arise in achieving real-life financial success.

2.  Inconsistency: It's not just about reading books; one must act consistently over a considerable period and implement strategies that require time and persistence.

3.  A narrow-minded disadvantage: Negative beliefs or restrictive thoughts can serve as obstacles to achieving financial goals. Even self-help books may not help a person overcome those mental blocks.

4.  Inability to take charge of finances: Making informed investment decisions and creating effective budgets are key factors in managing finances properly. Merely reading books may not provide this practical knowledge.

5.  Extraneous factors: An individual's financial life is influenced by economic variables, market fluctuations, and personal circumstances that may occur regardless of self-help efforts.

6.  Emphasis on short-term gain: Some self-help books focus on quick fixes or promises of overnight wealth, which can lead to unrealistic and unstable financial practices, ultimately affecting long-term success.

7.  Absence of a supportive network or mentorship: A support system or mentorship is crucial for providing guidance, fostering accountability, and encouraging progress toward one's goals.

8.  Procrastination or self-sabotage: People may procrastinate or engage in behaviors that sabotage themselves by creating barriers to their goals even when they are already knowledgeable through self-help books. Now, here are the reasons why a person may not have become a millionaire after reading those self-help books:

- Unaligned values: Financial success may be totally out of step with the individual's important values or may not be among their priorities, thus failing to motivate them to pursue it.

- Limited opportunities: Access to resources, education, and mentorship may vary among individuals, often determined by income, social class, and geography.

These factors can limit financial growth, regardless of self-help efforts.

Self-help books are valuable tools on a person's journey of personal development and empowerment through key touchpoints in life, from relationships to mental health and career success. Written by authors who have lived through these experiences or who are established experts in their fields, these books provide practical advice, exercises, and real-life examples that can help readers achieve their objectives and overcome difficulties.

Reading self-help books such as *Think and Grow Rich* by Napoleon Hill[63] and *The Success Principles* by Janet Switzer[64] profoundly influenced my life. These books inspired me to make firm decisions and set ambitious goals, reshaping my path. The techniques I learned—goal setting, journaling, and visualization—became the foundation for building several successful companies. These experiences ultimately led my wife and me to achieve financial independence.

Motivated by our journey, we felt compelled to share what we learned with others. That's why we wrote *Get Rich Like Instant Coffee: Unlocking Your Purpose for Financial Freedom*. Books like *Secrets of the Millionaire Mind* by T. Harv Eker[65] also taught me how critical mindset and belief are when it comes to achieving financial success. I hope our story and the lessons we share in this book inspire you to

---


63    Hill, *Think and Grow Rich*.

64    Jack Canfield and Janet Switzer, *The Success Principles: How to Get from Where You Are to Where You Want to Be* (HarperCollins, 2005).

65    T. Harv Eker, *Secrets of the Millionaire Mind: Mastering the Inner Game of Wealth* (Harper Business, 2005).

unlock your purpose and take the first step toward your own financial freedom.[66]

Besides personal experience, self-help books also touch on deeper psychological insights and practical tools that one can apply to daily life in order to enhance emotional wellbeing. I faithfully practice techniques such as affirmations and visualization, demonstrating how these methods can be seamlessly integrated into daily life to foster positive change and build emotional resilience. They provide strategies for managing such conditions as depression, anxiety, and PTSD both as a complement to professional therapy and as a resource unto themselves for personal development.

With regard to manifestation, or the idea of manifesting millions of dollars, manifestation is the process of believing in and visualizing an outcome with the purpose of making it real. Positive thinking and visualization can be helpful, but financial success is generally not achieved through manifestation alone. Manifestation typically requires knowledge, skills, effort, and persistence to become reality. It is highly unrealistic to manifest millions without concrete action and legitimate financial planning.

## The Power of Personal Mission Statements for Achieving Success

The concept of a personal mission statement, akin to a corporate mission, serves as a guiding light for individuals, offering inspiration and focus on the pursuit of positive change and impactful endeavors. Drawing from my personal experiences in launching multiple successful ventures, I emphasize the power of visualization and determination in achieving ambitious goals, including the creation of million-dollar

---

66    Ibid.

enterprises within a year. In forming the consultant mastermind group Xecutive 8, the mission extended beyond financial success to empowering others through education and entrepreneurship.

Inspired by the teachings of influential self-help books and my own personal insights, I cultivated a mindset of possibility, urging others to break free from their comfort zones and embrace faith and determination in their pursuits. This philosophy guided my team's journey from startup endeavors to multimillion-dollar enterprises, driven by a shared vision of helping others transcend financial limitations and manifest their aspirations.

Advocating for self-belief and positive thinking, I emphasize the transformative power of aligning one's thoughts with aspirations, echoing biblical teachings on the manifestation of desires through faith. I uphold the conviction that one's mindset shapes one's reality, encouraging readers to reject negative conditioning and embrace a path of personal growth and fulfillment. In summary, the journey I share underscores the transformative potential of a personal mission and faith-driven action. Through strategic planning, unwavering determination, and a commitment to personal and collective success, individuals can transcend adversity, achieve financial independence, and inspire positive change in both their lives and the lives of others.

## The "Biggest Millionaire" Goal

"You don't feel the need to fit in because you know that you play an important role here on Earth. The stronger you are emotionally, the more independent you become. When you feel the need to fit in, it shows that you are afraid to be yourself" (Donovan Barrett).

Mr. Banks, a memorable teacher, once imparted a crucial lesson on success: to achieve greatness, one must meticulously map out their goals and dreams, understanding the sacrifices, the timeline, and the unwavering determination required. This wisdom sparked a profound reflection within me, moving me beyond mere aspirations of wealth and fame.

I envisioned myself as a transformational personal development mentor, dedicated to guiding others in manifesting their ideal lives and building multimillion-dollar enterprises. This calling, rooted in a deep belief in God-given potential, inspired me to become a social entrepreneur with a legacy of storytelling and motivational speaking through successful seminars and workshops. Realizing that true success transcends material gains, I embraced the belief that our visions must rise above personal ambitions to impact the world positively. This journey required a profound shift in mindset and self-image, driven by continuous education and the acquisition of advanced knowledge and expertise. My wife's unwavering belief echoes that while fortunes and jobs may come and go, one's education and inner growth remain invincible, a testament to the enduring power of one's dreams.

Reflecting on historical figures like Dr. Martin Luther King Jr. and Mahatma Gandhi, who sacrificed their lives for noble causes, I understood the necessity of facing fears and overcoming obstacles to achieve monumental dreams. These leaders exemplified courage and resilience in pursuit of transformative change, inspiring others to challenge conventions and embrace new identities through renewed character, intellect, and actions.

Fundamentally, it is the path to the realization of the greatest human aspirations that requires more than ambition, a deep transformation in the cognitive sphere of thinking and acting. In tune with a higher power, as our goals become aligned with higher values and are strong enough to overcome hardships, we change not only ourselves but also leave our significant mark on the world, answering the divine appeal to lift humanity up through innovation, bravery, and unshaken faith.

## Vision to Reality: The Path to Success

David Strang's instant coffee serves as a powerful example of how ideas can be quickly transformed into executable plans, much like brewing a cup of instant coffee. The journey begins with ideation, symbolized by the "coffee bean," which is then gradually developed into actionable steps that lead to success. Whether it's a business venture, an online platform, or a community service project, the key is to identify the necessary resources and build an enthusiastic team to share your vision.

This concept echoes the discovery of the coffee bean itself. Ethiopian legend relates that a goatherd called Kaldi noticed that his goats were unusually energetic after consuming the red cherries of a particular tree. This led local monks to brew a drink to stay awake during their prayers, marking the beginning of coffee's long journey.

However, the invention of instant coffee came much later. In 1890, David Strang, a New Zealander, developed the first soluble instant coffee. This was followed by Satori Kato, a chemist from Chicago, who refined the process in 1901. However, it wasn't until 1909 that Constant Louis Washington, a Belgian chemist, perfected the technique and made instant coffee widely available to the public.

This whole transformation process, from an idea to a well-thought-out action to achievement, is essentially about how a vision turns into reality.

When your internal world aligns with your external reality, a harmonious flow emerges, bridging the gap between vision and reality and allowing your aspirations to manifest in the world around you.

And it is herein that the eternal wisdom of Napoleon Hill in *Think and Grow Rich* comes to light, showing how a money-conscious mindset can be truly transforming. It teaches that one should envision and live a life of wealth and prosperity so that self-talk impresses the inner subconscious mind, allowing desired manifestations to unfold.

This principle extends beyond financial gain to encompass holistic abundance, including health, happiness, and fulfillment—all rooted in unwavering faith and belief. Just as Hill's legacy continues to inspire generations, your steadfast commitment and clarity of purpose can together pave the way for enduring success.

Overcoming deep-seated poverty consciousness means that beliefs about money and abundance must be reprogrammed. What Jesus Christ tried to convey was the power of faith and the understanding that what one desired had already been accomplished. This perspective shifts an individual's perception from a place of lack to one of abundance. The next step is to attract and maintain wealth through intentional planning and purposeful action in the present.

## "Getting Rich Like Instant Coffee" Has Become a Popular Choice

In today's pursuit of financial success, the allure of get-rich-quick schemes parallel the appeal of instant coffee—quick, convenient, and promising immediate results. Yet just as instant coffee lacks the depth of a freshly brewed cup, the pursuit of quick wealth may not lead to lasting fulfillment or purpose. True prosperity lies in finding a balance between financial stability and personal growth, leveraging available resources to build a sustainable path toward both wealth and meaning.

The journey toward financial freedom requires more than expedient solutions; it demands the identification of passions and purposes that align with our capabilities and ambitions. By investing time and effort into ventures that resonate deeply, whether by starting a business or pursuing creative endeavors, individuals can cultivate a fulfilling life rooted in both financial security and personal satisfaction. This approach mirrors the deeper experience of savoring a thoughtfully brewed cup of coffee rather than settling for a quick fix.

The concept of creating wealth akin to David Strang's instant coffee extends beyond mere financial gain to encompass a holistic approach to success. It involves nurturing a mindset that combines ambition with patience, recognizing that sustainable prosperity develops through dedication, collaboration, and faith in one's abilities. Drawing from the biblical principles underlying human potential and the power derived from combined effort, the building of a cohesive mastermind group is instrumental in translating large ideas into tangible successes.

It allows individuals to transcend the constraints of their personal limitations by harnessing the collective intellect and creativity of a unified team, thus achieving incredible results.

Such synergy encourages various streams of income and entrepreneurial ventures while contributing to personal and communal growth in the process. Each venture, from landscaping to video production, represents a step toward creating residual and passive income streams that solidify financial independence.

Ultimately, the journey from rags to riches involves more than monetary gain; it embodies a spiritual and intellectual journey toward self-realization and collective prosperity. By aligning ambitions with purpose and leveraging the power of collaborative effort, individuals can build a legacy of meaningful achievements that endures beyond immediate gains. This comprehensive approach not only ensures financial stability but also cultivates a deeply fulfilling life marked by continuous growth and meaningful contribution to society.

## Note for you:

There is an important distinction to keep in mind as you move through this material. Faith is not passive, nor is it blind. It represents a conscious alignment of belief, thought, and action. When faith is rooted in awareness, it becomes a steady and stabilizing force, guiding decisions with clarity rather than urgency.

Self-manifestation invites reflection on the person you are becoming. Consider an image of your ideal self several years into the future, having reached meaningful milestones in your personal growth or entrepreneurial journey. This vision is shaped not only by accomplishments, but also by the qualities, discipline, and clarity that define who you are at that stage of life.

Visualization plays a role in reinforcing this inner alignment. When you imagine moments of success, fulfillment, or financial achievement, the emotions that arise offer insight into what truly motivates you. These feelings help anchor intention and strengthen belief.

The purpose of this chapter is not to offer instructions to follow, but perspectives to reflect upon. Faith, when practiced with patience and clarity, reshapes inner dialogue and influences outward experience. As understanding deepens, the ability to move forward with confidence, trust, and intention naturally expands.

# CHAPTER 9

# UNLOCKING THE HIDDEN WEALTH THROUGH GODLY WISDOM

*Consciousness is the infinite within us, and everything we see, and experience is an expression of that infinite essence.*

—Ernest Holmes

Godly wisdom transcends human understanding and is accessed through a deep connection with infinite intelligence and a sincere engagement with divine truth. As spiritual beings, we often underestimate the power of divine guidance, relying instead on limited perception and personal reasoning. True wisdom emerges when we recognize our connection to infinite intelligence and allow it to guide our thoughts, decisions, and aspirations.

The saying "behind every great achievement is a story" points to the quiet influence of godly wisdom at work beneath visible success. It reminds us that there is often more unfolding than what appears on the surface. Extraordinary accomplishments frequently reflect a deeper alignment with divine guidance, revealing the presence of a transcendent force that shapes outcomes and underscores the enduring role of godly wisdom.

Through moments of clarity, unexpected opportunities, and triumphs over challenges, we witness godly wisdom guiding us toward success. By fostering a deep bond with infinite intelligence and delving into divine teachings through prayer and spiritual alignment, we open ourselves to receive this profound and all-encompassing gift of wisdom. It's through this gift that we realize our accomplishments are not solely ours but a collaboration between our efforts and the divine wisdom guiding us toward fulfillment.

Trusting in this divine guidance and having faith that our desires are already within us is essential. By accepting our connection with cosmic consciousness and vibrating at its frequency, we manifest our deepest desires into being. Our thoughts and beliefs mold our reality.

While prayer and visualization have been fundamental in spiritual practices for centuries, their traditional use sometimes limits our potential to connect with our inner divine consciousness. Instead, we should be able to activate that power within us through meditation, self-reflection, and becoming self-aware rather than depending on the Universe. By adding prayer and visualization to spiritual alignment and action, one is empowered to co-create with the universe in manifesting our desires.

Stillness of mind and focus on intention during prayer connect us with our inner divinity, allowing us to visualize our goals vividly. Aligning our thoughts and actions with divine will creates a powerful energetic vibration that guides us toward manifesting our aspirations.

Taking practical steps toward our goals complements prayer and visualization, as action is integral to the manifestation process. This holistic approach not only allows us to receive guidance and support from the divine but also actively engages us in the creation of our reality. It deepens our self-awareness and strengthens our connection to the inner divine, thus leading to personal growth and fulfillment.

While prayer is not merely about seeking assistance, it also serves as a vehicle for inner strength and empowerment. By shifting our perspective from dependency to self-empowerment, prayer becomes a catalyst for personal growth and resilience. It allows us to connect deeply with our desires, motivating positive change and providing clarity and direction in life.

It is further a practice that nurtures inner peace, gratitude, and positivity; thus, it leads to the development of resilience and optimism amid adversities. Overall, there is also value in looking at prayer as a source of inner strength and alignment with the will of God in guiding us in how to live a meaningful life.

In other words, prayer and spiritual alignment that allow us to receive godly wisdom connect us with our inner divinity and push us toward personal growth and accomplishment. It is a transformational journey that releases our potential and brings our actions into alignment with divine guidance, leading to a meaningful and purposeful life.

It becomes clear that the belief in prayer combined with visualization can powerfully transform our lives. It is much more than asking for favors from the outside; rather, it is a matter of taking responsibility for our lives and living with purpose and intention.

At the foundation of letting our potential flow and lining up with the universe's abundance through the master key of prayer are the teachings of Wallace D. Wattles, Napoleon Hill, and Neville Goddard.

They redefine prayer as an act of gratitude and faith in knowing that our inner self can manifest a dream into reality. This harmony of our intent with cosmic forces through prayer and visualization allows the tangible manifestation of our desires. Through it, one is able to live a deliberate life, undeterred by the incidents encountered, being continuously convinced of one's ability to do great things. These practices make us more aware that our thoughts and intentions create our reality. When we align ourselves with divine guidance and visualize reaching goals as if they have already been accomplished, we send an extremely strong intention of success. This strengthens not only our connection to a higher power but also our inner resolve to pursue our dreams relentlessly. The journey is transformative because the emphasis shifts from looking for validation from external sources to cultivating the inner being, which eventually reveals one's truest potential and leads to living a life of profound fulfillment and purpose.

Self-trust is about placing trust in our own capabilities and aligning our actions with integrity, leading us on a journey toward self-conceptualization and self-empowerment. Prayer and visualization become most helpful aids in this search by teaching us to clear away external desires and tune deeply into our inner wisdom. It helps us better understand who we are and what to do, and it lights the path toward fulfillment and contentment from within. In this shift in perspective, the illusion of separateness falls away, and we are liberated to live authentically as an expression of the true self.

What this means, in essence, is that the journey of prayer and visualization is not one of fulfillment from without, but one where we find inside ourselves a deep inner potential and live a life authentic to what is most valuable. This reminds us that our truest needs lie in self-discovery and inner growth, leading to a life full of meaning and purpose. On this journey, we begin to realize that our inner self possesses the potency to manifest dreams into being and needs only faith and intention aligned with the universe to be activated.

The journey of coming to understand and accept who we truly are is a lifelong process. This involves rejecting outside validation and looking within to find inner strength and resilience. This self-development journey, in the words of Viktor E. Frankl, gives the bold order to "stop searching; the answer is within you." It's a matter of coming into contact with your authentic self, which, in a way, is a biblical concept: "know thyself" and "be transformed by the renewing of your mind." Central to this journey is the law of reversibility, which involves understanding that transformation can go in both directions. In nature, science, and psychology, this concept is related to every other law and principle. Similar to how cause and effect become interchangeable in physics, our thoughts can become actions and vice versa. It is also a clear example of interconnectedness, underlining the power we have through our thoughts and beliefs in shaping our reality.

Applied to the areas of prayer and visualization, as taught by influential thinkers like Earl Nightingale and Napoleon Hill, it becomes deeply transformative. To visualize our wants already fulfilled and to align our thoughts and emotions with this reality is an act of intentionality, not wishful thinking. First, it requires that our mind engage with our consciousness and heed the biblical wisdom, "As a man thinketh in his heart, so is he."

While prayer has traditionally been held as a form of communication from humanity to the divine, in manifestation, it is seen in a different light. It is the faith and confidence we exert in prayer that actually engage us in shaping our reality. Thought then shifts us from asking for blessings to believing that they are forthcoming. This puts biblical teachings like "Whatever you ask for in prayer, believe that you have received it, and it will be yours" into application.

Thus, the journey of self-discovery and actualization at hand involves not simply setting and achieving goals but also aligning our thoughts and beliefs with our deepest desires. It means applying the law of reversibility and the true power of prayer and visualization in creating a reality that reflects our inner truth and aspirations. As we reach the end of this journey, let it be reiterated that the power rests in our own hands to take control of our lives and live purposefully to the fullest.

We need to nurture mindfulness, thankfulness, and insight so that turning points, which are at times forcibly thrust upon us, can change our lives in the right direction. In the words of Viktor E. Frankl, "The search for meaning is a potent medicine indeed, a true elixir; it is a stabilizer in the gamut of neuroses and psychoses, from the neurosis of Sunday melancholy to the psychosis of Sunday neuroses." This process is therefore in tune with biblical exhortations to "know thyself" and "be transformed by the renewing of your mind."

Mindfulness grounds us in the present and makes us thankful for the little things that often pass unnoticed in life. It inspires gratitude, as mentioned in the scriptures, "Give thanks in all circumstances, for this is God's will for you in Christ Jesus." With mindfulness, we shift from chasing external recognition to valuing inner delight. It's about being aware of the self, knowing what exactly we think and feel. In doing so, we conduct ourselves in a manner commensurate with what we believe in and reflective of integrity.

In the words of Maya Angelou, "Courage is the most important of all the virtues because without courage, you can't practice any other virtue consistently."

This opens up a whole new arena, enabling our personal fulfillment and growth to flourish without societal pressures. In fact, this is a journey of moments: With each step forward, we live a life full of purpose and joy.

## Letting Go of Comparison and Societal Expectations

Having lived in a manner that has let go of such societal expectations and embraced a path of authenticity, this now serves as a poignant reminder. Indeed, as Maya Angelou astutely said, "Courage is the most important of all the virtues because without courage, you can't practice any other virtue consistently." By reflecting on personal growth and inner contentment, we free ourselves from the relentless cycle of trying to live up to others' expectations.

I faced my own limiting beliefs that were pulling me down in relationships, family life, and finances. Through affirmations and the knowledge given by gurus like Bob Proctor, I changed my mind. I took that sense of unworthiness and replaced those beliefs through affirmations: "I am deserving of eternal love; I am deserving of financial success." Because of this change, I truly have been able to develop deep, meaningful relationships in all areas of my life.

Transformation through affirmations: This indeed was a transformation that materialized after deep introspection. I came to realize that my subconscious belief was standing in my way. Whereas I had some outer successes in life, I inwardly struggled with self-doubt about whether I could be worthy of love and financially stable. The words of Bob Proctor really rang true, that our beliefs are like a thermostat, regulating what we manifest into our lives. Through daily affirmations and immersive study, I made a conscious decision to rewire my thought patterns. I released all affirmations related to lack and fear, and I fully committed myself to those that echoed my inner worth and my nature as a deserving-of-abundance human being. Repeating them with conviction, I could feel deep within my mind that it wasn't just positive thinking, but a union of beliefs aligned with desires and a preparation of fertile ground to allow positive change.

Aligning with universal principles: Prayer and visualization became pillars of my daily practice. They were no longer about pleading for external changes but about aligning my consciousness with divine abundance. One of the deepest impacts Neville Goddard has had on me was to "assume the feeling of the wish fulfilled."[67] He taught me to approach prayer not from a space of lack, but from a deep sense of gratitude and certainty that my desires were already fulfilled in the spirit realm. This subtle shift in perspective brought a new depth of peace and empowered me. I was aware that real praying did not involve asking for things; even more so, it was to feel in one's heart, now, that those things are already granted.[68] The principle falls in good resonance with some deep biblical teachings to trust in the unseen and have faith that our prayers are heard and answered in God's timing.[69]

Living authentically to life alignment: Living authentically means just letting go of all the societal conditioning and accepting myself for what I am. That takes courage: breaking from the expectations put on you by others, taking into notice whispers of one's own heart. It was indeed a tough journey to accomplish; in that journey of authenticity, every step made the life path clearer and more peaceful inside. This is what Napoleon Hill's concept of "faith" became for me: a guiding light in darkness, an invisible yet unshakeable belief in invisible forces at work and their magic around us.[70] It taught me to trust in the process and to let go into the higher intelligence that knows best about what is good for me.[71]

---

67    Goddard, *Feeling is the Secret*.

68    Horowitz, *The Miracle Club: How Thoughts Become Reality*.

69    Hebrews 11:1, The Holy Bible (ESV).

70    Hill, *Think and Grow Rich*.

71    Nightingale, *The Strangest Secret*.

Alignment and intention-setting allowed manifesting: By embracing mindfulness and intention each new day, I became a co-creator of my reality. Spending my time with individuals who share similar beliefs reinforces my journey and accelerates growth. This highlighted the importance of collective consciousness and community when manifesting our desires. Aligned with universal principles, thoughts, emotions, and actions merge to create that which is truly divine and abundant. Through harmony with divine abundance, I have positioned myself to attract opportunity, relationships, and experiences that reflect my highest aspirations.

Embracing our true selves and aligning with universal abundance will ultimately provide us with a life of purpose, joy, and fulfillment. The journey of self-discovery brings us every step closer to manifesting our deepest desires into reality. This is the path that, through inner guidance and faith, becomes a great unleashing of transformation, one that truly emerges from living authentically in concert with universal principles. Letting go of limiting beliefs and trusting in the abundance of the universe serves as a deep reminder of our innate capability to manifest desires and live a life filled with fulfillment and abundance.

It helps us to let go of negativity and move into a space of positivity and trust in the universe. We give thanks for our wants as if they already are part of our reality before their actual manifestation has taken place. The attitude of gratitude gives the boost for our aspirations and makes them come into life. It keeps on reminding us that with the right attitude and faith in the universe, everything is possible. Releasing ourselves from the mental chains that bind us, opening up to the abundance of the universe—in our inner power lies the ability to manifest our dreams in confidence and positivity. It encourages letting go of doubts and fears and replacing these attitudes with abundance and gratitude. Focusing on what we want, rather than what we do not have, naturally brings positive energy and opportunities into our life.

This is the essence of true prayer and visualization: a deep-seated want in us for a fulfilled outcome, envisioning as if our desired reality has already come forth and all is right in the world. It transcends mere requests to become a heartfelt expression of gratitude in advance. The spirit understands our emotions more profoundly than our words.

While words facilitate communication, they can sometimes limit our ability to convey the depth of our thoughts and feelings. Words are symbols of symbols; the true essence resides beyond their surface meaning. Therefore, it is through heartfelt emotions and vivid visualizations that we authentically connect with the divine and bring our desires into tangible reality. This understanding encourages us to approach prayer and visualization with sincerity and unwavering faith, confident that our intentions resonate with the universe.

True prayer necessitates vulnerability and surrender, trusting that the universe or a higher power is aligned with our highest good. Through this trust, we tap into an infinite wellspring of love and support, enriching our lives with deeper meaning and fulfillment. It's not about asking for material wants to be fulfilled but about aligning with the creative essence and divine will, affirming our interconnectedness with the universe. Prayer extends beyond reciting words or seeking a desired outcome; it embodies a powerful practice that engages visualization with profound emotions and faith. Feeling is integral to prayer, imbuing our intentions with depth and sincerity.

When we pray, we connect with our inner spirit and a higher consciousness, envisioning our desires in the spiritual realm with faith that they will manifest in our physical reality. Prayer is a synergy of visualization and spiritual conviction, linking our consciousness with universal energy. Through prayer, we manifest our deepest desires and forge a spiritual connection with our inner selves.

Prayer is a powerful, transformative tool that bypasses the comprehension and reasoning of our minds. It helps us to dig deep inside of ourselves and reflect upon our thoughts, our actions, and our desires. If we want to make effective use of prayer, then we must absolutely know that our prayers have been answered. This knowing, based upon the laws of assumption and attraction, always works for our good and not against it.

Embracing faith and trust in these universal laws manifests our desires and catalyzes change in life. Prayer is not a wish or plea; it is a means of connecting with the universe to fulfill inner potentials. In this manner, believing that our prayers get answered with unshaken faith is necessary, even at times of misfortune or adversity. As the scripture reminds us, "When you pray, believe that you have received it, and it will be yours."

Faith in prayer is encouraged unwaveringly through the Bible, as reminded by Luke 18:1: *Man must always pray without being discouraged.* This command underscores that prayer isn't merely an act but a connection to spirit itself; our spirit is prayer. When we pray, we should envision our desires as already fulfilled, without expecting reciprocity or seeking external validation. Our sole focus should be on expressing gratitude for the manifestation of our desires, confident that they are already unfolding. This is because the infinite intelligence, universal spirit, or God resides within us, and our consciousness shapes our reality.

Therefore, whatever we pray and visualize is already materializing in our lives. Ours is to stay in tune with our consciousness, keeping in mind an attitude of gratefulness, but always knowing that our prayers are going to manifest at just the right time.

Prayer is deep and profound; it connects us to our higher self, thereby opening the doorways to communicate with the divine. It is a means of expressing hope, desire, and thankfulness to a much higher power. There are times when we find ourselves in a quagmire of difficulties or, for that matter, disheartened for not getting what we wanted from praying. At these critical junctures, one needs to look upon prayer not as an end to an earmarked means but as a spiritual connection. We must trust in the power of our prayers and the spirit within, knowing they are always heard and answered in the best possible manner.

It's equally important to approach prayer without expectations or attachments to outcomes, as prayer itself signifies surrender and trust in the divine plan. Our thoughts and internal dialogue also carry power, serving as unconscious prayers. Therefore, let us make prayer a daily practice, trusting in its strength and remaining undeterred by perceived lack of immediate results. Through persistence and faith, we forge a powerful connection with the divine, manifesting our deepest desires through prayer.

In our journey of self-discovery, it is crucial to pray and visualize with clarity, avoiding unconscious intentions and actions. By monitoring our internal dialogue and emotional patterns, we consciously direct our thoughts and emotions toward the universe, transforming them into potent prayers. This underscores the significance of maintaining a continuous state of prayer, where every thought and emotion serves as a form of communication with the divine. Prayer isn't confined to isolated moments; it encompasses a perpetual state of being.

When we constantly pray, we align ourselves with the universe, inviting boundless blessings and opportunities into our lives. Whether seeking validation or guidance from the divine, we are already immersed in a state of prayer, magnifying the potency of our intentions and requests. Ultimately, prayer transcends words; it is an emotion flowing from within us, connecting with cosmic consciousness, and manifesting our desires. We must strive for perpetual prayer, realizing our goals and life purpose through intention.

Through personal experience, I have seen the power of gratitude to change and alter life. It has evolved into a constant prayer for me, one that reminds me each day to express thanks for all the blessings that come into my life. The mere expression of gratitude has brought so much joy, contentment, and peace into my life. It changed my mindset from one of lack to one of plenty, finding the beauty and blessing in even the littlest things I never paid attention to.

Gratitude also cultivated mindfulness and presence as I sit in reflection on the list of things for which I am grateful. This really broke into my disposition and character, infusing more positivity, humility, and compassion. Gratitude is fast becoming a big part of my daily activities and is remarkably improving my well-being. I am excited to be able to share this important lesson with other people and motivate them also to live their lives in gratitude. From my personal experience, I am genuinely assured that, indeed, gratitude can become the perpetual prayer of one's life, carrying peace, happiness, and fulfillment in the tide.

Gratitude, besides being a powerful tool, can make us living prayers that broadcast endless joy and fulfillment. In our lives, gratitude begins its vital role by allowing us to include practices in the daily pattern of living whereby abundance and blessings that come our way, however small, are acknowledged, accepted, and met with appreciation. This thinking gives birth to a strong energy of gratitude and appreciation, inviting positive experiences and blessings into our life. Gratitude therefore becomes an instinctive practice in our lives, whereby the whole person personifies a prayerful attitude.

Our desires align with this prayer of gratitude, and we become conduits for its manifestation. This prayer regulates our actions, thoughts, and intentions so we can live a life in a much more meaningful and constructive way. Ultimately, prayer and gratitude come together inside us, and our deep desires are bound to happen. Recognizing oneself as God entails a profound sense of power and responsibility. Understanding that we possess the ability to create and shape our own reality can be awe-inspiring. It is a humbling realization that ever Letting Go of Comparison and Societal Expectations.

Having lived in a manner that has let go of such societal expectations and onto a path of authenticity, this now serves poignantly. Indeed, as Maya Angelou astutely said, "Courage is the most important of all the virtues because without courage, you can't practice any other virtue consistently." We free ourselves, in pondering personal growth and inner contentment, from the relentless cycle of needing to live up to others.

I faced my own limiting beliefs pulling me down in relationships, family life, and finances. Through affirmations and knowledge given by gurus like Bob Proctor, I changed my mind. I took that sense of unworthiness and replaced those beliefs through affirmations: "I am deserving of eternal love; I am deserving of financial success." Because of this change, I truly have been able to develop deep, meaningful relationships in all areas of my life.

Transformation through affirmations: This, indeed, was a transformation that actually materialized after deep introspection. I came to realize that my subconscious belief was standing in the way. Whereas I had some outer successes in life, I inwardly struggled with self-doubt about whether I could be worthy of love and financially stable. The words of Bob Proctor really rang home, that our beliefs are like a thermostat, regulating what we manifest into our lives.

Through daily affirmations and immersive study, I made a conscious decision to rewire my thought patterns. I released all affirmations related to lack and fear, and I completely let myself go into those that echoed my inner worth and my identity as a deserving, abundant human being. Repeating with conviction, I could feel deep within my mind that it wasn't just positive thinking, but a union of beliefs aligned with desires and preparation for fertile ground to allow positive change.

Aligning with universal principles: Prayer and visualization became pillars of my daily practice. They were no longer about pleading for external changes but about aligning my consciousness with divine abundance. One of the deepest impacts Neville Goddard has had on me was to "assume the feeling of the wish fulfilled." He taught me to approach prayer not from a space of lack, but from a deep sense of gratitude and certainty that my desires were already fulfilled in the spirit realm. This subtle shift in perspective brought a new depth of peace and empowered me. I was aware that real praying did not involve asking for things; even more so, it was to feel in one's heart, now, that those things are already granted. The principle resonates well with some deep biblical teachings, to trust in the unseen and have faith that our prayers are heard and answered in God's timing.

Living authentically in alignment with life: Living authentically means just letting go of all the societal conditioning and accepting myself for what I am. That takes courage, breaking from the expectations put on you by others, taking into notice the whispers of one's own heart. It was indeed a tough journey to accomplish; on that journey of authenticity, every step made the life path clearer and more peaceful inside. This is what Napoleon Hill's concept of "faith" became for me: a guiding light in darkness, an invisible yet unshakeable belief in invisible forces at work and their magic around us. It taught me to trust in the process and to surrender to the higher intelligence that knows best about what is good for me.

Alignment and intention setting allowed manifestation: In allowing mindfulness and intention in living each new day, I became a co-creator of my reality. Spending my time surrounded by supportive people who share the same beliefs reinforces my journey and accelerates growth. This reminded me that collective consciousness and community are everything when manifesting our desires. In tune with universal principles, thoughts, emotions, and actions come together to bring into being that which is truly divine and abundant. Through harmony with divine abundance, I have aligned myself with inviting opportunities, relationships, and experiences into my life as reflective of my highest aspirations.

Embracing our true selves and aligning with universal abundance will ultimately provide us with a life of purpose, joy, and fulfillment. The journey of self-discovery brings us every step closer to manifesting our deepest desires into reality. This is the path that, through inner guidance and faith, becomes a great unleashing of transformation, one that actually emerges from truly living authentically in concert with universal principles. Letting go of limiting beliefs and trusting in the abundance of the universe holds within it a deep reminder of our innate capability to manifest desires and live a life filled with fulfillment and abundance.

It helps us to let go of negativity and move into a space of positivity and trust in the universe. We give thanks for our wants as if they already are part of our reality before their actual manifestation has taken place. The attitude of gratitude gives the boost for our aspirations and makes them come to life. It keeps on reminding us that with the right attitude and faith in the universe, everything is possible. Releasing ourselves from the mental chains that bind us, opening up to the abundance of the universe, in our inner power lies the ability to manifest our dreams in confidence and positivity. It encourages letting go of doubts and fears and replacing these attitudes with abundance and gratitude. The focus on what we do want, rather than on what we don't have, naturally brings positive energy and opportunities into our life.

This concept underlines the fact that the universe provides for us day in and day out, and with trust in its abundance, one is able to lead a joyful, peaceful, and contented life.

This is the essence of true prayer and visualization: a deep-seated want in us for a fulfilled outcome, envisioning as if our desired reality has already come forth and all is right in the world. It transcends mere requests to become a heartfelt expression of gratitude in advance. The spirit understands our emotions more profoundly than our words. While words facilitate communication, they can sometimes limit our ability to convey the depth of our thoughts and feelings.

Words are symbols of symbols; the true essence resides beyond their surface meaning. Therefore, it is through heartfelt emotions and vivid visualizations that we authentically connect with the divine and bring our desires into tangible reality. This understanding encourages us to approach prayer and visualization with sincerity and unwavering faith, confident that our intentions resonate with the universe. True prayer necessitates vulnerability and surrender, trusting that the universe or a higher power is aligned with our highest good.

Through this trust, we tap into an infinite wellspring of love and support, enriching our lives with deeper meaning and fulfillment. It's not about asking for material wants to be fulfilled but about aligning with the creative essence and divine will, affirming our interconnectedness with the universe. Prayer extends beyond reciting words or seeking a desired outcome; it embodies a powerful practice that engages visualization with profound emotions and faith. Feeling is integral to prayer, imbuing our intentions with depth and sincerity.

When we pray, we connect with our inner spirit and a higher consciousness, envisioning our desires in the spiritual realm with faith that they will manifest in our physical reality. Prayer is a synergy of visualization and spiritual conviction, linking our consciousness with universal energy. Through prayer, we manifest our deepest desires and forge a spiritual connection with our inner-selves experience and challenge in life is of our own design. In this state, prayer assumes a new significance. Rather than praying to an external deity, we direct our prayers inward, acknowledging ourselves as the ultimate creators and sources of existence.

This form of prayer is steeped in self-gratitude, recognizing the divine power within ourselves. It is an ongoing act of gratitude for our capacity to manifest and create our own reality. This gratitude transcends material possessions, encompassing emotions, relationships, and spiritual growth. As we embark on our journey as God, prayer serves as a constant reminder of our true nature and limitless potential within. It becomes a practice that reinforces self-love, self-acceptance, and self-awareness, fostering a deeper connection with ourselves and the universe.

With this understanding, prayer becomes a potent tool for cultivating a purposeful and meaningful life as God. Understanding prayer allows us to unlock its full potential as a transformative force for living a purposeful and fulfilling life. As we awaken to our connection with God, prayer becomes a pathway to aligning ourselves with the divine and manifesting our desires. By integrating gratitude into our daily prayers, we embody living prayers, radiating joy and fulfillment. It is essential to approach prayer with awareness, avoiding unconscious repetition and seeking validation. Instead, we should pray with intention, visualizing our desires and trusting the divine to guide us on our journey.

Let us embrace prayer as a daily ritual, a practice of connecting with God and inviting abundance into our lives. Through this practice, we open ourselves to limitless blessings and opportunities, enriching our lives in ways beyond imagination. Prayer transcends religious rituals; it is a universal language of the soul, uniting us with the divine and manifesting our dreams into reality. As we continue our spiritual journey, it's vital to remember that our assumptions and beliefs shape our true identity.

Amidst societal expectations, staying true to our inner voice and beliefs is crucial. Our thoughts profoundly influence our actions and shape our destiny. Delving deeper into our spiritual journey, let's always remember that aligning our thoughts and beliefs with our deepest desires and values allows us to manifest our true selves. Let us free our minds from all the adverse self-concepts of our mind and unlock the infinite potential inside us. Each step taken in this journey reinforces the belief that we are destined to be nothing less than our authentic, empowered, and complete selves. Since we are humans, we end up performing on the desires of the ego and outside world.

But when we learn to trust our consciousness, the catalyst for thoughts and actions, we can transcend these limitations. Our consciousness connects us to divine wisdom and guidance, enabling us to uncover our true potential and fulfill our earthly purpose. Trusting in this inner power over the ego frees us to navigate life's challenges with clarity and purpose, staying true to our authentic selves. Let's always trust in the power of consciousness to guide us toward our highest self and inner fulfillment. In prayer and visualization, the spirit plays a pivotal role.

Our spirit runs within us, carrying with it all our thoughts, feelings, and intentions. As we pray, we get in touch with a superior power through a search for light and support. The spirit combines our intellect and emotions with that desire, thus amplifying the energy of visualization. By focusing on our desired outcomes with conviction, the spirit manifests these desires through interconnected events and circumstances, following the law of cause and effect. Our thoughts and intentions create energy that resonates through our surroundings, influencing reality. When we visualize positive outcomes and pray earnestly, the spirit acts as a conduit, bringing these desires to fruition.

Understanding the spirit deeply enriches prayer and visualization, and comprehension of the cause-and-effect principle reinforces the impact of our thoughts and actions. Our intentions, when aligned with faith and belief, send positive energy into the universe, shaping our reality. Conversely, negative thoughts can manifest undesired outcomes. This awareness encourages mindfulness in our thoughts and actions, fully realizing their power to shape our experiences. Delving into the spirit reveals a very interwoven world whereby our thoughts and actions influence our reality. Prayer and visualization, coupled with spiritual understanding, heighten one's capacity to manifest desires and deepen one's linkage toward the spiritual realm.

Through our connection with Spirit, we acknowledge that our desires are known and understood. Immersed in the universal mind, our thoughts and intentions are part of a larger consciousness. This realization assures us that we are never alone; Spirit is ever-present, guiding us toward our true desires and fullest potential. Trusting this connection means that our deepest desires are heard and supported by the universe in their divine timing to come into manifestation. Alignment with Spirit lets us trust the flow in life and know that everything unfolding is for our highest good. Let us embrace this connection to Spirit, allowing it to guide us toward our truest desires and closer to living our most authentic, fulfilling lives.

The realization of our desires is achieved through spiritual growth and the visualization power of prayer. Our thoughts and intentions hold tremendous power, turning into reality based on our faith and belief. This process is hindered by doubt and negativity, which we must overcome by fully trusting our desires. We can only tap into the unlimited wisdom and power available to us when we relinquish control to a higher power; otherwise, realization becomes challenging. The ego seeks control, leading to doubt and fear.

Once these obstacles are cleared, creativity and realization become an effortless process of flow. Spiritual development and prayer visualization are methods by which inner power can transform one's intentions into reality on the path to fulfillment. Adding visualization to prayer enhances the spiritual experience and bridges the gap between the physical and spiritual realms. It allows us to connect with the divine through imagination and intention in deeper ways. This approach goes beyond traditional prayer by engaging us in harnessing our thoughts and emotions and directing them toward spiritual goals.

Coupling our prayers with visualization escalates the power of the prayers and deepens our connection with the divine. It is meant for everyone regardless of religious orientation and gives meaning to our prayer. This helps in building faith within us by assuring us that the divine is constantly at work in our lives to take us through life's hurdles. We need to cultivate visualization into our daily spiritual practice.

Praying through visualization enriches the prayer by allowing us to immerse ourselves in the experience of being closer to the divine. It enables us to envision ourselves bathed in abundance, love, and guidance, reinforcing our belief in the spirit's presence. Through visualization, we access profound spiritual insights by creating a sacred space for communion with the divine. This practice transforms prayer into a powerful tool for aligning our thoughts and emotions with spiritual truth, providing inner peace and purpose to our lives. By integrating visualization into prayer, we connect more deeply with our spirituality and engage with the divine on a more profound level, thereby enhancing our spiritual journey.

Prayer visualization is one of those transformative practices where the use of internal creative power and intention enhances the experience of prayer. This goes beyond conventional methods because it allows us to creatively envision our wants and align them with spiritual truth. By cultivating faith and belief in our prayers, we unleash the power of visualization for the manifestation of our deepest desires. The technique helps us connect more deeply into the universe and provides an ability to concentrate our intentions for spiritual growth and fulfillment.

Prayer is not an asking for earthly things but a communion with the spirit whereby one realizes oneself and understands one's divine nature. Thus, including visualization in prayer helps one better understand spirituality and further fortifies the connection to one's source.

By adding visualization to prayer, we deepen and enrich our spiritual connection, enhancing our capacity for manifestation. Engaging the subconscious mind through visualization transforms how we approach our thoughts, behaviors, and lifestyle. With continuous practice, our consciousness shifts from negative beliefs to positive affirmations, promoting a mindset of upliftment.

Additional practices such as meditation and yoga support this process, providing relaxation and mindfulness. With dedication and persistence, we can reprogram the inner mind to reconnect with our true essence, ultimately moving toward a more fulfilling and positive life.

Praying with visualization enhances our spiritual life by serving as a bridge between the physical and spiritual planes. By creating a vivid mental image during prayer, we cultivate a closer relationship with the divine. This practice helps align our thoughts and feelings with spiritual truth, thereby empowering our prayers. Through faith and intention, the power of realization is activated, deepening one's connection with the divine through visualization.

This is a very different kind of transformation from the way prayers have traditionally been said. It is a deep spiritual practice nourishing faith and inner peace.

Prayer visualization is a very powerful method that clothes our connection with the divine, adding depth to the spiritual experience.

That means clearly visualizing with intention and feeling; one aligns one's thoughts and emotions with spiritual truth and materializes one's most important desires. It triggers the power of visualization to channel positive energy toward meaningful changes in life.

Through the addition of visualization to prayer, we are developing faith and coming closer to divinity. It is a transformational art in which the mind and heart are empowered to anchor their thoughts and intentions on spiritual truth, producing wholeness and peace in one's life. Prayer visualization opens us up to infinite possibilities of the universe so that we can manifest our highest ideals. Infinite intelligence continuously guides and leads us on our life journey. As we tap into this intelligence, we access perfect health, and the law of harmony operates within our minds and bodies.

Surrounding us are beauty, love, peace, and abundance, all ours to embrace.

Understanding and accepting the principles of right action and divine order allow us to live a life guided by love and fullness rather than fear. It's crucial to release fear projections onto situations and instead extend love toward them, as love is the most powerful force in the universe. Our lives are governed by this infinite intelligence, and by acknowledging its love and abundance, we manifest joy, peace, and abundance in all aspects. Trusting in this guiding force and embracing its principles enables us to live harmoniously with ourselves, others, and the world around us. Through imagination and recognition of the love within us, we experience a life filled with infinite blessings and possibilities.

# CHAPTER 10

## THE TRIAD OF SELF

Imagination is more important than knowledge. For knowledge is limited, whereas imagination embraces the entire world, stimulates progress, gives birth to evolution.

—Albert Einstein

In a symbolic dialogue between consciousness, conscience, and the subconscious mind, the universe is represented as infinite intelligence, Adam embodies conscience, and the woman represents the subconscious, often described as the inner creative mind. Consciousness reveals how positive thinking attracts positive outcomes through the laws of attraction and assumption. Conscience counters by suggesting that negative thoughts can also manifest, yet consciousness reminds him of the power of choice and the principle that what we believe, we receive. This realization leads conscience to release blame and accept responsibility for his own thoughts, opening the way to a more fulfilling and intentional life.

The woman, symbolizing the subconscious, emphasizes that the unconscious mind and the reticular activating system (RAS) can sometimes mislead perception. This exchange highlights the importance of awareness and accountability in shaping experience. The subconscious is portrayed as a powerful source of inner strength and deeper understanding, often viewed as mysterious yet essential for growth and transformation. By depicting the unconscious as feminine, the narrative underscores its nurturing and intuitive qualities, inviting trust in inner wisdom as a guide toward self-discovery and fulfillment.

The story emphasizes the profound impact of our thoughts on our lives. By consciously choosing positive thoughts and beliefs, we attract positivity. However, acknowledging our subconscious mind's role in shaping our actions is essential. Negative unconscious patterns can hinder growth, but awareness allows us to change them.

Engaging fully in the present moment is a profound practice; it encourages complete immersion with genuine passion. This practice opens our eyes to the beauty and possibilities present in each moment, even amidst an ocean of distractions. It cultivates greater sensitivity to our environment, feelings, and thoughts, enabling us to make mindful decisions toward a fulfilling life. It teaches us to cherish every instant, helping us release regrets of the past and ease anxiety about the future.

Being aware of these distractions allows us to appreciate the beauty of life. Mindfulness is all about living in the present moment, neither anxious about the future nor dwelling on the past. This kind of perspective opens up a whole new world before our eyes, a world where the seemingly trivial moments of life become sources of joy and fulfillment.

Similarly, to live in the modern world, one has to adapt and learn to cope with life's stresses while keeping inner peace intact. Techniques such as deep breathing, meditation, and nonjudgmental observation help tame racing thoughts and reduce stress. All these practices bring inner stillness, clarity, and a sense of peace that is crucial to living mindfully.

Being present in the moment enhances our experiences and relationships, making life more fulfilling. Immersing ourselves in the present allows us to interact with the world fully and appreciate each moment. Peace and contentment arise from reducing stress and anxiety by letting go of unhelpful thoughts. Intentional and mindful living promotes meaningful connections and experiences; therefore, the practice of being present becomes invaluable. The effective art of communicating with the unconscious mind begins by leading the life one desires. One should be aware of their thoughts and beliefs and let go of negative ones by replacing them with positive affirmations. Repeating affirmations daily, preferably in a meditative state, sends clear messages to the subconscious. Visualization techniques and the practice of feeling the positive emotions associated with a desired life are powerful tools. Have faith in the process, act toward your goals, and maintain consistency and persistence. Remember, you have all the power, and your subconscious mind shapes your reality; therefore, communicate with it intentionally to lead the life you have always envisioned. Undeniably, being present in the now is one of the strongest methods for creating a life of success and abundance.

By combining a positive mindset, tapping into the universe's infinite intelligence, and taking purposeful actions, we can bring our desires into reality. Our thoughts and beliefs hold immense power and directly influence our actions. By understanding and utilizing universal laws such as the law of attraction, the law of abundance, and the law of realization, we can shape our reality. Our emotional state plays a crucial role in the realization process. Releasing emotional resistance and aligning our thoughts and actions with our desires creates an emotional state that harmonizes with our mental constructs, bringing our dreams into existence.

The secret to effective goal mapping lies in the ability to live fully in the present. It requires mindfulness, an awareness of our thoughts, feelings, and surroundings, free from judgment and distraction, which allows for clearer focus on our goals. In the present, we can identify beliefs that may hold us back or negative thought patterns that obstruct our path. This process helps us release past regrets and future fears, freeing our energy to act now. By connecting with our desires and intentions, being present while mapping out our goals opens a world of new possibilities for growth and success.

Achieving success with the personal law of attraction and the law of assumption requires being fully present in the moment. Immersing ourselves in the moment and blocking out distractions or negative thoughts helps us focus our energy on our desires and align with their frequency. This mindfulness and presence are essential for manifesting our goals and attracting what we truly desire. Setting clear, specific goals through goal mapping provides guidance toward success through intentional visualization of desired outcomes.

The metaphor of life as a tree, with fruits representing our thoughts, is one of the strongest illustrations of the creative process and the realization of desires. Like a tree growing from a seed, our creative potential is limitless. Our thoughts, like fruits, are manifestations of our creativity and can bring our desires into existence. Nourishing these thoughts with positivity aligns them with our intentions, leading to favorable outcomes.

The story of Moses and the burning bush symbolizes the divine connection between creativity and divine guidance. Our bodies, like the burning bush, are made of heat but not consumed by it, symbolizing our ability to hear divine guidance through our thoughts. Jesus is often referred to as the Word, representing creativity, thereby teaching the manifestation process through its use. We need only tap into our thoughts and desires to manifest them. Understanding Jesus as "the Word" reminds us of His divine creativity and the miraculous manifestations that flowed from it.

When we unleash the creative force within and make it work for us rather than against us, it gives us the power to create transformation in our lives and manifest our deepest desires. This implies that we can access the deepest parts of our mind, intellect, and creativity to realize the unlimited potential needed to achieve our dreams. Just as Jesus performed miracles through "the Word," we too can manifest our desires through our thoughts and words, thereby shaping our reality. This highlights the profound capacity of the mind to create through thought and imagination and underscores the importance of positive thinking.

Jesus, viewed as an expression of this powerful Word, connects us with our divine nature and allows us to express our full potential in manifesting a life that is complete, loving, and purposeful. Regardless of religious path, Jesus as the Word reminds us that we can manifest, indeed create, our desires and shape our reality through creativity. Embracing a life full of positivity, love, and fulfillment can transform not only our lives but also the world around us.

Stories of extraordinary individuals such as Abraham, Moses, Jesus, and His disciples, who made a significant impact, demonstrate that these principles represent humanity at its best. By embodying love and spreading positivity throughout our lives, we influence others in ways that create a ripple effect, ultimately contributing to a more harmonious world. Living by these principles allows us to realize our full potential and the true meaning of our lives.

Adam, Eve, Moses, and Jesus in the Bible are powerful symbols of creation, consciousness, and divine awareness. Through their actions and words, they reveal a profound understanding of existence. For example, Moses envisioned his people living freely from slavery and, through his close connection with God, led them to the Promised Land. His consciousness inspired others through love and compassion. These individuals remind us that we all have the potential to use our consciousness and creativity for good and achieve extraordinary outcomes.

Beyond the physical world lies a realm of spiritual consciousness and creativity that adds depth and mystery to our existence. This realm is deeply connected to our lives through energy, which drives physical processes and life itself. Despite scientific advancements, many aspects of this realm remain unexplained, fueling curiosity and the quest for knowledge. Its vastness and complexity inspire exploration and remind us of endless possibilities.

Our spiritual consciousness, though beyond full comprehension, plays a significant role in shaping our reality. It guides us toward deeper connection with ourselves and the universe, providing purpose and meaning. Experiences of spiritual awakening, inner peace, and connection to a higher purpose highlight this power. Just as the pillar of fire symbolized divine presence and guidance during the parting of the Red Sea, our spiritual consciousness represents the divine force within us, inspiring awe and reverence.

The parting of the Red Sea can also be seen as a metaphor for the unifying force of shared knowledge in achieving success. Just as the Israelites crossed the parted sea by relying on collective faith, we can overcome obstacles by harnessing our creative power and trusting our subconscious mind. This reassures us that unity, shared purpose, and collective wisdom can bring our ideas into reality.

The concept of creation "in the image of God" emphasizes the value of our creativity in shaping our reality. Genesis states, "Let us make man in our image," suggesting that humans possess divine creative abilities. This connection between humanity and the divine implies that we can use creativity to unlock limitless potential and manifest our deepest desires. Understanding this allows us to use our emotions as guides, distinguishing between feelings of limitation and empowerment. When harnessed correctly, this power enables us to create positive experiences for ourselves and others.

Our emotions, though often viewed as short-term or uncontrollable, can be powerful guides in our lives. By becoming aware of our emotions and understanding how they influence our thoughts and actions, we can use them as a compass to realize our purpose. It takes determination and strength to maintain a positive mindset in the face of adversity, especially in conditions of disease or poverty. Yet those who cultivate this mindset often rise above such circumstances and become masters of their fate, leading lives of health, prosperity, and abundance. Therefore, recognizing our emotions and allowing them to guide our actions is essential when seeking to make a meaningful impact in the world.

The core understanding required for realization is that there is a single thinking substance from which everything is created. Every thought held in this substance becomes a form, and by impressing our thoughts upon it, we can bring them into reality. As Bob Proctor said, "The secret to getting our wants is through belief and knowing our wealth thermometer." This insight is crucial because our feelings act like a thermometer of alignment, indicating the degree to which we are internally aligned to bring about what we want. Rather than simply managing our thoughts, we must learn to work with our emotions, which are the most powerful tool in creating the life we desire. We can implement the practice of daily self-checks using what I call an "emotional thermometer," helping us make adjustments and realign our experiences with our goals.

It is easy to get wrapped up in life nowadays amid the hustle and bustle and forget to check in with ourselves. Creating a better life requires asking ourselves throughout the day how we feel in the present moment and incorporating healthy habits into daily life, such as regular exercise, proper nutrition, meditation, journaling, and reading. When practiced consistently over time, these habits can make a significant difference in a person's life and support personal growth, professional success, and balanced living.

The word *manifesting* can feel intimidating, but it simply means projecting positive thoughts and emotions to attract positivity and abundance into our lives. The future becomes brighter when we care for our emotional needs. Our emotional well-being deeply affects our physical and mental health, our relationships, and our overall quality of life. Paying closer attention to and nurturing our emotional health can lead to greater happiness and success. We must learn not to suppress or repress our feelings but to understand them, allowing us to unleash their full potential as a creative force in manifestation.

It would be misleading to suggest that realization is some kind of secret, as it is an internal and deeply personal journey of self-discovery and empowerment that each of us can undertake. Emotions play a crucial role in this process of realization. When we tune in to and emotionally align with our desires, we create a clear, coherent signal that the universe can recognize and translate into physical reality.[72] Realization isn't about bypassing your emotions; it's about understanding and working with them to harness their power. It's akin to learning to dive off a diving board: Realization requires practice and courage. As Gabrielle Bernstein teaches, when we have a strong sense of connection and certainty regarding our desires, it's time to

---

72    Murphy, *The Power of Your Subconscious Mind.*

share the vision with the world and enjoy the process.[73] The universe resonates with the energy we emit; thus, our imagination should be coupled with positive feelings. This is why Jack Canfield says, "See what you want, get what you see."[74] When thinking and feelings align with our desires, anything can be brought into existence.[75]

By mastering the principles of vibration, an individual goes a step ahead to understand the vibratory paradigm—to take control of one's life and design the desired reality. This paradigm takes a different look at atoms from the traditionally accepted notion and introduces them as intelligent information in a cloud form. By using vibratory powers, we are able to manifest our wants and make wealth creation part of our lives. The cause-and-effect principle due to consciousness proves the fact that anyone is capable of becoming wealthy in their way if done in a specific manner. It indicates the intricate and dynamic nature of human thought and perception, whereby the importance of our consciousness stands out in shaping our reality.

Consciousness is an elaborate and fascinating part of human existence studied within the fields of psychology and neuroscience. Principles such as subjective experience, self-awareness, attention, intentionality, and perception help explain our thoughts, feelings, and behaviors. Once understood and applied, these principles can shape our reality and bring our manifestations into a life of abundance and fulfillment. Ongoing research and debate remind us that there is still much to learn about this complex aspect of our lives. Understanding and utilizing the principles of vibration and energy allow us to tap into the universe's unlimited potential. Our nutritional choices affect both

---

73 Gabrielle Bernstein, *The Universe Has Your Back: Transform Fear to Faith* (Hay House, 2016).

74 Jack Canfield, *The Success Principles: How to Get from Where You Are to Where You Want to Be* (HarperCollins, 2005).

75 Hill, *Think and Grow Rich.*

our physical health and energetic well-being, as different foods carry varying vibrational patterns. By becoming more conscious of what we consume, we can refine our vibration and create a harmonious state within ourselves.

This concept extends beyond nutrition and encompasses all aspects of our vibratory universe. Living in alignment with this understanding enables us to reach our fullest potential, opens the door to a world where abundance is shared by all, and allows every living being to thrive in mind, body, and soul.

The law of attraction and the law of assumption play the most prominent roles in manifesting our desires. Our thoughts and feelings act as magnets that determine the reality we experience and what we draw into our lives. In other words, for any desired outcome to manifest, our thoughts and emotions must align with what we seek. By connecting with positive thoughts and feelings, we invite harmony, abundance, and prosperity into our lives, benefiting both ourselves and others. As Napoleon Hill stated, it is the "infinite intelligence, the spirit of consciousness" within us that allows us to will and act.

Many people believe they remain poor because others have monopolized wealth, yet new opportunities are always available to those willing to seek them. Rather than competing solely within established industries, we can direct our attention to emerging fields such as electric railways and aerial transportation. Even when employed by large corporations, it is possible to achieve wealth and independence by following a purposeful path and taking consistent action. By focusing on what we desire and believing in success through diligent effort and persistence, we can remove limiting barriers and create meaningful success.

Most people are so preoccupied with daily problems that it never really dawns on them that their thinking and beliefs bring into manifestation their reality. With the law of coherence, all thinking and vibrational energy attracts similar energies.[76] In order to make changes, we must change our thoughts and the story we have created. Dr. Joseph Murphy indicates that a method to release inner fears and negative thoughts is to make a conscious choice to place one's attention elsewhere.[77] We have the option to design our lives by using empowering thoughts and beliefs, a life full of joy, abundance, and success.

*Power vs. Force* by David R. Hawkins delves deep into the recesses of human consciousness and the potential within it for increasing happiness and satisfaction in our lives. Despite the title suggesting a conflict between opposing forces, Hawkins's primary focus is on measuring and elevating consciousness. He explains that everything is made of energy, each possessing a unique frequency shaped by our thoughts and emotions. As we elevate our level of consciousness, we begin to relate to a universal consciousness that brings greater positivity into the world around us. Hawkins also indicates that language cannot fully describe or accurately denote inner feelings and states of consciousness.

Therefore, the author encourages readers to interact more deeply with their pure emotions to improve their lives and the world in general. The book offers a deep exploration of consciousness from both religious and scientific viewpoints, revealing that current technology still falls short of fully measuring or capturing the energy inherent in all things. Hawkins, supported by physicists, anticipates that as technology evolves, our understanding and measurement of energy will also expand. He found that an individual's energetic calibration reflects their belief system, explaining why different people can interpret the same event in various ways. By understanding our

---

76    Napoleon Hill, *Think and Grow Rich*

77    Ibid., 102.

own level of consciousness, we gain insight into the broader paradigms of others and their experiences.

Emotions play a crucial role in manifesting new realities, but labeling them with words can limit their power. Hawkins suggests tapping into pure emotions free from preconceived definitions to create positive changes in life. This unconventional yet powerful approach can be effective with dedication and understanding. It is our emotions, coupled with the law of attraction and the law of assumption, that dictate how we view the world and infinite intelligence consciousness, or God. The law of attraction helps us understand that whatever we think about and believe in is what we attract into our lives. The law of assumption explains how our beliefs become our reality.

Our thoughts and beliefs, as influenced by our emotions, can either be limiting or expansive in our understanding of the world and our connection to a higher power. If we approach life from a positive, loving, and trusting place, we attract experiences that are in harmony with such thinking. On the other hand, negative emotions and limiting self-concepts block us from connecting with higher power. By becoming more conscious and intentional with our emotions, we can create a better reality and deepen our understanding of infinite intelligence consciousness.

This process goes beyond mere acceptance of others and their differences; it requires active awareness and intentional emotional engagement. When emotions are consciously guided, relationships become richer, and society becomes more tolerant and understanding. Infinite intelligence consciousness deepens through intentionality, allowing us to live harmoniously within ourselves and with all that surrounds us. We become more compassionate by being aware of and intentional with our emotional states, thereby creating a ripple effect in the world.

## When You Experience a Mirage or Déjà vu

Experiencing déjà vu and mirages is easy to relate to; they feel familiar yet inexplicable, as though you've seen them before, although that can't be possible. Maybe this feeling isn't a trick of the mind but instead a manifestation of the incredible strength of your imagination. The subconscious mind is a powerful tool that shapes our beliefs and perceptions. When we strongly believe in something, our subconscious can bring it into reality, and the thin line between reality and fantasy becomes blurred. It could also mean that what feels like déjà vu is simply the manifestation of a deeply held belief or visualization coming to life. With creativity and belief in the subconscious, we may conjure desires and thoughts into being. Indeed, this reminds us of how deeply our thoughts and beliefs shape our experiences and lives. So when you feel déjà vu or see a mirage, it might be your own beliefs and creativity at work.

## Entrepreneurial Journey:
## Embracing Innovation and Risk

Ecclesiastes 10:19 says, *"A feast is made for laughter, and wine maketh merry: but money answers all things."*

Being an entrepreneur means initiating a business venture and taking significant risks with the potential for extraordinary rewards. Entrepreneurs are innovators; they create something new, including thoughts, products, services, and methods of doing business. Imagine yourself doing exactly what you love, traveling, networking, and communicating with successful people. It is crucial to offer something of value to attract customers and generate profit. Remember, we are not just physical beings, but also sources of energy meant to experience life and love.

As the Bible says, "Give, and it shall be given unto you," emphasizing the importance of creating wealth and happiness for others, not just yourself. Avoid envy of others' possessions; we all have the potential to build our reality. To be a true entrepreneur, shed the poverty mindset instilled by circumstances and upbringing. Embrace thoughts of wealth, prosperity, happiness, and good health. Form a mastermind group of trusted, honest individuals who support your goals, and avoid those who criticize or belittle your decisions. Learn from successful CEOs and set realistic, attainable goals. Be enthusiastic about calculated risks and influence others without imposing power. Adaptability, respect, and trust are key, along with strong communication skills, including the ability to present ideas effectively.

Possess a range of skills, from finance to marketing, and be prepared to eliminate negative influences from your team. Envision yourself as a multimillionaire, embedding this desire deeply within your subconscious. Financial freedom, prosperity, happiness, and good health should be your driving forces.

Experience is the best teacher for entrepreneurship, but learning from others and taking notes are beneficial. Robert T. Kiyosaki, in his book *Rich Dad Poor Dad*, emphasizes financial literacy, independence, and investing in assets. Consider franchises for established systems and support, but beware of taking on too much work alone, which can harm your company's reputation.

Set clear timelines and balance your workload to avoid burnout. Ultimately, it is dedication, perseverance, and a positive frame of mind that allow you to realize your entrepreneurial dreams and build a successful, enriching life.

# Lifestyle Entrepreneur:
## Merging Passion with Sustainable Income

A lifestyle entrepreneur founds their venture first and foremost out of passion, integrating their personal interests, competencies, and abilities with income generation in a sustainable way. Unlike entrepreneurs focused on selling to shareholders, lifestyle entrepreneurs aim for long-term viability in fields they are passionate about, such as hobbies or specialized expertise. They often seek self-employment for personal freedom, family time, and the pursuit of inspiring projects. Many lifestyle entrepreneurs maintain control over their ventures, opting not to scale aggressively, which helps ensure a healthy work-life balance without external shareholders. Common in creative and tourism industries, lifestyle entrepreneurship values passion-driven business goals over strict profit motives, often leveraging digital platforms for global reach.

## Embracing Change and Moving Forward

"Faith is the ability to see the invisible and believe in the incredible, and that is what enables the believer to receive what once seemed impossible" (Clarence Smithson).

I look back at my life and find that I've often encountered stumbling blocks and obstacles that once seemed impossible to overcome. Then, one day, the inevitable happened: I realized that I needed to stop focusing on the past. Reflecting on past circumstances only created more challenges and limited my self-worth and potential. It hindered my path to success and stability for my family. Instead, I focused on how far I'd come and where I wanted to go, aiming for wealth, financial freedom, and security.

I learned from experiences, like my wife fixing her old car named MacGyver, which taught me about the power of persistence and adaptation. Reading *The Power of Your Subconscious Mind* by Joseph Murphy helped me understand how past experiences influence our future.[78] I realized my own subconscious beliefs were holding me back, stemming from childhood struggles and setbacks like prison time.

Changing my mindset and emotional reactions, alongside affirmations, started to improve our circumstances.[79] Yet challenges persisted, like my wife's battle with cancer and job instability due to reduced hours. It highlighted the precariousness of relying on employment benefits. That's when I saw the value in being self-employed—creating stability and security for my family, even in uncertain times. Planning with financial strategies like 401(k) and life insurance became crucial, ensuring we were prepared for emergencies. I also focused on developing business ideas to generate additional income.[80]

My journey included periods of homelessness and mistakes in business ventures due to poor location choices and lack of capital. But moving to Phenix City, Alabama, changed everything. It was there that I discovered the right opportunities and experienced a mindset shift that guided me toward financial freedom and happiness.

I realized that transforming my thoughts and habits around money was key. It's not just about wealth but about achieving true freedom, security, and the ability to give back. I came to understand the importance of financial consciousness and its impact on life satisfaction and community support.

---

78  Murphy, *The Power of Your Subconscious Mind*, 105.

79  Ibid., 108.

80  Hill, *Think and Grow Rich*, 96–97.

I also reflected on my journey and realized that I always wanted more from life. I relentlessly pursued education, entrepreneurship, and personal growth despite facing numerous challenges and setbacks. Setting ambitious goals and persistently pursuing them transformed my life. It wasn't easy, but by optimizing my lifestyle and income strategies, I made significant progress.

Along the way, I learned to save aggressively, starting by saving 30 percent and eventually saving up to 90 percent of my income. This disciplined approach not only secured my financial future but also empowered me to take control of my destiny.

Today, I encourage people to break the chains of limitation within their beliefs, embrace change, and focus ambitiously on their dreams. Life is one of growth, endurance, and creating possibilities that align with our deepest aspirations. We can manifest a dream life through a change of mind and a commitment to action.

STEP 1: Plan your business. Before you can invest in or take on your business venture, you must plan it. Determine what product or service you are offering and whether people will want it. Writing in *Start Your Own Business*, the staff of Entrepreneur Media, Inc. states, "A sound business plan will also help you stay focused on your mission and objectives, establish a framework for management and marketing, and serve as a yardstick against which you can measure your actual performance."

In fact, 79 percent of businesses that have a business plan survive their first year, compared to those that do not.

Writing a business plan is not just about survival; it is about growth. While 75 percent of companies with a well-defined plan expect growth, only 17 percent of companies without a business plan foresee growth. Many studies, including one by AT&T, prove that a formal business plan can make all the difference. Business owners who have taken this step claim that a formal business plan contributes greatly to their success.

That is the foundation for everything, from starting a side hustle to launching a full-fledged enterprise. *Start Your Own Business* leverages the collective experience of over forty years of Entrepreneur Media, guiding budding entrepreneurs through every step, from financing a venture to turning a brand into a household name. This proper planning lays a sound foundation that will sustain growth and help guarantee success. Welcome ideas and approaches in this guide from people with sound business experience and successful entrepreneurs. This is your first step toward realizing your dreams on your own terms.

- Avoid analysis paralysis when launching a business.

- Specify and research your target audience.

- Test ideas with your target group before going to market.

- Pitch your research to secure funding from venture capitalists, apply for loans, and manage cash advances.

- Research how your workspace should be organized to best benefit your company and brand.

- Run successful social media and Google ads as part of your marketing campaign by using influencers to help promote your brand.


STEP 2: Create a legal entity. When starting your business, the most important step is creating a legal entity to protect you and your endeavors. There are many legal liabilities associated with business, and proper research is essential. Ensure that your location is free from liens and hidden fees that could later create serious financial consequences. The most critical action to take as you begin making your business a reality is to protect yourself legally. You will safeguard your personal assets and your venture from unknown risks by building a solid legal entity. This step sets the groundwork for stability and resilience in your business operations.

Always remember to consult experts and adhere to legal guidelines specific to your industry and location. *Start Your Own Business* emphasizes the importance of proactive legal measures to secure your business's future success. Take these precautions seriously to navigate the complexities of business law and establish a firm foundation for growth.

STEP 3: Register for taxes.

STEP 4: Open a business bank account and credit card. Check with your local banks for discounts and incentives for opening new business accounts.

STEP 5: Set up business accounting.

STEP 6: Obtain necessary permits and licenses. Contact your local Chamber of Commerce for assistance with permits and licenses and to support networking opportunities.

STEP 7: Get business insurance.

These insights reflect my journey, a path that spanned over eighteen years of learning and growth. It all began with my writing journey in May 1999, a time marked by pauses caused by overwhelming negative emotions that led to serious mental health challenges. Amid fears of failure and the threat of poverty, my struggles evolved into profound contemplation about life and its meaning. I grappled with existential questions about God's purpose for my life. These introspective moments were pivotal, guiding me toward understanding and embracing my personal journey with faith and perseverance.

"The greatest of all remedies for the fear of death is a burning desire for achievement, backed by useful service to others" (Napoleon Hill).

In my journey, a pivotal moment came when a doctor, not a preacher but a physician, remarked, "Mr. Clemer Leggett, your illness resides only in your mind. All sickness begins there, often rooted in fear and unforgiveness." This revelation around 2010 reignited my passion for writing. Inspired, I began compiling wisdom from physics, science, theology, and self-help, drawing from thinkers such as theoretical physicists and philosophers.

Meditating on life's meaning and exploring the universe's consciousness, I realized that success lay in reprogramming the subconscious mind. Thus, I meticulously crafted a diary akin to sacred scripture, where daily affirmations and profound quotes from the world's wisest minds became my guide. What could be more precious than communing daily with such wisdom?

Within my diary, I penned quotes and affirmations spanning diverse cultural backgrounds and historical eras, including philosophical views on God, intellect, consciousness, and the power of the subconscious mind.

These quotations by journalists, philosophers, scientists, and authors, some known and some unknown, are intended to impact your life in a deeply fundamental way, as they have mine.

On our journey to unlock the fullness of our potential and come into prosperity, it is necessary to look a little deeper at personal motivational and strategic issues. Take a moment to reflect upon these questions to clarify your direction and tap into your inner reserves:

1.  What are my deepest desires and aspirations, and how can I align my actions with those goals while overcoming limiting beliefs and fears?

2.  What unique talents, skills, and passions do I possess that I can utilize in the process of wealth creation, and what actions can I take to embrace a mindset of abundance and prosperity?

3.  What tools, assistance, and daily habits will attract opportunities into my life, help me keep my energy high, and allow me to tap into my subconscious mind for the manifestation of my financial dreams?


The time spent reflecting on these questions may bring great insight and set one on the path toward living a more satisfying and successful life.

# CHAPTER 11

## GENIUS AND CREATING YOUR DESIRED REALITY

As Earl Nightingale once stated, "Genius is simply the ability to put into effect what is on your mind." This perspective challenges the belief that genius is solely inborn, proposing instead that greatness can be cultivated through intentional use of the senses. By engaging sight, hearing, touch, taste, smell, and intuition, and anchoring them in unwavering faith, we gain deeper perception, creativity, and understanding of the world around us.

Through conscious engagement of these senses and a commitment to faith in oneself and a higher purpose, individuals can move beyond perceived limitations and unlock their full potential. Neville taught that faith is the certainty of what is hoped for and the evidence of what is not yet seen, a guiding principle that mirrors the process of nurturing desires through focused thought, belief, and purposeful action.

Yet I've witnessed a common struggle, a spark of hope kindled by the idea of coaching, only to be dimmed by logistical worries. It's a dance of progress hindered by doubt, a delicate balance familiar to many. Overcoming doubt, fueled by fear and uncertainty, is key.

Dr. Martin Luther King Jr. illustrated this in his "I Have a Dream" speech, championing faith as the catalyst for realizing dreams and overcoming obstacles. His belief in the transformative power of faith echoes across generations.

Reflecting on my own journey, which included earning my GED and an associate's degree in the arts, I've seen how genius and faith synergize. Genius unlocks our potential; faith aligns us with the universe's plan. The law of attraction underscores this synergy, where our thoughts manifest into reality. By embracing our inner genius and trusting in the law of attraction, we invite abundance effortlessly.

Our limiting beliefs act as barriers to attracting abundance and success in life. These beliefs often stem from past experiences, societal conditioning, and self-doubt. Yet by recognizing these barriers and replacing them with empowering beliefs, we can attract abundance more freely. This process isn't about divine reward or punishment, but about having faith in our true identity as divine beings. As the Scriptures affirm, faith is having confidence in what we hope for and assurance in what we do not yet see, a testament to the profound influence of our thoughts and beliefs on our reality.

Business leaders like Bill Gates and cultural icons like Shahrukh Khan exemplify success rooted in a deep belief in their worthiness. Conversely, those struggling with poverty or lack of success may be held back by limiting beliefs. Brian Mayne, a prominent personal development expert, emphasizes the transformative power of belief and deservingness. By replacing limiting beliefs with empowering ones, we expand our capacity to attract greatness in all areas of life. Tapping into our inner genius is pivotal in attracting abundance and success, a potential inherent in each of us. However, ingrained beliefs can create barriers and limit our sense of deservingness. By replacing these with empowering beliefs, we activate invisible forces that turn our desires into reality. Our subconscious mind plays a crucial role in this process, acting like a "thermostat" that regulates our life experiences.

Gratitude is a major key in this process. As stated in the Scriptures, "Give, and it shall be given unto you." Gratitude pertains not only to what we already have but also to what we are going to receive. By cultivating gratitude and desire within ourselves, we align with abundance on all levels of our lives. Research shows that happiness precedes success, making gratitude a powerful tool in achieving desired outcomes. It shifts our perception away from fear and toward happiness, creating fertile ground for manifesting our desires through the power of thought.

Combining gratitude, desire, and faith creates a powerful mindset for achieving happiness and success. Thankfulness helps us appreciate what we have today while desire fuels our ambition. When faith is added to both, it becomes the catalyst that turns dreams into reality. It enables us to believe that all things work for good and to tackle adversity with determination. As Raymond Holliwell notes in *Working with the Law*, desire ignites the power that drives our actions toward success. By cultivating a mindset of abundance and positivity, we attract more opportunities and blessings into our lives. Gratitude, as Florence Scovel Shinn observed, counters fear, which is an inverted form of faith in negative outcomes. We unlock our inner potential for happiness and success by substituting faith for fear and trusting in the universe.

Unfortunately, fear confines us within self-imposed limits and prevents us from seizing opportunities and allowing our dreams to flourish; faith liberates us from these constraints and enables us to tap into our inner genius and truly live life. "Decisions determine destiny." Self-trust and trust in the universe are essential for unlocking our full potential and removing limitations from our lives. By replacing fear with faith, we embark on a journey toward success, happiness, and abundance.

This involves practicing unconditional gratitude and being thankful in advance, not only after achieving something. This concept of inner awakening teaches us that everything we focus on becomes part of our reality and continues to grow. The universe is inclusive and brings forth what we focus on; it does not exclude. By shifting this mindset and realizing that our attitudes toward money may be what holds us back, we break old paradigms and allow ourselves to embrace lives of prosperity and abundance. This literature is intended to guide readers toward embracing the laws of attraction and assumption as powerful keys to genuine freedom and fulfillment.

This may sound simple, but it is rarely taught in schools. By understanding and applying the truth that freedom and wealth exist within, through self-awareness and contentment, we can mobilize the power of our thoughts to create the life we desire. Let us turn the page and stop obsessing over negative thinking; instead, let us foster a mindset that keeps us moving toward success and fulfillment. This approach focuses more on touching the core of who we are than on what we want; therefore, it mobilizes our inner strength to reach full potential. The universe neither excludes nor denies; it simply responds to our energy and thoughts. By keeping our focus on positivity and gratitude, we can confidently move forward on the path to success and growth.

People who think about their problems all day and focus on what they don't want tend to maintain and amplify those issues because that is where their attention lies. Conversely, while focusing on what we don't want hinders progress, the upside is this: By focusing on what we do want and practicing gratitude in advance, we can manifest those desires into being. This understanding comes from the realization that our experiences are shaped by our thoughts and beliefs. True liberation and fulfillment arise when we actively place our trust in ourselves and the universe. Rather than dwelling on our struggles, we should focus on cultivating a positive mental attitude (PMA). PMA combines faith, integrity, hope, optimism, courage, and unselfishness. Those who possess a positive mental attitude set high objectives and strive conscientiously to achieve them. As Napoleon Hill stated, "A person with a Positive Mental Attitude sets high goals and constantly strives to achieve them." With a positive mental attitude, we overcome barriers and create a life without limitations.

## Rags-to-riches stories are eternal.

They are the very fairy tales that have inspired people since time immemorial, from stories about Roman Abramovich and Mohed Altrad, who struggled through unimaginable adversity to attain phenomenal success, to discussions about the potential of franchise businesses as a key to success. Such tales remind us not to give up on our dreams. These individuals are successful and remind us that our circumstances have nothing to do with our potential. Hard work and perseverance lead to greatness. However, as much as franchise businesses may be viewed as a path to success, it is ultimately the will of these individuals that determines their results.

These motivational stories also challenge the assumption that not wanting to be rich is synonymous with laziness, as there can be many reasons behind one's priorities and personal definition of success. Over time, these individuals become role models, encouraging us in the pursuit of our goals and reassuring us that success is possible regardless of origin or circumstance. The book *Icons & Innovators* presents seventeen billionaires who rose from poverty-stricken backgrounds and further cements the idea that with willpower, hard work, and a degree of luck, any person can rise above adversity and go on to do incredible things.

When viewed together, these stories drive home the premise that no matter one's background or challenges, anything is possible when pursued relentlessly. They illustrate the power of the law of attraction, the law of assumption, and imagination. These universal laws demonstrate how our thoughts and beliefs shape our reality. The ideas stored within our consciousness, conscience, and subconscious mind can be consciously accessed, allowing our deepest desires to find expression. These stories encourage us never to give up on our dreams or stop believing in ourselves and our ability to overcome obstacles along the path to our goals.

These inspiring tales invite us to keep an open mind and embrace new possibilities, as unexpected paths often lead to the greatest successes. Ultimately, they serve as beacons of hope and motivation, reminding us that nothing is impossible if we dare to believe in ourselves and our dreams.

One of the most amusing and inspiring success stories I have encountered is about a man named Kevin. He always wanted to be a stand-up comedian, and after years of practicing jokes in front of his mirror, he finally gathered the courage to perform on an open-mic night. Things did not go according to plan, as the audience did not utter a word or show even slight amusement. Instead of quitting, Kevin chose to make the best of the situation and relied on his quick wit and comic timing to improvise. He joked about the awkwardness of the moment and even impersonated James Brown, which left the audience in stitches.

Not only did he save his performance that night, but he also earned a place in the club's regular lineup. From that moment on, Kevin became a stand-up comedian known for transforming challenging situations into comic moments. This story illustrates the power of perseverance and how humor can turn a near failure into remarkable success.

It is often said that whatever happens occurs for a reason and that we are all born with the potential for success in one way or another. Throughout life, we encounter moments when we are tested and face obstacles that seem unconquerable. In such moments, it is easy to forget that these challenges are meant to test our strength and determination.

They shape and mold us into who we are meant to become and provide guidance that ultimately leads us toward success. When you look at people who appear successful, remember that their journeys were also filled with ups and downs, much like our own. We are all meant to have success stories, though the paths we take will differ. It is often said that for every success, struggles and failures are necessary because they teach valuable lessons and make success more meaningful. Rather than comparing our achievements to those of others, we should reflect on our own journeys and trust that our stories are unfolding exactly as they are meant to.

This idea takes on significance if you are an entrepreneur or business owner and wish to scale up your business by expanding its reach. This can be achieved by creating a robust web presence representative of your brand's values and personality, including developing a complete website, maintaining strong social media profiles, and producing blog or video content that is relevant to your target audience. By doing all of the above consistently, individuals can create an online image of a credible and trustworthy professional with whom others can confidently collaborate to run their business successfully. Having a compelling online persona can also attract a wide audience, from prospects to clients, because people may connect with it and feel comfortable as they get to know it better.

For this reason, every individual should make their utmost effort to pay attention to their online persona; it is not only their personal brand at stake, but their business as well.

By carefully curating an online persona, individuals can position themselves and their businesses for success.

For better or worse, technology and social media have created a radical shift in how we present ourselves to the world. In today's digital era, one's online presence carries greater significance, as it can substantially affect both personal and professional success. This, in turn, gives us the ability to mold and shape how we are perceived by carefully managing our online persona and building a personal brand that distinguishes us from others in our field. This applies not only to celebrities but also to individuals and businesses at all levels. Strategic use of social media, websites, and other online tools allows people to project their best qualities and unique strengths, establishing credibility as influential or leading figures in their industries.

This does more than improve professional reputation; it can also open opportunities in the form of collaborations, partnerships, or clients. What was once the domain of the rich and famous has now become an essential tool, without which personal and professional lives can struggle to thrive. By taking responsibility for our online presence and intentionally creating a personal brand, we position ourselves more effectively for career and business success.

This process begins with deep introspection and self-discovery, including understanding our values, beliefs, and goals. Knowing ourselves and clarifying our aspirations help align our actions with our true selves. This stage may also include seeking role models and mentors who inspire us to become our aspired selves. Integrity and authenticity are required to envision an idealized self and to have the courage to strive toward it. Deciding who we want to be is not about complying with societal expectations but about staying connected to our true passions and life purpose. This lays the foundation for personal growth and development, allowing us to live more fulfilling and purposeful lives.

This process also helps identify the market we need to reach, which is critical in building a successful personal brand. In the modern digital era, it is important to establish a strong online presence through blogging, website development, and the creation of key social media profiles. I am reminded of what my college professor once said: Post frequently and carefully avoid personal posts that do not align with the brand. Knowing who we want to be is therefore the first step in understanding ourselves and living a meaningful life. This decision is not only important for personal growth and development but is also crucial to our careers and businesses.

What having a brand truly means is being deliberate about how we show up and using that presence as a vehicle for personal growth and success. This same concept applies to leadership, where the principle of positive command takes center stage. Command positivity refers to a person's attitude and method of directing or guiding others, whether at work or in everyday life, in the most positive way possible.

This is an essential element of effective leadership and can lead to improved performance and overall success. One powerful way a leader demonstrates effectiveness is through the practice of "command positivity." To be truly effective, leadership goes beyond giving orders and making decisions; it includes communicating purpose, motivation, and meaning so others can unite around a common goal.

It paves the way for authenticity and vulnerability, thereby creating meaningful connections and relationships. This has the added advantage of allowing leaders to create a positive atmosphere and supportive environment that enables teams to achieve great results. Moreover, it allows everyone to be understood as they truly are, beyond achievements or titles. Leaders should put command positivity into practice because it benefits both the team and the organization while also making people feel valued and understood. This results in a stronger, more cohesive, and motivated team, which ultimately leads to better results and overall success. As leaders, we must ensure that the work environment is positive and enables employees to develop feelings of empowerment and motivation for their personal goals within the framework of the organization's greater mission.

Command positivity enables us to do this by building valuable connections and relationships. This leads to a happier and more successful team. Strive to be leaders who prioritize and practice command positivity, as it benefits ourselves, our teams, and our organizations. As businesspeople, it is essential to build healthy relationships with others to move forward successfully while also maintaining a healthy relationship with ourselves. By using imagination, visualizing what we want and believe in, and reinforcing our subconscious, we gain deeper self-awareness and become better able to connect with others on a meaningful level. This involves cultivating creative thinking regularly, remaining open to new ideas and perspectives, and challenging ourselves when it is necessary to change limiting beliefs and thought patterns.

Through reflection and self-examination, self-awareness is nurtured, and a confident individual begins to emerge, which is essential for both business and personal relationships. This growth also enables us to relate to others through mutual respect and understanding. As entrepreneurs, a strong sense of self, combined with deep inner and outer relationships, forms the core of success in the business world. By prioritizing these relationships, we can establish firm connections and create a support system that enables us to achieve our life goals and progress beyond our current position.

As demonstrated by Simon Sinek, bestselling author of *Start with Why*, success lies in understanding the purpose or belief behind what we do and communicating it effectively. Sinek emphasizes that people are not drawn to products or services themselves, but to the "why" behind them. More importantly, in today's market, where nearly everything can be replicated, understanding one's "why" is critical. Successful leaders and organizations begin with a clear sense of purpose or belief, which becomes the driving force behind their actions and inspires others to support and follow them. When we operate from a strong "why," connections and customer loyalty grow stronger. This leads to differentiation and the ability to stand out in the marketplace. Sinek's message reminds us that true success comes from a clear sense of purpose and from building meaningful relationships with our audience. This energy of purpose radiates outward, clearly communicating our "why" to others.

The forbidden truth behind every successful person lies in the fact that they refused to let go of unyielding determination and an unshaken belief in the power of positivity. Take, for example, Jack Canfield, a world-renowned American author, motivational speaker, and entrepreneur. Most popularly known as the cofounder of the *Chicken Soup for the Soul* series, which has sold over 500 million copies worldwide,[81] Canfield's road to success was filled with rejections and setbacks of every kind. He never faced disappointments due to these challenges; instead, he worked in the direction with great determination. Canfield believes in clear and particular goal setting, visualization of the target to be achieved, and works consistently

---

81    Jack Canfield and Mark Victor Hansen, *Chicken Soup for the Soul* (Health Communications, 1993).

on it.[82] He also credits success to an unremittingly positive mindset and belief in the law of attraction.[83] Through books, speeches, and workshops, he has continued to inspire others to take on their own roadblocks and claim all they are capable of achieving.

His story serves to remind us that with hard work, determination, and a positive attitude, anything is possible. Now, let's talk about how to get wealth overnight. Impossible it may seem, but indeed, it's possible with the right strategies. Indeed, many FOBs and billionaires shared their success stories, and what runs in common is their sheer determination for work.[84] They took calculated risks, faced setbacks, and looked for growth opportunities relentlessly. Whether it's wise investments, lottery jackpots, or ingenious ideas, the following stories are a source of inspiration and a reaffirmation that everything is attainable with effort and a correct approach. They valued the opportunity to invest their money wisely and to be around people who could support them.[85] These strong truths create a background for the very real possibility that anybody can gain financial abundance in a very short period of time, given they are able to give the required effort in the right direction and make strategic decisions.[86]

Wealth isn't just about money; it's about living a meaningful life. These stories go to show that anyone can overcome poverty through firm resolution, hard work, wise decisions, and strong supportive systems.

With a PhD in psychology, Weinschenk has accumulated over thirty years of experience, making her a recognized authority on how

---

82   Jack Canfield, *The Success Principles: How to Get from Where You Are to Where You Want to Be* (HarperCollins, 2005).

83   Byrne, *The Secret*.

84   Hill, *Think and Grow Rich*.

85   Eker, *Secrets of the Millionaire Mind: Mastering the Inner Game of Wealth*.

86   Bernstein, *The Universe Has Your Back: Transform Fear to Faith*.

people think, learn, and behave. She studies the factors that account for success in every aspect of life: from business to relationships. She has authored books and numerous articles on the science of success, which are very practical insights and strategies for individuals and organizations to become all they can be. Weinschenk's work has been widely acclaimed and recognized for its timeliness and relevance that makes her a highly demanded speaker and advisor for companies and people seeking the key to realizing their full potential. Through this vast knowledge, Weinschenk freed the individuals with a bag of tools and techniques that helped them to unleash all hidden potential for attaining successful results. Weinschenk's expertise in imagination, visualization, the law of attraction, and assumption gave any individual some tools and techniques that help people unlock their full potential to achieve success.

She emphasizes the power of the mind in envisioning ideas and transforming creativity into reality through visualization. Additionally, the work of Weinschenk may also incorporate the law of attraction, suggesting that positive thoughts and beliefs help attract positive results. Weinschenk also highlights assumptions and how they shape our perception and, therefore, our actions and results. Through this understanding, she empowers individuals to take charge of their own lives and strive for whatever degree of success they wish to achieve. Through her insights, she has shown people how to harness their inner creativity and imagination, visualize desired outcomes, align their thoughts with the frequency of the law of attraction, and make empowering assumptions that support their goals and aspirations. As a result, she has become a valuable resource for individuals seeking personal growth and success.

A business opportunity is an investment package that allows a buyer to set up a business using established technology and financial structures. This type of opportunity ranges from franchises to other forms of businesses. Though franchises offer a systemized business model, not all business opportunities are considered franchises; therefore, not all require rigid structures, leaving room for creativity and innovation. Those who want to start a business can explore different opportunities, choose the one that best suits their skills, interests, and financial capabilities, and move forward accordingly.

Business opportunities provide a pathway for individuals to become entrepreneurs and contribute to the economy by creating jobs and providing goods or services to consumers. Today, with advancements in technology, these opportunities have become more accessible and diverse, making it easier for people to enter the business world. Business opportunities serve as a vehicle for individuals who wish to succeed independently and create a niche for themselves. Packages or investments facilitate the use of technology, enabling owners to turn passion into a money-making enterprise. In the modern digital era, a strong integration of technology is essential in the corporate world, and therefore, business opportunities are extremely valuable.

While franchises are the most common form of business opportunity, other options are vast, ranging from online stores to investments in technology firms. However, it is essential not to commit to any venture without proper research into the associated risks and benefits. By carefully selecting business opportunities and utilizing them effectively, entrepreneurs can make a meaningful impact in the evolving business world and achieve their entrepreneurial aspirations.

## The Secrets of Success Unveiled

Success may be perceived as an elusive thing, but what if I told you it lies within each and every one of us, merely waiting to be tapped into through our infinite intelligence and consciousness? This may seem like a bold statement, but this is the pure truth. Our inner selves hold the key to our potential, guiding us toward our goals and helping us overcome obstacles. We can harness all our potential and, therefore, true success by tapping into our inner wisdom, intuition, and creativity.

Success isn't just an outward act; there must also be inward growth through a connection with self and confidence in infinite intelligence. This process instills inner wisdom within us, provides a better understanding of ourselves, aligns our actions with our true purpose, and helps us overcome obstacles. By practicing these fundamental principles consistently, we open the door to endless possibilities and enable ourselves to lead a fulfilling life.

## The Ten Principles for Unlocking Success

1. I am promising: Keep your word to yourself and others. Fulfilling promises instills confidence and reliability, reinforcing integrity and honesty in all spheres of life.

2. Integrity in action: Align your thoughts, words, and actions with your values. Pay attention, adapt, and develop beliefs that enable you to live a fulfilling life.

3. Clear-cut goals and a healthy lifestyle: Set realistic goals while maintaining a healthy lifestyle to improve energy, reduce stress levels, and increase productivity, enabling a better quality of life.

4. Continuous learning and an extraordinary personality: Continuous learning, combined with an extraordinary personality, builds strength and uniqueness of character. Proper planning, execution, and personal distinction facilitate success in all areas of life.

5. Psychology of excellence—know your value: Adopt a positive approach and strive for excellence. Recognize your worth and contribute something unique to the world; your individual strengths inspire confidence and drive success.

6. Nonnegotiable habits and persistence: Build healthy nonnegotiable habits through consistency and persistence while focusing on your goals and your own definition of success.

7. Open mind: Embrace new ideas and perspectives and remain open to change. This promotes diversity, inclusivity, and empathy, allowing continuous growth and a deeper understanding of the world.

8. Uncomfortable situations and financial control: Face difficult situations directly and maintain financial control. This proactive approach ensures stability and demonstrates responsible practices, building trust among stakeholders.

9. Now-and-win strategies: Life is meant to be lived now, and realistic goals must be set. Take intelligent risks, continually learn and adapt, and take time for reflection and maintenance to maintain balance and prevent burnout.

10. Creative power encompasses knowledge: Imagination, as Albert Einstein said, "is more important than knowledge." Imagination and creativity drive innovation beyond what was once thought possible. Unleash your inner creative genius and dream big.

Success is within reach for anyone willing to connect with their inner wisdom, trust their infinite intelligence, and follow these guiding principles. Embrace your own consciousness, harness its power, and unlock the secrets of success in all areas of your life.

The future does not exist anywhere but in your mind.

Through my journey of self-discovery, I've realized that I am a pure expression of consciousness, experiencing both spiritual and physical realms. This realization has made it clear that I embody infinite intelligence, often referred to as God. I understand myself as part of the creative consciousness, a messenger of divine truth, and a manifestation of eternal perfection, representing the universal mind. I possess a soul because I am life itself, and I have come to see the soul as an idealized concept of infinite intelligence, a divine self-creator. Consciousness, which is the essence of God's infinite intelligence, manifests through our physical experiences. My name, which is merely an ego identifier, sets me apart from other expressions of consciousness. At my core, I embody love and presence, reflecting the all-encompassing consciousness of infinite intelligence.

In creating my diary, I expanded it to double its size and spent months avoiding newspapers, magazines, and television, which improved my well-being.

This period heightened my awareness of societal ignorance and superficiality. Our education should focus on preserving the cultural heritage of our ancestors, including great thinkers, philosophers, and scientists. Unlike conventional self-help books, I organized my ideas by specific themes for different periods, writing daily on topics such as God, intellect, love, divine law, human nature, faith, temptation, self-sacrifice, eternity, and unity with God.

Each entry begins with an open thought, includes relevant quotes, and ends with my reflections. I wrote stories, affirmations, and quotes inspired by renowned philosophers and entrepreneurs. On November 2, 2023, I created a significant work intended for a global audience, aiming to offer timeless guidance. This guide integrates the wisdom of religion, philosophy, and literature, serving as both a spiritual and practical manual to promote peace, success, and community contribution.

My aim is to share wisdom widely, particularly in times of heightened spiritual need. I have compiled diverse thoughts, affirmations, and stories, properly crediting their original authors and translating them to enhance clarity and unity.

My goal is not to provide literal translations but to offer an accessible reading experience that inspires readers to create their ideal lives. As Gerald Schroeder noted, "The mind creates a deity when it transcends all understanding."[87] I present quotes and philosophies to help you succeed and realize your desires. Napoleon Hill and Neville Goddard emphasize that "if you didn't believe you could have it, you wouldn't desire it."[88]

Understanding the reticular activating system is crucial. The RAS filters information based on our focus and emotions, reinforcing doubts or positive intentions.[89] For example, in a noisy environment, you focus on important conversations, filtering out irrelevant distractions. Similarly, the RAS filters information that aligns with your goals. By visualizing and reprogramming your subconscious mind, you align your intentions with your purpose, achieving success.[90] This work is a gift meant to elevate and inspire readers. As Gerald Schroeder said, "The mind becomes the creator of a deity when it surpasses all comprehension."[91] This guide helps you realize your potential, harness

---

87   Gerald Schroeder, *The Hidden Face of God: Science Reveals the Ultimate Truth* (Free Press, 2001).

88   Hill, *Think and Grow Rich*; Goddard, *Feeling is the Secret*.

89   Murphy, *The Power of Your Subconscious Mind*.

90   Nightingale, *The Strangest Secret*.

91   Schroeder, *The Hidden Face of God*.

infinite intelligence, and achieve your desired life. Bob Proctor stated that "a conscious idea or goal, when repeatedly pursued with intense desire, is taken over by the inner self and acted upon through any available means."[92]

Recognize that you are deeply connected to the universal energy through your body and your inner mind. Exploring these connections helps you manifest your desires. I used to meditate before sleep, focusing on aligning my body's vibrations with the universal energy, which facilitated abundance and manifestation. Understanding this connection is key to overall well-being and success. Reconnect with your body and subconscious, feeling the universe's energy flowing through you. The answer lies in our belief systems. Erroneous beliefs hinder progress toward our goals and dreams. Our beliefs, formed in childhood and influenced by our environment, shape our actions and destiny. As Mahatma Gandhi said, "Your beliefs become your thoughts, your thoughts become your words, your words become your actions, your actions become your habits, your habits become your values, and your values become your destiny."

Our thoughts significantly impact our emotions, behaviors, and reality. Our predominant thoughts shape our outcomes, so directing our mental focus is essential. By consciously choosing positive rather than negative thoughts, we create a more fulfilling existence. Training the mind involves acknowledging and managing negative thoughts without letting them dominate. Instead, we should focus on constructive and empowering thoughts. This practice empowers us to foster resilience and productivity. Through deliberate thought management, we can shape a positive future.

---

92    Bob Proctor, *You Were Born Rich: Now You Can Discover and Develop Those Riches* (McCrary Publishing, 1984).

Every day presents a mix of thoughts, but we have the power to choose which ones to cultivate. By actively curating our thoughts, we enhance our well-being and outlook. Our thoughts are seeds in our minds, influenced by experiences and nurtured by attention. They evolve into ideas and actions that shape our reality. This process transforms fleeting thoughts into significant contributions.

Our ideals, born from these thoughts, drive meaningful change. By nurturing these ideals, we harness their transformative potential, impacting both ourselves and others. Embrace this power to shape your destiny. By fostering positive thoughts and ideals, we enrich our lives and positively impact the world. Through conscious choice and belief, we can create a future filled with positivity and purpose.

*"And the LORD answered me*: '*Write the vision; make it plain on tablets, so he may run who reads it. For still the vision awaits its appointed time; it hastens to the end, it will not lie. If it seems slow, wait for it; it will surely come; it will not delay*'" (Habakkuk 2:2–3).

In Indian philosophy, the **Vaiśeṣika** identifies nine fundamental substances shaping our reality: earth, air, water, fire, ether, space, time, soul, and mind, each with unique qualities. Ātman, the inner self, witnesses bodily changes, distinguishing between finite and infinite consciousness. I delve into the laws of attraction, assumption, attention, cosmic knowledge, cosmic consciousness, Holy Spirit, vibration, and scripting. My studies in physics, theology, quantum physics, and engineering have revealed their profound interconnections and implications.

The law of attraction uses imagination, emotions, and senses to manifest desires, moving beliefs from the conscious to the subconscious. The law of assumption transcends sensory perceptions, relying on will, perception, reasoning, intuition, imagination, love, and belief.

The law of vibration shows that our thoughts and emotions emit frequencies that affect our reality. Positive vibrations attract positive experiences while negative vibrations bring unfavorable outcomes. This law works in conjunction with the law of attraction and the law of assumption.

The laws of Spirit connect us to abundance, wealth, health, and success through the Holy Spirit. Invoking the spirit taps into our potential to manifest desires. This divine connection predates creation, guiding us toward fulfillment and aligning us with universal intelligence.

Understanding this spiritual connection enables us to manifest desires confidently, overcoming limiting beliefs and embracing our role as creators aligned with the universal order. Throughout history, including in the Bible, it has been recommended to write down desires clearly so they can be understood. Whether you write the same vision daily or vary it, repetition reinforces belief and brings desired outcomes within reach.

Scripting, a powerful tool for achieving goals, involves writing scenes in the present tense as if they have already happened. This practice helps replace limiting beliefs with empowering ones, clarifies desires, and increases the likelihood of success. I aim to share effective ideas that will help you realize your dream life. Emotional management is crucial, as stress and anxiety impede progress. Our subconscious mind responds to daily challenges and emotions much like background programs on a computer. Just as too many open programs can slow down a computer, negative thoughts and emotions can hinder us. Through autosuggestion techniques, we can replace negative patterns with positive affirmations, thereby building new thought patterns.

Affirmations, though simple, are powerful tools for aligning with our beliefs and desires. They condition the inner self mind to realize these beliefs. The emotional state during affirmations, whether positive or negative, affects their effectiveness. Rational thoughts can counteract anxiety by focusing on reality rather than negative assumptions.

Creating a vision board or using visual imagery complements affirmations by reinforcing goals. Regularly viewing images related to goals helps bring them into reality. Imagining desired outcomes prepares us mentally by associating words with images and emotions to empower the subconscious. This approach not only accelerates progress but also fosters a relaxed and confident state, optimizing performance.

Furthermore, integrating these practices into a daily routine enhances their effectiveness. Regular engagement with affirmations and visualization solidifies their impact, making the process more intuitive and ingrained. Developing a habit of checking in with your emotional state and adjusting practices accordingly can significantly amplify results. Consistent application of these techniques, combined with heightened emotional awareness and thoughtful management, supports goal achievement. Remember, the subconscious mind does not differentiate between true or false; it materializes what we consistently think, visualize, and believe. Effective and consistent application of these techniques, combined with emotional awareness and thought management, leads to successful outcomes.

Affirmations are straightforward yet powerful self-suggestion tools. By repeating affirmations that align with beliefs and desires and genuinely feeling their truth, we condition the inner self mind to bring them into reality. It is important to monitor emotions during affirmations; positive emotions support goals while negative ones can undermine them.

## The 369 Method: A Closer Look

The 369 method, often attributed to Nikola Tesla, incorporates spiritual practices such as visualization, affirmations, and focused intention. This technique involves writing your goal three times upon waking, reading it six times around noon, and repeating it nine times before bed. Although there is no scientific evidence directly linking Tesla to this method, his deep fascination with the numbers 3, 6, and 9 suggests an appreciation for their symbolic significance. Proponents believe that this method can help set intentions and manifest desires through concentrated effort and repetitive focus.

Scripting, a concept explored by psychologist Silvan Tomkins, enhances this approach by encouraging detailed scene construction in the present tense. This practice helps replace limiting beliefs with empowering ones, fostering a mindset that embraces uncertainty and possibility. With our minds processing up to eighty thousand thoughts daily, we occasionally encounter inspired solutions. This insight emerged during my scripting practice, which involved internal dialogue and sparked a motivation to share effective strategies for achieving one's dreams. Emotional management is crucial, as stress can hinder manifestation, similar to how a computer slows down when too many programs are running. Autosuggestion techniques can replace negative thought patterns with positive affirmations, reinforcing a desirable mental state.

Affirmations play a crucial role in this process as powerful self-suggestion tools. Repeating affirmations that align with our beliefs conditions the subconscious mind to support realization. Emotional awareness is essential; positive emotions enhance realization while negative emotions obstruct it.

Vision boards and visual imagery complement affirmations by reinforcing goals through regular visualization. Imagining desired outcomes prepares the mind by linking words, images, and emotions to empower the subconscious. This practice accelerates realization and fosters a confident, relaxed state conducive to optimal performance. The 369 method and similar techniques require dedication and belief. While realization requires time, consistency and effort can expedite results. By aligning with the universe through structured practices, we invite our desires into reality.

Maintaining a daily diary supports reflection and serves as a valuable tool for realization. It can include quotes, affirmations, and goal planning to help achieve dreams effectively. By internalizing wisdom and applying it through structured, consistent practice, affirmations and strategic planning can support a fulfilling and abundant life. This approach merges spiritual principles with practical methods for realizing dreams, emphasizing personal growth and achievement.

In addition to the 369 method, several other numerical techniques can enhance manifestation and self-improvement. The 555 method involves writing your specific desire fifty-five times for five consecutive days, deepening your mental and emotional connection to your goal. The 7×7 method requires writing your affirmation or desire seven times in the morning and seven times at night for seven consecutive days to help anchor the habit. The twenty-one-day method involves daily affirmations or visualizations, based on the principle that twenty-one days are needed to form a new habit. The thirty-day Challenge involves clearly identifying what you want to achieve and performing small daily actions or affirmations for thirty days while tracking progress in a journal.

The 3-6-9 cycle is similar to the 369 method, requiring you to write your desire three times in the morning, six times in the afternoon, and nine times in the evening over a set number of days. The 12-12-12 method involves writing your desire twelve times at 12:00 PM and again at 12:00 AM for twelve days, aligning with focused intention. The 10-10-10 method requires committing to writing your goal or affirmation ten times in the morning, ten times in the afternoon, and ten times in the evening for ten consecutive days, building consistency and commitment.

Most of these techniques use numerical patterns and structured practices to support manifestation and raise self-awareness. Choose the approach that resonates most with you and aligns with your personal goals for the best results.

Imagine a prisoner gazing out at the world from behind bars. Despite physical confinement, he dreams of freedom, wide-open spaces, and the feel of the wind. Though surrounded by darkness, he still has the power to focus on the light of his dreams.

This illustrates the concept of manifestation, showing that we can not only create the life we desire through our thoughts and actions but also mold and shape it, much like clay.

Consider this analogy: We all possess a deep reservoir of potential, often obscured by layers of doubt and fear. By writing a letter to yourself, an earnest declaration of your desires, such as envisioning a judge reevaluating your case and granting freedom, a boss offering a long-awaited promotion, or life with a special person in your ideal home with the cars you've always wanted, you begin to bring buried dreams to the surface.

Even in the face of limitations, such as confinement in prison, the mind remains free. You always have the choice to remain within current constraints or to envision and move toward a life beyond them.

Manifestation is the way to envision living your best life by transcending one's problems and struggles, not turning a blind eye to them. For instance, if you don't like your job, you write to yourself on the perfect work environment you are to be in, what inspires you to work, and what difference you would want to make.[93] This letter is used to bridge thoughts and inspirations to make aspirations reality. Read this letter several times a day and build a momentum of emotion, excitement, and gratitude, and watch as your subconscious mind and the spirit of cosmic consciousness go to work in your favor.[94] Even when surrounded by barriers, your mind can soar. By actively envisioning your ideal life and expressing your desires in writing, you unlock your potential and move closer to creating a reality that truly reflects who you are.[95]

These methods utilize numerical patterns and structured practices to help manifest desires and improve self-awareness. Choose the approach that resonates most with you and aligns with your personal goals for the best results.

"Riches begin in the form of thought! The amount is limited only by the person in whose mind the thought is put into motion. Faith removes limitations!" (Napoleon Hill).[96]

---

93    Murphy, *The Power of Your Subconscious Mind.*

94    Hawkins, *Power vs. Force: The Hidden Determinants of Human Behavior.*

95    Hill, *Think and Grow Rich.*

96    Ibid.

The collection of speeches by Neville Goddard offers a treasure trove of wisdom and knowledge.[97]

While the authorship of all speeches remains uncertain, they impart profound insights into the law of realization and the creative power inherent within us. Goddard emphasized the crucial role of feeling and imagination in realizing desired outcomes.[98] Going deeper into his teachings, it becomes evident that he transcended mere individual realization, delving into the concept of infinite intelligence as the creator of the universe.[99]

His teachings speak about how to awaken our consciousness and subconscious mind in order to connect with this universal consciousness in every life moment and be in contact with the divinity inside us.[100] This perception is furthered by Napoleon Hill, in his landmark of a book, *Think and Grow Rich*, where he shows how the power of thought and imagination brings our ideas into being.[101] He underscores that these mental faculties, when coupled with strong emotions, can materialize into reality.[102]

This concept resonates with biblical wisdom that suggests God's thoughts and ways surpass human understanding, reflecting the profound nature of our internal hidden self-mind and the universe.[103] Neville Goddard, known for his mysticism and teachings on the laws of assumption, believed fervently in the transformative potential of ideas into reality.[104] He viewed our imagination as the creative power

---

97  Goddard, *Collected Speeches: The Law and the Promise*.

98  Horowitz, *The Miracle Club: How Thoughts Become Reality*.

99  Goddard, *Feeling is the Secret*.

100  Hawkins, *Power vs. Force: The Hidden Determinants of Human Behavior*.

101  Hill, *Think and Grow Rich*.

102  Nightingale, *The Strangest Secret*.

103  Isaiah 55:8–9, The Holy Bible (ESV).

104  Goddard, *Feeling is the Secret*.

of God within us, capable of shaping our destinies. His teachings continue to inspire individuals to unlock their full potential and create meaningful lives.[105]

In challenging times, traditional employment may not always suffice, prompting the need for imaginative solutions. Our imagination, boundless and unrestricted, becomes instrumental in overcoming obstacles. For instance, through visualization, even someone confined to a wheelchair can envision themselves running on a beach, potentially facilitating physical healing through the power of belief.[106] Realizing desires involves immersing oneself fully in imagination, envisioning the desired outcome as a present reality. This creative act, akin to planting a seed, germinates into tangible results. Trusting in the process and maintaining faith in one's imagination is key, allowing natural means to unfold without undue concern for logistics. Recent reflections on Alexander Crummell's pioneering efforts in founding the American Academy underscore the transformative potential of imagination and higher consciousness.[107]

Amidst prevailing scientific racism, Crummell envisioned an institution dedicated to African American education and equality.[108] His bold initiative met with skepticism, serves as a testament to the power of innovative ideas and unwavering determination in combating societal injustices. Crummell's vision for the academy, which attracted diverse scholars like W. E. B. Du Bois,[109] transcended conventional norms, championing intellectual pursuits and fostering societal

---

105 Horowitz, *The Miracle Club: How Thoughts Become Reality*.

106 Murphy, *The Power of Your Subconscious Mind*.

107 Dickson D. Bruce Jr., Alexander Crummell: *Pioneer in African-American Thought* (University of Georgia Press, 1991).

108 Alexander Crummell, *The Greatness of the African Race* (Cornhill Press, 1898).

109 Du Bois, *The Souls of Black Folk*.

change.[110] Their collective endeavor epitomizes resilience and the transformative impact of education in challenging systemic racism.[111]

Imagination and higher states of consciousness are what Neville Goddard preached,[112] then Alexander Crummell and W. E. B. DuBois concretely put into practice, which hold the key to manifesting dreams and effecting positive change in society. This reminds us that with audacious ideas combined with iron determination, we can reshape our realities in striving toward a more just and equitable world.[113]

## Power of Infinite Intelligence

Napoleon Hill stated, "A mind dominated by positive emotions becomes a favorable abode for the state of mind known as faith. A mind so dominated can, at will, command the subconscious mind, which it will instantly accept and act upon." In every chapter of Napoleon Hill's book *Think and Grow Rich*, the principles required to lead a useful and meaningful life are carefully presented. Hill underscores the significance of nurturing a burning desire, cultivating self-belief, training the subconscious mind, and meticulously planning to achieve success.

As I immersed myself in this profound work, I came to grasp that our reality is profoundly shaped by our thoughts and imagination, whether consciously or unconsciously. These thoughts, acting as vibrations, stimulate our subconscious, which in turn connects with the infinite intelligence of the universe. Through the power of imagination, we are able to create wealth and abundance in our lives.

---

110    Bruce Jr., *Alexander Crummell: Pioneer in African-American Thought*.

111    Bruce Jr., *Alexander Crummell: Pioneer in African-American Thought*.

112    Goddard, *Feeling is the Secret*.

113    W. E. B. Du Bois, *The Education of Black People: Ten Critiques, 1906–1960* (Monthly Review Press, 2001).

I think of imagination as a kind of divine builder, almost like God as depicted in various forms of imagery, an artisan potter working with clay, as taught through the writings of the prophet Jeremiah.

As the potter molds the clay, so do we possess the ability to mold our destinies through imagination and the force of the universe's cosmic consciousness. This understanding has become deeply important to me, especially the realization that positive thoughts and emotions that fill my mind that attract abundance into my life. The human imagination holds within itself a mysterious and powerful force, one that shapes not only our thoughts but also our reality. It is a creative power that molds our deepest desires and aspirations into tangible forms.

In those moments, when passion and clarity are high, this creative part of ourselves brings us into a definitive purpose or idea. Often, this process is accompanied by a profound feeling of assurance; we feel that we have reached something transcendent. It is described by Canadian psychiatrist Richard Bucke as cosmic consciousness, an extraordinary state in which one attains immense joy, a sense that the meaning and purpose of the universe have been revealed, belief in immortality, and freedom from fear of death.

In this higher state of existence, social concepts such as sin are washed away, and one perceives the unity of all that exists. Our imagination opens the door to higher consciousness, creating an advanced capacity to experience life in fuller ways than we might have dreamed. It is a gift and one worth developing. Indeed, as it develops, it guides us along a path of self-discovery and enlightenment. Thus, by applying our imagination, we begin to realize our inherent potential and create a reality filled with endless possibilities.

For Hill, synthetic imagination is the faculty by which we take old ideas, concepts, ideals, plans, or theories and combine them into new and improved forms. One notable example is Booker T. Washington's founding of the Tuskegee Institute in 1881. Despite having to overcome numerous obstacles as an African American leader during a time when racial discrimination was rampant, Washington's imagination and determination propelled the institute to greatness. Born into slavery and self-educated, his experiences at Hampton Institute and Wayland Seminary gave him a vision for an institution that would provide agricultural education for Black Americans.

Selected to lead the Tuskegee Institute with General Armstrong's backing, Washington was able to strategically use his prior experiences and knowledge to create a new type of institution. Although there were significant setbacks and resistance from the outset, Washington worked tirelessly to promote the institute across the nation, reassuring white patrons that its goals would not pose a threat to white supremacy or economic competition.

Under Washington's leadership, the Tuskegee Institute emerged as one of the finest schools of its time, boasting more than 100 well-equipped buildings, 1,500 students, a faculty of 200 teaching 38 trades and professions, and an endowment of nearly 2 million dollars at the time of his death. His philosophy infused the curriculum, emphasizing patience, enterprise, and thrift as essential principles for the financial advancement of Black Americans. Washington believed that through diligence, economic self-sufficiency, and cultural development, African Americans could attain acceptance and respect within broader society.

His steadfast commitment to these principles helped transform Tuskegee into a prestigious center of education and advancement for African Americans, leaving an indelible mark on American history. Thus, Napoleon Hill's insights on harnessing imagination and Booker T. Washington's example of visionary leadership at Tuskegee underscore the transformative power of ideas and perseverance. Together, they illuminate the potential of imagination not only to conceive visions but to actualize them, overcoming obstacles and contributing to the creation of a better world for all. These lessons resonate deeply with me, inspiring personal growth, societal progress, and a deeper understanding of our true creative potential.

## Unleashing the Power of Creative Imagination for Transformation

Napoleon Bonaparte, one of France's most illustrious military and political leaders, strongly believed in the limitless possibilities of human imagination. He espoused the idea that creative imagination serves as the workshop where our ideals take shape. According to him, our thoughts and plans are initially crafted by imagination and then transmitted to the depths of the subconscious mind. Through this process, our desires and impulses are imbued with form and action, ultimately materializing into reality. Contrary to common belief, physical limitations do not hinder our creativity or ability to manifest; rather, it is our awareness and openness to the flow of energy that define our experiences.

Our consciousness interprets this energy flow, shaping both our physical reality and our imagined constructs. Our subconscious mind plays a pivotal role in defining these experiences, relying on our ability to perceive and comprehend them accurately. Thus, everything we encounter is a blend of physical and imaginative aspects, profoundly influenced by our consciousness.

Our physical bodies and the world in which we live are manifestations of the realities we have brought into being. This is important: We must accept and take ownership of our experiences as our reality and not simply as perceptions. Our feelings ground us in the present moment so that we do not become lost in imagined worlds. They act as a channel for transforming creative vision into manifested reality. We need to be forthright about our intentions and motivations since what once seemed improbable can become inevitable through the power of creative imagination.

Understanding our own consciousness and that of others provides insight into thoughts, beliefs, and perceptions. Yet it is important to recognize that our creations may not always mirror our true consciousness due to past experiences and present circumstances. Our creative imagination represents our ideal self and the life we aspire to live, underscoring the need for a positive and intentional mindset to manifest these truths into physical existence.

The faculty of creative imagination, as Napoleon described it, yields remarkable rewards, potentially surpassing the earnings of highly educated professionals such as lawyers, engineers, teachers, and doctors. This faculty serves as a conduit to infinite intelligence, channeling intuition and inspiration that guide us toward extraordinary success. Creative imagination thrives when the conscious mind resonates at higher frequencies, driven by powerful desires. It also facilitates communication with the subconscious mind and with mastermind groups of like-minded individuals, amplifying mental capacity and achievement.

The notion that creative faculties sharpen through active development is profound yet often overlooked in today's fast-paced world. This insight underscores the importance of contemplation and reflection before action, highlighting how great leaders and artists achieve greatness by actively nurturing their creative imagination. The compilation by *Benton Spirit News*, published in February 2022, underscores the undeniable connection between our thoughts and reality, guided by the spirit of infinite intelligence within us. Through imagination, visualization, and emotion, we translate thoughts into tangible forms, shaping the fabric of the reality we perceive. The list showcases significant contributions by Indigenous peoples, particularly African Americans, throughout history who have influenced and advanced society.

The encyclopedic roster of "divine geniuses" of the human race bears a deep mark on history, demonstrating how human ingenuity has profoundly impacted a wide array of fields. The long succession of brilliant minds, such as Albert Einstein in physics, Leonardo da Vinci in the arts, and William Shakespeare in literature, has left an enduring imprint on society through epochal changes in ideas and thought. Their achievements have inspired future generations to recognize the limitless potential of human creativity and the power of inspiration. Historical examples such as the Wright brothers' pioneering flight highlight the transformative power of persistent imagination and focused effort. Despite skepticism and setbacks, their dream of flight remained constant and ultimately reached its pinnacle at Kitty Hawk, North Carolina, forever changing human history.

Lonnie Johnson's invention of the Super Soaker water gun is a powerful example of how brilliant ideas can arise from the most unexpected situations. While working on an experiment related to his contributions to a NASA mission, the idea struck him. The eventual result was a highly popular toy that delighted people around the world. His journey, from conceiving the idea to successfully marketing the product, underscores what imagination, persistence, and hard work can achieve.

Madam C. J. Walker was an extraordinary example of resilience and entrepreneurship. Born to parents who had once been enslaved, orphaned at a very young age, and later suffering from hair loss,

Walker became the founder of the first line of hair care products for African Americans. Her entrepreneurial drive and commitment to helping others earned her recognition as one of America's first self-made female millionaires, leaving an enduring legacy in the beauty industry. In the end, the words of Napoleon Bonaparte on creative imagination, along with the inspiring stories of innovators such as the Wright brothers, Lonnie Johnson, and Madam C. J. Walker, truly affirm the power of human imagination and determination.

These stories remind us that through visionary thinking, persistence, and connection to our creative potential, we can shape reality. They inspire us to cultivate a mindset of possibility and resilience that unlocks both personal and collective growth toward the realization of our dreams.

John Deere (1804–1886), a blacksmith, saw an opportunity to improve agricultural production by recognizing how inefficient most plows were in prairie soil. He turned this insight into reality by manufacturing and selling nearly one thousand plows by 1846 and partnering with Leonard Andrus to keep up with growing demand.

Thomas Alva Edison (1847–1931) was one of America's greatest inventors, leaving an indelible mark on history through innovations such as the incandescent light bulb and the phonograph, which helped shape modern communication and power generation.

Hedy Lamarr was an Austrian-American actress and inventor who pioneered foundational technologies that later became Wi-Fi, GPS, and Bluetooth, proving that intellect and innovation extend far beyond the silver screen. Ruth Handler cofounded Mattel Inc. and, despite widespread skepticism, created Barbie, a revolutionary doll for girls around the world. Her entrepreneurial vision later expanded into innovative medical products, such as the "Nearly Me" prosthetic breast, designed to support cancer survivors.

One of the most famous Black educators in American history, Booker T. Washington (1856–1915), was born into slavery. In 1881, he founded the Tuskegee Normal and Industrial Institute, now known as Tuskegee University, to provide training in agricultural and industrial skills, as well as academics. Through his vision and leadership, the institution became a premier center of learning that placed strong emphasis on education and economic enterprise for African Americans.

## The Seven Levels of Social Classes Based on Capital Wealth

Examining the seven levels of social classes defined by capital wealth in America, as analyzed by Christy Bieber, offers a valuable framework for evaluating one's financial mindset and potential for wealth accumulation. This chart helps individuals assess their current position in the pursuit of financial success and reflect on their existing financial status.

People operate at various frequencies depending on their comfort and familiarity with their financial situation. This familiarity can sometimes lead to hesitation or fear when aiming for higher levels of wealth, due to uncertainty about one's ability to succeed.

Utilizing this chart can provide valuable insight into one's financial goals and position relative to desired wealth. It underscores the importance of recognizing one's current standing and empowering oneself to overcome limitations, thereby progressing toward greater financial prosperity and security.

- Lower destitute: Characterized by extreme poverty and a lack of basic possessions and resources. For example, a destitute elderly person.

- Lower poor class: Refers to the bottom 20 percent of earners, with an income at or below $15,007.

- Lower class: Includes the bottom 20 percent of earners with incomes ranging from $15,008 to $28,008.

- Lower middle class: This includes those in the twentieth to the fortieth percentile of household income, ranging from $28,009 to $55,000.

- Middle class: Includes households in the fortieth to the sixtieth percentiles, with incomes ranging from $55,001 to $89,744.

- Upper middle class: Consists of those in the sixtieth through to the eightieth percentiles, earning between $89,745 and $149,131.

- Upper class: Represents the top 20 percent, earning $149,132 or more, reflecting significant wealth.

Understanding where our subconscious mind sets expectations for success, income, and wealth is crucial, as highlighted by Christy Bieber's chart. These figures provide a snapshot of current earning potential, not a fixed or unchangeable state, but one that can evolve over time depending on actions and mindset.

The chart clearly shows that middle upper and upper classes generally possess a much higher net worth compared to those in lower or lower middle classes. For example, while the median net worth for those earning $149,132 or more is approximately $805,400, the median for the lower class is around $12,000.

# Brain Waves, Hypnosis, and the Benefits of Using Subliminals

"The subconscious mind comes into play in various brain waves, including beta, alpha, gamma, theta, and delta. These brain waves have also been shown to activate when individuals are laughing, daydreaming, meditating, singing, dancing, or moving spontaneously" (James Morcan).

Through personal exploration, I've delved into brain waves and hypnosis, employing subliminal message recordings and affirmations to reprogram my inner creative subconscious mind. This practice involved listening to recordings during meditation and playing them while I slept. I even experienced dreams in which affirmations echoed back to me, indicating that I was actively absorbing these frequencies.

According to Dr. Jan Philamon, PhD, BA, brain waves are detectable through electrodes placed on the scalp, much like tuning into radio frequencies. EEG technology measures these waves across gamma, beta, alpha, theta, and delta bands, all of which are essential for mental performance and information processing. Harnessing these frequencies through recordings and affirmations has noticeably enhanced my mental acuity and overall well-being.

My research aligns with studies (Karremans et al., 2006; Verwijmeren et al., 2011, 2013; Strahan et al., 2002; Mudrik and Koch, 2013; García-Orza et al., 2009; Van Opstal et al., 2011; Sklar et al., 2012; Karpinski et al., 2016; Kawakami and Yoshida, 2015; Reber and Henke, 2012; Mudrik et al., 2014) that highlight the impact of brain wave frequencies on cognitive abilities. Understanding bandwidth, the capacity to transmit information within a given timeframe, is pivotal for mental agility and retention.

Subliminal messages, which operate below conscious awareness, can significantly influence decision-making and behavior, integrating into long-term memory after repeated exposure. This integration enhances their effectiveness in shaping choices and behaviors. By incorporating positive subliminal affirmations, such as "I am grateful for all the abundance that surrounds me in my life," we can create powerful shifts in mindset toward prosperity and well-being.

Brain waves, according to Dr. Jan Philamon's classification, fall into categories such as gamma, beta, alpha, theta, and delta, each playing a vital role in mental function and productivity. Gamma waves, in particular, enhance focus, memory, and problem-solving abilities. Understanding and leveraging gamma waves can optimize concentration, clarity, and emotional stability, which are essential for overall mental health. Techniques such as meditation help rebalance brain waves and restore cognitive resilience.

In summary, mastery of these insights allows us to develop a mindset open to abundance and prosperity by fully utilizing the brain's innate capacities for optimal mental and emotional well-being.

Gamma: These waves are produced when you are deeply focused or "in the zone." According to WebMD, individuals who produce more gamma waves tend to be happier and better able to concentrate. Lower gamma activity may explain difficulties with attention or focus. Gamma waves represent peak concentration and aid in information processing. Brain waves range from very fast to very slow, with gamma waves occupying the fastest end of the spectrum.

Beta: Beta waves are present when we are mentally alert and engaged. This state supports clear thinking and analytical problem-solving and commonly occurs during activities such as studying or working on challenging tasks.

Alpha: These waves occur when you are relaxed, daydreaming, or meditating. Research shows that increasing alpha activity can reduce depression, ease anxiety, and enhance creativity. Alpha waves are ideal for learning and memorization, reflecting a calm yet alert mental state.

Theta: Theta waves occur during light sleep, as well as during moments just before sleep or upon waking. They are also associated with deep relaxation, creativity, intuition, and meditation. These states are conducive to forming memories and learning new skills.

Source: National Library of Medicine, Biotech Information. The National Center for Biotechnology Information advances science and health by providing access to biomedical and genomic information.

Delta: Delta waves are the slowest brain waves recorded in humans and are associated with deep sleep, profound relaxation, and restorative healing. Delta activity is often observed in cases of brain injury, learning difficulties, or severe ADHD. Suppression of delta waves can lead to poor sleep and impaired rejuvenation of the body and brain. Adequate delta activity promotes deep rest, immune system support, and natural healing.

Various techniques can enhance and regulate brain waves. Meditation and breathing practices can stimulate gamma activity. Diet, such as incorporating nuts like pistachios, may support gamma and delta waves. Music, including binaural beats, has been shown to boost alpha and theta wave activity.

| Frequency band | Frequency | Brain states |
| --- | --- | --- |
| Gamma (γ) | >35 Hz | Concentration |
| Beta (β) | 12–35 Hz | Anxiety dominant, active, external attention, relaxed |

| Alpha ($\alpha$) | 8–12 Hz | Very relaxed, passive attention |
| Theta ($\theta$) | 4–8 Hz | Deeply relaxed, inward-focused |
| Delta ($\delta$) | 0.5–4 Hz | Sleep |

## Unlocking Learning Potential Through Scripting and Mind Mapping

Scripting, or jotting down notes in your journal, is akin to training a muscle, the brain. Just as physical exercise strengthens muscles, scripting sharpens your mind by engaging the reticular activating system (RAS), a crucial part of the subconscious **mind**. The RAS prioritizes what demands immediate attention, filtering out distractions and aiding in the processing of knowledge into memory.

While some may find journaling tedious, the mental benefits are profound. It serves as a tool to process events, providing a safe outlet to vent and express inner thoughts and ideals. Moreover, it enhances cognitive function through regular memory recall and reflection.

Your brain, much like a muscle, thrives on regular training. Journaling doesn't necessitate stress or upheaval; even brief notes can yield significant benefits. Whether recording accomplishments, reflecting on mistakes, or chronicling daily occurrences, each entry contributes to mental agility and clarity.

Conscious mind mapping is another powerful technique. It involves centralizing an idea and branching out with related thoughts and connections. This method enhances comprehension and retention by visually organizing information around a central theme or objective. Manifesting desires involves harnessing the inner consciousness's ability to connect with infinite intelligence consciousness. By programming the inner consciousness through repetition and visualization, we can align our lives with our aspirations. The inner consciousness operates in the present and is incapable of distinguishing between reality and imagination, making it a potent tool for realizing our goals.

In essence, by integrating scripting, journaling, and mind mapping into daily routines, we engage our brain's capacity for growth and transformation. These practices not only foster mental clarity and creativity but also empower us to manifest our ideal lives through deliberate subconscious programming.

## Understanding the Three States of Consciousness: 3D, 4D, and 5D—a.k.a.

This exploration unveils deep insights. It delves into the 3D, 4D, and 5D states of consciousness and further reveals our connection with reality, a connection that extends beyond the conventional physical world. We traditionally perceive reality in three dimensions: length, width, and height. However, theories in quantum physics suggest the existence of additional dimensions, including time and consciousness, which contribute to a richer understanding of the universe.

These dimensions embody spiritual or metaphysical levels of consciousness and existence. 3D consciousness pertains to our immediate physical reality, experienced through the senses and material existence. It is characterized by a linear perception of time, material focus, and dualistic thinking that divides reality into opposites such as good and bad or success and failure. This polarized mindset often leads to ego-driven behavior rooted in fear and scarcity.

Transitioning to 4D consciousness deepens our understanding of time, which becomes more fluid and interconnected. Here, time is perceived as cyclical rather than linear. Emotion, intuition, and the subconscious dominate. This growing interconnectedness dissolves rigid dualities and creates a more holistic view of reality. In this state, individuals may experience heightened intuition, greater awareness of synchronicities, and deeper spiritual insight. This shift fosters emotional healing, empathy, and self-understanding.

5D consciousness represents a significant expansion of awareness. Time is no longer experienced as a sequence but as an integrated continuum. In this dimension, a profound sense of unity with all existence emerges, diminishing the sense of separation and ego. Sensitivity to energy and vibration increases, and qualities such as unconditional love and joy become more prevalent. Actions are guided by intuition, oneness, and consciousness, fostering harmony in relationships and supporting spiritual growth.

The transition from 3D to 4D involves tuning into deeper emotional and psychological patterns, often marked by introspection and personal transformation. Moving from 4D to 5D signifies an ego-transcending state in which unity and spiritual awareness flourish, resulting in meaningful shifts in perception and interaction with reality.

Central to this exploration is the understanding that the human brain functions as a communicator, receiver, and broadcaster of information. It operates as a data processor and energetic circuit, much like a brain computer interface. Through sine waves and amplitude modulation, brain frequencies transmit information intricately linked to manifestation and our connection to cosmic consciousness.

Within these states of consciousness lies immense potential for personal and collective transformation. Each state represents a distinct dimension of reality, and movement through them enhances our understanding of ourselves and the world. This journey toward higher consciousness unveils infinite possibilities and invites alignment with deeper truths and aspirations.

Consider Raimon Samso's metaphor of the mind as a 3D printer. Just as a 3D printer transforms digital designs into physical objects, the mind converts thoughts into behaviors and lived experiences. This analogy highlights the inherent creativity within us. When one dwells intensely on an idea, it can become an experience.

Our intentions and thoughts act as creators of reality. The emphasis lies not on imagination alone or even the law of attraction, but on intent. In the 3D printer analogy, intent is the central force. A person's ability to believe in something can give rise to a solid reality born from that belief. This metaphor also parallels the Neurath ship, where construction occurs layer by layer while remaining within the real world.

As we navigate these dimensions, mindfulness and intentionality are cultivated, sharpening our awareness of thought. This awareness reveals how beliefs shape reality. By choosing empowering thoughts, we create experiences aligned with our deepest desires.

Embracing interconnectedness enhances compassion and understanding. As consciousness expands, we recognize that our actions influence collective energy. This realization inspires positive contribution, unity, and harmony.

The journey through dimensions is both personal and collective. By expanding consciousness, we align with a greater cosmic narrative that fosters growth and transformation. The benefits extend beyond the individual to humanity and the universe itself.

The Kybalion states, "As above, so below; as below, so above."

Throughout my journey, I have researched and studied manifestation extensively. One key principle is mentalism, the projection of thought into the universe. Through this principle, we learn to harness the power of the mind to shape reality within infinite intelligence.

Correspondence aligns with mentalism and teaches that what we hold in thought and subconscious awareness becomes reality. It explains levels of existence through varying vibrational frequencies and how they interact.

By deepening awareness, we observe how conscious thoughts impact reality. To align with our highest good, we must identify and release limiting paradigms. This allows harmony with the manifestation of infinite intelligence and cosmic consciousness.

Vibration exists in all things, physical and spiritual. Each carries a frequency, and we can influence our vibration through thought and emotion. Higher vibrations support positive manifestation.

The principle of polarity teaches that opposites are degrees of the same spectrum, like water and ice. Physical and spiritual energies are similarly connected, with spiritual energy vibrating at a higher frequency.

Rhythm reflects life's cycles of highs and lows. By focusing on growth and forward movement, we maintain a higher rhythm.

Gender exists in all creation as masculine and feminine energy. These forces operate across all planes of existence.

Energy is emotion in motion. Masculine and feminine energies must balance within the brain and consciousness, unified through love. When both hemispheres of the brain vibrate harmoniously, creation is optimized across physical, intellectual, and spiritual planes.

All manifestation originates from a single source of consciousness and follows universal laws. According to the principle of correspondence, the "I am all" creates the universe mentally, and human consciousness mirrors this process through mental imagery.

Creative energy enables innovation and expression. Artists, inventors, musicians, and writers channel this force naturally. Creativity can also be cultivated through serene environments, music, or nature. Observing children at play reminds us of imagination lost through adulthood.

The Temple of Wisdom symbolizes the pursuit of knowledge and enlightenment, representing a state of inner reflection and higher learning.

The sixth sense refers to heightened awareness such as intuition, clairvoyance, and spiritual perception, connecting us to universal truth.

Aligning with God consciousness involves embracing positive self-emotions and releasing negative ones. God consciousness embodies qualities such as love, peace, abundance, confidence, joy, and strength. Negative emotions like fear, doubt, poverty, and sorrow hinder connection with the higher self.

Recognizing these patterns allows conscious choice. Choosing positivity elevates vibration and creates fulfillment while inspiring others.

Aligning with God consciousness requires commitment through meditation, gratitude, and self-reflection. These practices release negativity and allow divine qualities to flourish.

Understanding interconnectedness fosters compassion, healing, and unity. This journey of self-discovery unlocks potential and leads to a life of joy, purpose, and abundance, encouraging us to share our gifts with the world.

In confronting subconscious negativity, acknowledging emotions such as fear, sorrow, or inferiority is essential. Awareness clears the path for positive energy and abundance.

Overcoming these obstacles aligns us with higher purpose and inspires others. Contributing to collective consciousness through love and positivity transforms both individual and collective experience.

## Raise the Thought to Reach the Result

Lift up the thought to reach the result, this concept is a powerful reminder of how mindset and determination play critical roles in shaping outcomes. This statement highlights that our thoughts and beliefs are powerful forces, serving as the foundation for our actions and results. Elevating our thoughts requires us to rise above limitations in pursuit of desired outcomes. The phrase emphasizes that success demands not only positive thinking but also hard work and diligence. It encourages us to cultivate a growth-oriented mindset, where continuous improvement and innovation propel us forward rather than settling for mediocrity.

Success demands determination. Determination strengthens resolve and commitment toward goals, enabling us to overcome obstacles and challenges. By aligning our thoughts with our aspirations, we unlock our full potential and achieve remarkable results. This serves as a powerful reminder that success is not merely a matter of luck or talent but also the result of developing the right mindset and maintaining relentless determination to translate thoughts into action and realize desired outcomes. This approach inspires us to strive higher, believe in ourselves, and persist in the pursuit of our dreams.

The vibrational chart below can help us understand and increase overall vibration and energy. To use the chart, first locate where you are on the scale, from low-vibrational feelings at the bottom to high-vibrational feelings at the top. Note the emotions and behaviors associated with each level. This heightened awareness helps clarify how thoughts, feelings, and actions influence overall vibration.

From there, set intentions to rise into higher vibrations through practices such as gratitude, self-care, and positive thinking. Balance is essential, as one cannot remain in a high vibrational state at all times. Regular reference to the vibrational chart helps maintain awareness and supports intentional adjustments toward a more positive and aligned life. This tool serves as a guide into higher states of being, consistently attracting greater abundance and joy through continued use and intention.

This process involves shifting your mind and beliefs to become a vibrational match for the things you desire, including wealth, prosperity, perfect health, financial freedom, and enjoyment of life.

Release negative thoughts about money and success and let go of limiting beliefs. Focus on abundance and practice gratitude for what you already have. Visualize yourself living in financial freedom and enjoying optimal health, fully experiencing the joy and excitement it brings. Taking action toward your goals includes setting financial objectives, developing budgets, and investing in well-being, all of which support becoming a vibrational match to prosperity. Surround yourself with positive and successful people to elevate your vibration. As you practice self-care and self-love, your sense of worthiness grows, attracting even more abundance into your life.

Believe that the universe holds infinite abundance and that you deserve wealth, prosperity, perfect health, financial freedom, and enjoyment. By aligning your thoughts, feelings, actions, and beliefs with abundance and positivity, you naturally become a vibrational match for your desires. An ignited vision is the first step toward achieving success and creating the life you desire. It involves vividly imagining what you want to accomplish and persistently pursuing it with passion and determination. However, visualization alone is not enough; your vibration must also align with your vision.

Align thoughts, feelings, and actions with your vision, emitting the positive energy you wish to attract. Thoughts are the origin of results; they generate feelings that drive actions and ultimately determine outcomes.

You control your thoughts and can choose positivity over negativity. Use the chart below as a guide to align yourself with your vision and manifest desired outcomes. By consciously choosing positivity and taking consistent action toward your vision, you can materialize your aspirations and create a fulfilling life. Eckhart Tolle wisely noted that focusing on negativity or complaining only intensifies problems. Instead, one must either change the situation, accept it, or walk away.

Maintaining focus and motivation toward your vision is essential for success and fulfillment. This mindset frees you from negative thoughts and self-pity that hinder goal attainment. Aligning thoughts and actions with an ignited vision allows manifestation to unfold, fostering progress through determination and enthusiasm. This optimistic outlook reveals possibilities rather than obstacles, paving the way toward a purposeful and rewarding life.

With positive thinking, you can achieve meaningful success and cultivate a life filled with joy, fulfillment, and achievement. Such a mindset is vital for success in both personal and professional spheres. By remaining focused and motivated, obstacles are overcome and progress continues toward goals. Refer to the chart below to understand the power of positive thinking in guiding a rewarding life. Ultimately, nurturing an optimistic and determined mindset is key to achieving success and creating a meaningful life.

**Chart Instruction:**

Please refer to the attached letter regarding the Emotional Spectrum Chart and follow the instructions outlined in that document.

**Circular Graph: Embracing Positivity Refusing Negativity**

A circular graph acts as an effective visual aid. It represents emotional vibrational states and depicts the choice of positivity over negativity. The graph arranges emotional data along a circular scale, with high-frequency emotions at the top and low-frequency emotions at the bottom.

The graph serves as a visual representation of human emotions and allows an individual to track their feelings in real time. Users can color-code various emotions and, in doing so, patterns begin to emerge. Over time, these patterns can encourage reflection.

For instance, one can assess whether negativity always occurs at the same time of day or whether positivity consistently happens during a particular activity. By recognizing these patterns, users can make informed changes.

The graph also provides support at the present moment. When an individual is struggling, all they need to do is look at the graph to see a real-time visual representation of their emotional state.

This alone can be soothing. It can offer grounding and serve as a much-needed reminder, a reminder that things are not always this bad and that positivity may be just around the corner.

Overall, the graph can be a powerful tool in the journey toward better mental health. Is it a substitute for professional help? Definitely not. However, it can still be worth trying. It also offers a way to find emotional footing and build greater self-awareness.

# Graph Structure

Center of the circle:

Focal point of the core: It is a central graphic point symbolizing your chosen vibrational stance. Classify it simply as "Vibrational Choice."

Outer circle: Emotional spectrum, mapping emotional frequencies. Positive emotions at the top and negative emotions at the bottom.

Circle points: Place the points in order of vibrational frequency. Include new, powerful numerals. Utilize the labels and descriptions provided in the presentation.

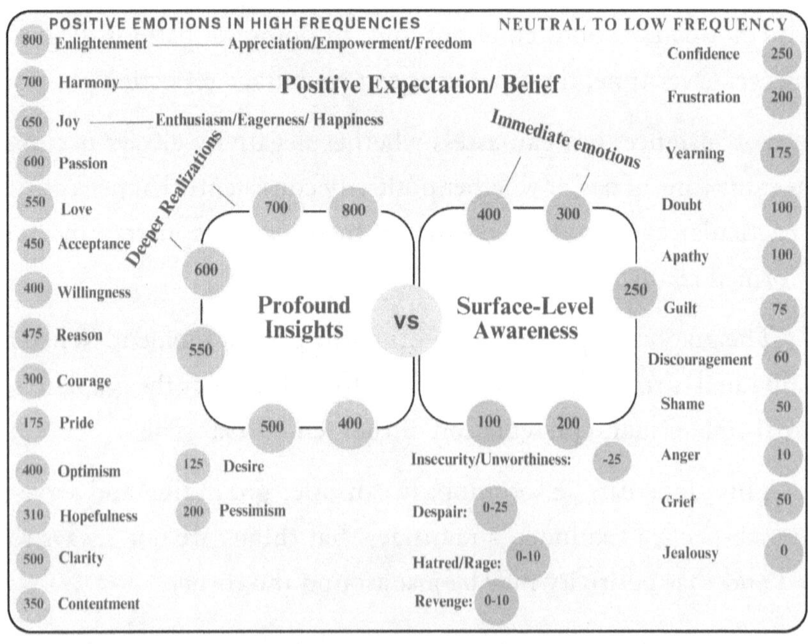

# Positive Emotions in High Frequencies

800: *Enlightenment.* Not a state of confusion, but one of profound clarity. You can perceive things remotely and engage with their true nature. You see all that is happening in the here and now. It is a powerful state. Hold it close. Embrace it fully.

700: *Harmony.* A mental state of balance and inner peace. Natural order. Free of opposition. Homeostasis. Balance of thought, spirit, and mind. Harmony, such a beautiful word. Sit with it for a moment. Bask in it. Close your eyes and feel the sense of balance. It is all within you.

650: *Joy.* An emotion of intense happiness. Exhilaration. Delight. Bliss. It is radiant. Fill your heart with joy, a gift to the soul. Channel that joy, that lightness. It is a sense of upliftment from within.

600: *Passion.* Is it intensity? Is it enthusiasm? Is it fervor? Yes. It is the fire that ignites within. Energy. Drive. It powers you. It is the force behind action and creativity. Passion. Feel it. Embrace it.

550: *Love.* What is this emotion? Is it a feeling, an attachment, an attraction? Love. It is deep compassion and unconditional acceptance of others. Feel it. Feel the emotions that come with it. Love.

500: *Clarity.* Is it a pure emotion? Perhaps not. It is a state of mind and a state of thought. Clarity. Insightful understanding. Clear. Lucid. It washes over you. Put aside muddled thoughts. Embrace clarity.

450: *Acceptance.* It is embracing life's events without judgment. Acceptance. It is a liberating feeling. Do not fight it. Accept it. It is what it is. It means the world. It is simply acceptance.

400: *Willingness.* It is openness to opportunities, new experiences, and fresh possibilities. Openness to growth, change, and fulfillment.

Willingness. It is welcoming what is next and what is to come. It is positivity. It is readiness. It is willingness.

300: *Courage.* It is boldness in facing fears and challenges. It is inner strength. Fear becomes smaller. Challenges become conquerable. It is courage. It is a lion's heart. It is fearlessness. It is courage.

## Neutral to Low Frequency

250: *Confidence.* Description: An unwavering belief in oneself and firm conviction in one's abilities.

200: *Frustration.* Description: Intense feelings of being hindered or blocked, accompanied by a sense of unfulfillment.

175: *Yearning.* Description: An insistent feeling of need for improvement and a strong desire for change.

150: *Anxiety.* Explanation: An unsettling feeling of uneasiness, marked by worry about future events.

100: *Apathy.* Description: An absence of concern and a lack of participation in life.

75: *Guilt.* Description: A feeling of sorrow or remorse for past actions.

50: *Shame.* Description: A painful feeling of unworthiness and deep self-judgment.

## Low Frequency (Negative Emotions)

25: *Despair.* Description: A sense of utter hopelessness and profound loss.

10: *Anger.* Description: Unrelenting frustration accompanied by destructive tendencies.

0: *Jealousy.* Description: Feelings of inadequacy and resentment toward others.

-25: *Insecurity.* Description: Uncertainty about self-worth and personal value.

-50: *Grief.* Description: Deep sorrow and disappointment.

## Visual Representation

Circle segments: Each segment embodies an emotion. Segment size conveys the intensity of vibration. Higher frequencies occupy the top while lower frequencies reside at the bottom.

Color coding: A gradient color concept illustrates the emotional spectrum. Warm, vibrant tones signify positive emotions while cool, muted shades represent negative emotions.

Connecting lines: Draw lines from the core point to each emotion. This reflects the journey from negativity toward positivity.

## Key Takeaway

Message: This graph visually captures a range of emotional vibrations. It emphasizes conscious choice to engage with higher frequency emotions. Moving to the top of the circle aligns you more closely with positivity and empowerment This leads to a more fulfilling and enriched life.

*"If you get into the picture, into the energy of the good you desire, you can't help but manifest it"*

*(Albert Einstein).*

Our world today is profoundly shaped by two essential faculties, the programming senses and the vibrational nervous system. These faculties enable our minds to interpret vast amounts of data, continually shaping our experiences and beliefs. As infinite intelligent spirit consciousness, we tap into cosmic consciousness, becoming aware of our subconscious and unconscious thoughts and beliefs.

By comprehending and reprogramming our mental paradigms, we can alter our self-programming circle and mold our ideal self-image. With our reticulated activating system operating online, we have the capacity to make conscious choices about what we want to perceive, believe, and know. This process dictates how we feel about ourselves, others, and the world in general. By positively managing perception, reasoning, intuition, imagination, and visualization, we can create a more elevated reality not only for ourselves but also for those around us.

The following chart represents the many aspects of the mind that hold untapped potential for exploration and utilization in furthering individual development and achieving a deeper understanding of the world. The human mind possesses tremendous capacity for growth and evolution. By leveraging these faculties, we can continually expand both self-awareness and our understanding of the world.

From feelings and thoughts to fantasy and intuition, all these aspects of the mind play an important role in how we perceive the world. Introspection allows us to dive deeply within, gaining profound insight into ourselves and our surroundings, thereby developing as individuals.

By exploring these different aspects, we more fully realize our humanness and expand our potential for learning and understanding the world around us. The following chart reminds us of the limitless opportunities hidden within our minds, all waiting to be tapped for personal growth and development.

Since the dawn of inquiry into the capabilities of the human mind, each accomplishment has revealed more about who we are and the world we inhabit. By embracing the complexities of the mind, we unlock new dimensions of personal growth and understanding, enriching life through increased awareness, creativity, and fulfillment.

## I AM INFINITE INTELLIGENCE

| THOUGHTS | CONSCIOUSNESS | SPIRIT |
|---|---|---|
| Perception | Cosmic Consciousness<br>Perception<br>Conscience<br>Subconscious<br>Unconscious | |

| BELIEFS | PROGRAMS |
|---|---|
| Conviction | God<br>Self<br>People<br>World |

| EXPERIENCE | CONSCIOUS |
|---|---|
| | Choose<br>Will<br><br>RAS<br>Reticular Activation System<br>Gatekeeper<br>Conscious<br>Subconscious<br><br>Will<br>Perception<br>Reasoning<br>Intuition<br>Imagination<br>Visualization |

| REPROGRAM | IDEAL SELF-IMAGE |
|---|---|
| | Self-programming Cycle |

| PARADIGMS | |
|---|---|
| Thoughts<br>Belief<br>Conviction | Change<br>Belief |

# Intuition and Dream Symbol Exercises

Intuition and dream symbol exercises are some of the most powerful tools that allow people to tap back into their imagination, subconscious, and inner spirit. Such practices include learning how to tap into our inner knowing that always seems to be present and using dream symbols as a form of communication with our subconscious mind. As one refines their intuition and interprets dreams more intentionally, one can learn quite a bit about oneself and one's aspirations.

The following exercises open a doorway to our creative abilities, allowing us to reconnect with our inner spirit, which is sometimes overshadowed by the burdens of everyday living. If one could release the chains of logic and reason, a power would be unleashed that allows imagination to become the guide. Such processes develop greater awareness, clarity, and direction in life.

By listening to our intuition and learning to interpret the symbolism in our dreams, we tap into deeper states of consciousness, thereby uncovering hidden wisdom. This opens new levels of self-awareness, connecting us with universal knowing that resides deep within ourselves.

In the end, intuition and dream symbol exercises become powerful catalysts for personal growth, extending deeply into ourselves and connecting us with everything that surrounds us. Symbols and images can be highly influential on our inner selves and subconscious processes without our conscious awareness. They are able to elicit deep resonance within our hearts, creativity, intuition, and authenticity in a singularly profound way. Whether experienced in waking life or in dreams, these symbols speak to us about something important, offering insight into our path of self-discovery.

With an open heart, free from judgment and excessive rationalization, we may actively explore these experiences in a responsible manner and take full advantage of what they can offer in transforming our lives. Recurring symbols are a powerful tool for accessing the deeper layers of the self and gaining insight into the subconscious operation of the mind. Letting go of inhibitions and trusting that symbols exist to guide us in personal growth and spiritual journeys unlocks their full potential. It is very important to stay focused on selected symbols, as this allows us to gain deeper insight and prevents our potential for self-discovery from becoming clouded.

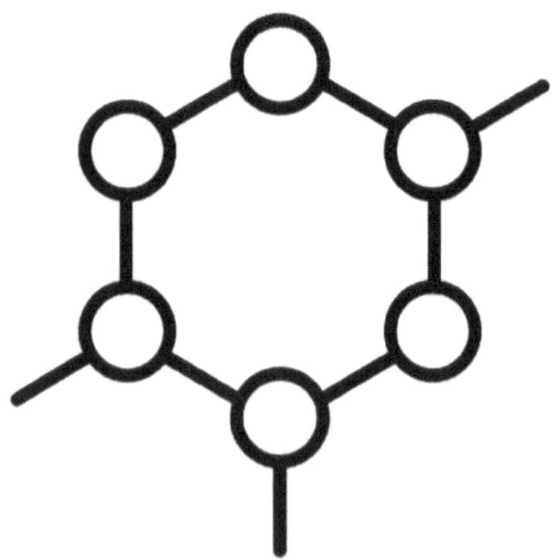

These steps guide someone toward directly connecting with themselves and their intuition in a systematic manner. Take about five minutes to meditate, and try to center yourself. Find a comfortable position where you can close your eyes and focus on your breathing. Imagine distractions fading away like ocean waves, calming into a serene pond. This tranquil space serves as a sanctuary for quieting the mind and accessing inner calm, available whenever needed.

As you repeat affirmations, invite your subconscious mind to reveal insights. Embrace any symbols or objects that intuitively come to mind as gateways to deeper understanding. Avoid analyzing these impressions; instead, accept them with trust and openness to what they may signify. Choose an image, symbol, or object that resonates as a portal to your heart and intuition. Draw this symbol in the center of a six-pointed shape, with circles at each point, and encircle it with lines. Without prompting, jot down qualities associated with the symbol. This exercise encourages unexpected connections and insights to emerge naturally.

Select the phrase that resonates most deeply and transform it into a question or a personal request. By responding spontaneously and without overthinking, you can uncover practical actions aligned with your inner guidance. This process facilitates self-discovery and deeper insights into your true self.

The resulting six-pointed shape serves as a tangible reminder of this transformative process. Display it prominently to reinforce your commitment to ongoing self-exploration and growth. Enter the process of unlocking this hidden wisdom within, fostering a closer relationship with your intuition and inner spirit.

## Self-sabotage and How to Unlock Full Manifestation Potential

*Lazybones*, noun, refers to a do-nothing. When people perceive someone as not doing anything with their life, they may use words such as bum, deadbeat, good-for-nothing, goof-off, idler, laggard, lay-about, indolent, loafer, lackadaisical, lounger, slothful, malingerer, moocher, shirker, slacker, sloth, or sponger. A miser is someone who hoards their wealth and doesn't share or spend any of it. If you remember the old saying, "You can't take it with you," then you won't end up acting stingy like a miser.

Self-sabotage is one of the major hindrances to success. It is a pattern of behavior in which an individual knowingly or unknowingly hinders their progress and success. These behaviors can manifest in many forms, such as procrastination, self-doubt, fear of failure, negative thoughts and habits, lack of discipline, and more. Self-sabotage can stem from deep-rooted beliefs and fears that prevent an individual from taking risks and achieving goals. It can also result from low self-esteem and fear of success, leading to behaviors that prevent one from reaching full potential.

Self-sabotage can lead to missed opportunities, unfulfilled potential, and a vicious cycle in which an individual struggles to live a successful life.

Breaking negative trends and patterns is the gateway to a better life and success. It requires deep self-examination, seeking help, and intentional effort to turn negative thoughts and behaviors around. Once the chains of self-sabotage have been overcome and replaced with a positive mindset, true potential can be unleashed and success can be achieved.

It is the power of actualization that comes from within the spirit in us, which materializes the biggest dreams and desires. The power of this energy can be witnessed in how it connects us with the universe, linking our minds with desired outcomes through endless possibilities. What it takes to bring our wants into being is the fusion of thoughts, beliefs, and actions with that inner spirit. It is essential to understand one's intention while also believing in guidance from one's spirit. At times, one's spirit combines with desires to form a powerful magnetic attraction, drawing opportunities, people, and circumstances into our lives to fulfill our goals. Inner connection to the spirit places us in a position to co-create our destiny and live the life we have always dreamt of. By listening to and caring for our spirit, we have the power to unleash our limitless inner potential and turn our thoughts into tangible reality.

Manifestation involves the concept that thoughts and beliefs shape reality. However, a crucial element in the actualization of anything is the spirit itself. The spirit, or soul, energizes the mind and emotions to work continually toward achieving goals. Its power can help manifest our wishes when the spirit within aligns with our goals and beliefs. The spirit bridges the conscious and subconscious mind by harmonizing thinking and behavior. The spirit inspires us and energizes action toward our dreams. Our spirit also aligns us with a higher source of guidance and wisdom, allowing us to tap into universal energy and achieve even more meaningful and impactful desires. As we cultivate alignment with our inner spirit, the doors to limitless possibilities open, and the actualization of goals into physical reality becomes far more accessible. In this sense, nurturing and paying attention to the voice of the spirit is an integral part of true realization of our potential.

Pamela's self-sabotaging behavior pattern greatly affected her relationships and overall success in life. While she tried to maintain a healthy and satisfying relationship, problems and conflicts repeatedly arose, eventually destroying her partnerships. This stemmed from a lack of self-worth and fear of intimacy, which led her to push away people who cared for her. Professionally, Pamela also sabotaged her chances of success through procrastination and lack of self-confidence. Consequently, she let opportunities slip away that she was fully capable of pursuing. Pamela knew she was undermining her own growth, but she did not find it easy to break the cycle. It wasn't until she sought therapy and built stronger self-esteem that she was able to overcome these patterns and find true happiness in both her relationships and career. She came to understand that self-love and acceptance were essential because they allowed her to release destructive patterns and embrace a more positive outlook. Through this, Pamela became more successful, avoided negativity and toxic relationships, and built healthier relationships grounded in mutual trust, communication, and **connection**.

## Tapping into the Power of Role Models to Establish Self-esteem

In today's world, the impact of role models on an individual's self-concept, confidence, and level of manifestation is significant. Hollywood stars, athletes, and even historical figures can be powerful sources of inspiration for building inner confidence. Yet as much as role models may boost self-confidence, the true spark of confidence must come from within. Confidence is one of the strongest attributes that shapes success and happiness, and it can be strengthened through guidance from positive role models. Whether through family, friends, teachers, or public figures, role models encourage us to realize our potential by believing in our own capabilities.

True self-confidence does come from within, and it takes time to grow. We overcome obstacles and fulfill desires by developing the confidence that already exists inside us. While role models can inspire and point the way, self-belief remains essential. Trust your abilities, find strength in positivity, and let that be your foundation. Confidence is the foundation of a well-lived life, and when it is strengthened by the influence of role models, inner strength can carry us toward our goals with determination and certainty.

Congratulations for hanging in there and sticking with it.

These past few chapters have been informational and light on exercises. I have no doubt, though, that you've been continuing the visualizations, affirmations, and journaling. Now it's time to give you space for reflection on what we have discussed so far. Take a moment to consider the following questions and write your responses in your journal:

How do you think this has been reflected in your life through the positive role models that might have influenced your perception of yourself and your confidence? Name times in your life when a role model made a deep impact.

What could you do to develop and strengthen your inner confidence and self-belief without depending on outer influences such as role models?

Can you think of a time when you questioned yourself or felt insecure, and how it might have been different if you had acted with the confidence inside you, like the role models you admire?

I encourage you to look at their life experiences. What role has confidence and self-belief played, and how can you tap into your inner strength in service of your goals?

# CHAPTER 12

# THE POWER OF DETACHMENT AND UNIVERSAL PRINCIPLES FOR FULFILLMENT

Change the way you look at things and the things you look at change.

—Wayne Dyer

It becomes clear that wealth is not solely about accumulating money but about understanding the deeper connections among physics, science, and psychology that shape our experience of prosperity. Many struggle to achieve financial success because these connections are overlooked, often attributing limitations to a lack of capital. In reality, the true barrier often exists within the conscious mind, reflecting patterns formed in our inner world.

By intentionally engaging our creative power through daily imagination practices, we activate the law of imagination, a principle echoed by thinkers such as Einstein, who valued imagination beyond mere knowledge. This practice is not idle daydreaming; it is a disciplined spiritual exercise and an act of self-awareness that releases divine creativity, supporting detachment, clarity, and deeper fulfillment.

It is through the visualization of goals, combined with relentless effort, that one moves closer to wealth. Many people are bogged down by restrictive perceptions and negative affirmations about money, thereby never realizing their potential. To be free, one must break loose from such chains by replacing these constraints with abundance, allowing the mind to experience financial freedom.

Great minds, from Napoleon Hill to modern-day visionaries, have affirmed throughout history that the key to destiny lies in the mind. They understood that as humanity learns to govern the mind and align it with positive ideas and motives, possibility becomes limitless in every avenue of life.

Such vivid envisioning, on a personal level, as demonstrated by Jim Carrey's approach of seeing success as an already completed reality, illustrates this principle clearly. Persevering through painful and untrue circumstances, along with inherited beliefs, I continued to picture a different future. That resilience, an enduring characteristic I learned from the difficult experiences of my family, became a valuable teacher in determination and the power of imagination.

It has been a misconception for some to believe they are not creative or that creativity is not meant for them. In truth, all reality is rooted in the power of visualization and higher consciousness. Creativity is not a gift reserved for a few. Recent scientific understanding shows that creativity extends beyond genetic limitations and the constraints of the physical world. Our creative faculties free us from material limitations and launch us into exploring new frontiers and possibilities.

Consciousness also plays a pivotal role in shaping our reality, as thoughts and beliefs directly influence experiences. Harnessing the power of visualization and higher consciousness allows us to surpass physical limitations, unlocking deeper creativity and understanding. Far from being a weakness, imagination emerges as a powerful tool for elevating insight and creation beyond the mundane.

The concept "if you can dream it, you can achieve it" underscores the transformative power of imagination. It reminds us not to restrain our potential by refusing to dream, but instead to use imagination as fuel to unlock our fullest potential.

The power of thought and imagination creates the blueprint for the future, forming the platform upon which tangible achievements are built. Action is equally essential because without it, dreams remain fantasies rather than realities.

Thus, this process is not whimsy but a fundamental dynamic that shapes our lives. It is through balancing imaginative vision with directed action that a path is set toward a better future for ourselves and those around us.

When combined with deliberate action and unwavering belief in our goals, imagination transforms ideas into tangible achievements, paving the way for genuine success and fulfillment.

The distinction between a great mind and a conventional mind lies in their approach to problem-solving and critical thinking. Conventional minds often adhere to established norms and patterns, relying heavily on sensory perception and logical reasoning. In contrast, great minds question the status quo, guided by curiosity and driven by a desire for deeper understanding. They integrate logic with intuition and emotion, recognizing a broader spectrum of intelligence that includes intuitive and emotional insight.

Conventional minds seek to understand and relate to the world through that which is tangible: sensory data and logical deduction. Great minds, however, understand the wisdom of the heard and the strength of Intuition, as conventionally disregarded, draws upon emotional intelligence and experience for insights unreachable by logical reasoning alone.[114] True knowledge would thus involve, apart from the intellect, an emotional resonance that is built from personal experiences, empathy, and depth in insight.[115]

In the world we live in today, which is dynamic and interconnected, being able to actualize our fullest potential involves far more than intellect. It involves emotional intelligence, the imagination that can be a source of vision, and the deepening of contact with others.[116] Imagination, so highly stressed by Neville Goddard and many others, plays a core role in the materialization of wishes.[117] By vividly imagining our goals as already achieved, we align our energies with their realization.

Whenever people come together in harmony, merging energies and insights toward one objective, the end result is something no single person could achieve: a collective intelligence greater than the sum of its parts. Such an idea is underlined by in-depth research conducted by Napoleon Hill into the power of collaborative effort and shared vision.[118] Our own mastermind group exemplifies this synergy, leveraging diverse perspectives and resources to accelerate personal and professional growth.

As we continue to explore and apply these principles, we deepen our understanding of our boundless potential and our capacity to shape our destiny. Our mastermind group becomes a very powerful conduit to harness the transformational power of the imagination

114   Hawkins, *Power vs. Force: The Hidden Determinants of Human Behavior.*

115   Daniel Goleman, *Emotional Intelligence: Why It Can Matter More Than IQ* (Bantam Books, 1995).

116   Hill, *Think and Grow Rich.*

117   Goddard, *Feeling is the Secret.*

118   Hill, *Think and Grow Rich.*

for the creation of a successful life, wherein all dreams can spring into reality. The often-underestimated power of imagination acts as the connecting link between our thoughts and the physical world, enabling us to envision and materialize our desired outcomes.

Within our mastermind group, we deeply understand and actively harness this power of imagination to propel us toward our goals. We believe staunchly in the fact that any vision one can fathom is attainable. My diverse team combines a wealth of perspectives, knowledge, and resources that nurture collective understanding and accelerate progress even faster.

The effectiveness of the group depends on members trusting one another, communicating openly, and not disclosing any information outside the group; hence, it is a safe space where members share challenges and receive invaluable feedback. Through our shared imagination and inner vision, we've witnessed dreams turn into tangible realities, fostering both personal and professional growth.

Our mastermind group stands testament to the profound impact of effectively utilizing imagination. We continue, through the help and encouragement of other sojourners, to avail ourselves of that power to create more valuable and meaningful lives for ourselves and others.

Neville's teachings remind us that imagination is the bridge between our current state and desired reality. It's not about fretting over how our imagined state will materialize, but rather about trusting in its creative force. By dwelling in our desired future state and allowing a sequence of events to unfold, we align ourselves with the fulfillment of our desires. This process isn't about wanting alone but about believing and embodying our desires. Imagination, when actively engaged, allows us to assume the consciousness of our desired state, gradually manifesting it into tangible form.

In essence, success hinges on our unwavering faith in the creative potential of our imagination. It begins by believing in ourselves and knowing that our imagination is one of the most powerful tools to manifest dreams into practical achievements.

First, one must clearly identify their goal and then develop a plan to achieve it. As the saying goes, "two heads are better than one"—highlighting the power of collaboration in problem-solving and goal setting. Visualization and imagination play key roles in plotting, strategizing, and organizing objectives.

Breaking goals into smaller, achievable steps allows one to track progress and build momentum along the way.

Success means admitting to oneself a positive attitude of mind and building on what he believes in himself or his capability. Indeed, this is of prime importance when one has to make his way against the odds that are sure to threaten his determination, and the obstacles that scar the road to success. This allows us to see challenges as opportunities for growth and to believe in ourselves, enhancing our resolve to continue in the midst of hardship.

The third step emphasizes building a network of like-minded individuals who can support and encourage one another. Having supportive people with similar passions and aspirations offers immense guidance, encouragement, and accountability in large measures. Such peers offer great support—not only in realizing our journey but also in inspiring and pushing us toward excellence. Their presence fosters a positive, nurturing environment where mutual success is celebrated, and progress is accelerated.

The fourth step underscores the continuous learning and pursuit of knowledge and skill enhancement to help the individual self-development of having a growing mindset.

This way, embracing a growth mindset and remaining open to new ideas and perspectives are essential. Through ongoing learning, individuals stay adaptable and ahead of evolving trends, ensuring relevance and competence. In a mastermind group setting, this step is enriched by collective insights and experiences, further enhancing personal and professional development.

The sixth step advocates for discipline and focus, which are crucial for averting distractions that derail progress. It necessitates setting boundaries, prioritizing tasks, and maintaining organizational clarity. With unwavering commitment to goals and a steadfast resolve to resist temptations, individuals ensure the efficient use of time and energy, key ingredients for sustained success.

Perseverance through challenges defines the eighth step, recognizing setbacks as inevitable but transient. True success requires resilience and determination to weather storms and emerge stronger. Each obstacle surmounted builds character and expertise, propelling individuals closer to their ultimate goals.

Finally, the ninth step encourages celebrating accomplishments as milestones of progress and sources of motivation. Recognizing and commemorating achievements not only boosts morale but also fuels ambition for future endeavors.

In conclusion, these mastermind steps provide a comprehensive framework for navigating the journey toward success.

In the simple passive state, the imagination does appear somewhat cliché and unoriginal as it simply emphasizes over and over images or scenes from our past. When we were kids, we liked to compare our thoughts to sand and how thoughts are like grains of sand, when focused, gather other sands to form shapes and become useful to others when shaped creatively With creative minds as children, we tried to explain next how thoughts can be compared to energy particles, focusing light particles to construct something tangible. This principle, often referred to as the law of attraction suggests that we attract results in our lives depending on our thoughts, feelings, beliefs, and actions. Yet often our thoughts are grounded in past experiences rather than our true aspirations, perpetuating cycles of repetition rather than innovative creation.

To unleash true creativity, we must transcend the confines of past experiences and allow our imaginations to create without boundaries. Our imagination holds immense power to shape our reality and manifest our deepest desires. By tapping into its boundless potential, we expand our horizons and form synergistic mastermind groups that introduce fresh ideas, collaborators, and resources. However, many of us limit our imagination by dwelling on past experiences.

To harness this power effectively, we must engage in present-moment visualization, seeing our aspirations as already fulfilled. This proactive approach allows us to operate from the end state of our goals, transcending present circumstances.

With the laws of attraction and assumption in action, we possess the capacity to co-create a reality that resonates with our true desires. Our imagination serves as a transformative tool to craft a life of profound fulfillment.

In the realm of personal development, it's crucial to understand that our beliefs either limit or expand our potential for growth and success. These beliefs can either align with our desires and enhance our deserving capacity, known as growing beliefs, or hinder our progress with limiting beliefs.

This transformative journey requires self-awareness, intentionality, and trust in our ability to release limiting beliefs and harness the power of our minds. Through our thoughts and beliefs, we possess the innate ability to shape our reality and manifest our dreams.

As we navigate this journey, we must remember that every thought we hold shapes the fabric of our reality. By aligning our thoughts with our desired outcomes and persistently taking action toward them, we emulate the resilience and determination exemplified by pioneers like Charles M. Schwab.

Each day presents an opportunity to focus on our desired outcomes and persevere in the face of challenges, guided by our inner Sherpas, the navigators of our dreams.

## The Power of Detachment: Ascending the Levels of Consciousness

Gayle sat in quiet reflection on a park bench, embracing the power of detachment amidst the daily barrage of negative emotions. She realized that the journey toward achieving desires is a transformative process, integral to personal growth and ascending to higher levels of consciousness.

As a dreamer, Gayle understood that mere dreaming wasn't enough to manifest her desired life. She recognized the law of attraction at play—aligning thoughts and emotions with desires to manifest them into reality. By releasing resistance and focusing on positive thoughts, Gayle saw how this approach not only brought her closer to her goals but also shaped her into the person capable of achieving them.

Detaching from external markers of success, Gayle found peace through meditation and letting go of the need for control. She discovered that true happiness lies in detaching from external validation and embracing inner peace and clarity.

Committing to daily detachment, Gayle liberated herself from approval-seeking and fear of failure. She embraced uncertainty as part of life's constant flow, experiencing growth and change with calmness and clarity. Each challenge overcome propelled her to a higher level of consciousness, deepening her connection to herself and the world.

Through detachment, Gayle unlocked a life of fulfillment and inner peace, free from external expectations and societal pressures. Trusting in the universe's timing and surrendering control, she found certainty and purpose.

Detachment liberated Gayle, allowing her to embrace her true, and authentic self, free from societal norms.

## Essential and Necessary Letting Go

The soothing sound of rain gently hitting the windowpane formed a backdrop to the tumultuous thoughts swirling within me as I sat on the edge of my bed. To surrender, an essential step toward growth and happiness, demanded immense courage, strength, and vulnerability. Despite understanding the concept in theory, I failed to achieve these goals in practice, and it became one of the toughest challenges I had ever faced. I used to hold grudges and focus on negative thoughts and patterns of behavior that were no longer helpful to me as a person. At some point, I could no longer bear the burden. I took a deep breath and let go. It was akin to removing a bandage long stuck to my skin, painful yet liberating. With each release, I felt lighter and freer, ready to embrace a new chapter in my life.

"I am" serves as a powerful affirmation in this process of letting go, a declaration of our power and ownership over our actions and emotions. It is about relinquishing attachments to people, things, or situations that hinder our present and future.

Saying "I am" as an affirmation of letting go liberates us from negative emotions such as anger, resentment, and regret, which impede present fulfillment. It creates space for new relationships, experiences, and opportunities that enrich our lives.

It teaches us to trust life's unfolding and believe in its purposeful direction. By releasing what no longer serves us, we welcome fresh beginnings and endless possibilities across all facets of our journey.

To live meaningfully, we must embrace the unknown with open arms, using "I am" to affirm the release of attachments and to wholeheartedly embrace the journey ahead with confidence and trust.

## Surrendering Our Worries and Attachments

After class, Latrice approached her instructor, a wise old woman named Sophia, and poured out her heart. Sophia listened closely, nodding knowingly as Latrice spoke of her struggles and fears. Then, with a soft smile, she said, "My dear, the key to finding peace and happiness lies in releasing and letting go. Free yourself from worries and attachments, and trust in the journey that lies ahead."

At first, Latrice felt somewhat shocked and concerned by Sophia's words, but deep inside, something resonated with their truth. She knew she had to make a change in her life, to let go of her need for control and perfection, and to allow the flow of life to take over.

And so, Latrice began her journey of release. She started by releasing her need to be a people pleaser and her tendency to try to be perfect in every aspect of her life. She allowed herself to make mistakes and learn from them, embracing the fact that she was only human. The more she released, the more peace and contentment filled her heart.

With each passing day, she felt lighter and freer, as though a weight had been lifted from her shoulders. She learned to see the beauty of the world around her and the small miracles that had always been part of her life but had been overlooked while she was trying to control it.

In the end, Latrice knew that letting go and releasing were not signs of weakness but signs of strength. Disengaging from control and trusting in the unknown took courage, but through it came a peace and fulfillment she had never known.

That is the frightening yet liberating aspect of letting go of our worries and attachments. Every time we stay tied to our worries, clinging to our attachments, we limit our growth and potential. But once we release these burdens, we open ourselves to new opportunities and experiences.

Freeing ourselves from our worries allows us to let go completely and trust that life's journey will see us through and that all will be well. Similarly, letting go of our attachments frees us from material things or relationships that may be holding us back.

Allow yourself to let go of your woes and attachments, knowing that you are always looked after. Ultimately, it is a balance of attachment and detachment in our relationships that allows us to fully experience love and connection without being bound by expectations or fears.

### Keep Manifesting Your Dreams!

Here's my open letter for you.

*Dear readers,*

*It is empowering when you start using your emotions while creating your vision board and when you are journaling about your dreams or aspirations which are very powerful steps toward manifesting your dreams into reality. By engaging in these activities, you're not only setting intentions but also actively aligning your thoughts and actions with your desired outcomes.*

*Again, this is just a reminder, manifestation is a journey that requires persistence and belief in your own power to create change. Here are a few tips to help you continue on this transformative path:*

*Consistency is key in helping you dedicate regular time to visualize and reflect on your vision board.*

*It is also said that consistency strengthens your intentions and keeps your goals at the forefront of your mind.*

*Embrace the process: Trust that every step you take toward your goals, no matter how small, is progress. Manifestation often unfolds in unexpected ways, so stay open to opportunities and lessons along the way.*

*Celebrate your wins: Acknowledge and celebrate each manifestation or positive change that comes into your life. Recognizing your achievements boosts your confidence and reinforces your belief in your ability to manifest.*

*Connect with community: Share your journey with others who are on a similar path. Whether it's through any discussing your vision board creations or journal entries, connecting with like-minded individuals can provide encouragement and new perspectives.*

*Reflect and adjust: Use your journal to regularly reflect on your experiences, insights, and any adjustments you may want to make to your goals. This self-awareness helps you stay aligned with what truly matters to you.*

*Remember, you have the ability within you to realize your dreams and desires. Believe in yourself, maintain concentration on your objectives, and keep fostering your dreams deliberately.*

*Dry the tears, let the light of belief and determination to get what you need fill your heart here and now and you'll see you can have a purposeful, joyful and fulfilled life.*

*Warm regards,*

*Clemer Leggett*

## Before you turn the page, here's the breakthrough concept you need to know.

My journey into understanding the power of the inner mind and its influence on our reality began with a simple desire: to manifest my deepest desires and reshape my life. I embarked on a quest for self-discovery, rigorously testing the capabilities of my mind. Writing down my goals and actively pursuing them became my daily ritual.

In exploring this process, I discovered a profound truth: Sickness often originates in our consciousness before manifesting in our physical bodies. By cultivating beliefs in robust health and rejecting negativity, I experienced a notable improvement in my well-being. The financial aspect also revealed its own wisdom. Rather than fixating on bills and debt, I learned to shift my focus toward investing in assets.

This journey has underscored the paramount importance of nurturing a positive mindset and fostering a healthy self-relationship. As Napoleon Hill aptly noted, a clear goal is crucial for success, steering us away from aimless drifting and toward purposeful transformation.

To navigate challenges with steadfast determination, we must clearly articulate hopes for our aspirations and craft actionable plans to achieve them. Surrounding ourselves with our tribe and close confidants—supportive, like-minded individuals who inspire and encourage us—becomes instrumental in staying on course.

Yet amid this pursuit, the concept of detachment emerges as essential. Letting go of outdated selves and limiting beliefs liberates us from past failures, opening us to new perspectives and pathways for growth. It's about shedding old skins to embrace change boldly, expanding our horizons beyond the confines of comfort.

In this journey, faith and perseverance play crucial roles. Trusting in the process and maintaining an unwavering belief that what's meant for us will come to fruition, we find ourselves on a path of continuous growth and self-discovery.

As we embark on this transformative odyssey, let's cherish each step with intentionality.

## Navigating the Path to Success: Principles of Growth and Fulfillment

The principles guiding self-improvement and success emphasize more than just positive thinking—they also underscore the importance of taking action, resilience, and continual learning. Each individual's journey toward success is unique, requiring a personalized approach rooted in setting clear goals, adapting to challenges, and nurturing a strong work ethic.

As we delve into these principles, it becomes evident that success isn't a one-size-fits-all concept but rather a dynamic pursuit shaped by our choices and commitments. By embracing a proactive mindset and persisting through obstacles, we can propel ourselves toward our aspirations.

However, success isn't solely about mental strategies; it's also about practical steps, resilience in adversity, and continuous self-improvement. The "snowball financial plan visualization," blending practical financial planning with spiritual wisdom, offers a unique tool for aligning monetary goals with biblical principles of stewardship and contentment.

This holistic approach fosters not just financial stability but also a deeper spiritual connection and overall life fulfillment. By cultivating a positive mindset, practicing gratitude, and setting meaningful goals, individuals attract abundance into their lives while staying aligned with their faith and values.

Ultimately, success is about more than material achievements, it's about living authentically, in harmony with our values and purpose. By embodying these principles and embracing a growth mindset, we not only enhance our personal lives but also contribute positively to the world around us.

In a serene town nestled among rolling hills lived Nicky, a young woman on a quest to manifest her desires and live a fulfilled life. Nicky, deeply rooted in the teachings of the Christian Bible and guided by principles of the infinite intelligence, found solace in her unwavering faith and obedience to God's plan.

Yet Nicky also felt drawn to the practical wisdom of the twenty-one possible principles that promised a path to worldly success and fulfillment. She saw the value in setting goals, practicing gratitude, and cultivating kindness, principles that resonated with her aspirations for personal growth and achievement. Navigating life's complexities, Nicky found herself torn between these two sets of principles. One day, in a moment of clarity, she realized the key lay in integrating both. She understood that she could embrace the infinite intelligence principles as her moral compass, guiding her toward spiritual well-being and eternal rewards. Simultaneously, she could incorporate the twenty-one possible principles into her life, using them as practical tools for personal growth and self-improvement.

With this newfound understanding, Nicky embarked on a journey to harmonize these principles in her life. She practiced gratitude, set actionable goals, maintained a positive attitude, and adapted to changes with resilience.

As Nicky walked this integrated path, she felt a deep connection to both sets of principles, realizing they were not mutually exclusive but complementary. Over time, she witnessed her desires manifesting, leading her toward a life of true fulfillment.

In the end, Nicky understood that by embracing both the principles of infinite intelligence and the twenty-one possible principles, she had unlocked the full potential of her life. She found that true fulfillment came from harmonizing faith with practical action, and spiritual growth with personal development.

By integrating these principles into our own lives, we too can manifest our desires and find fulfillment. The principles provide a strong spiritual foundation, guiding us toward righteousness and faithfulness in accordance with God's will.

Simultaneously, the twenty-one possible principles offer practical strategies for success and personal growth. They encourage self-care, goalsetting, positivity, and resilience, promoting virtues like gratitude, kindness, and openness. By embracing these principles, we learn to prioritize self-improvement, embrace diversity, forgive, live in the present, seek wisdom, and contribute positively to our communities.

By harmonizing these principles in our lives, we can achieve a balanced and fulfilling existence, aligning spiritual fulfillment with personal success. Mindful of our impact and guided by wisdom, we can become the best versions of ourselves, fulfilling our desires while remaining true to our faith and values.

## These Are the Laws of Reality

The law of assumption—so termed law of attraction—is the universal law that our thinking and beliefs attract into our life experiences and conditions that match those thoughts and beliefs. The law is closely associated with the law of divine one—yes, all about embracing the opportunities and possibilities coming from the universe. On the other hand, low vibrations or negative energy hinder the manifestation of our desires. The law of cause and effect helps us to remember that our present experiences are brought about by our thoughts and actions in the past.

Underlying them all, however, is the principle outlined in "Principles of Mind and Identity": that our thinking and beliefs bring about our reality. To be able to manifest our desires, however, there has to be more than a passive thinking of those things; there has to be action motivated by inspiration, and there has to be faith.

As outlined in the law of perpetual translation of energy, energy is constantly in translation and can be applied to our purposes.

The law of correspondence would thus infer that what happens within us is reflected in the without. The law of relativity simply teaches that challenges may be perceived from different levels and, therefore, from different perspectives, with no judgment being placed on right or wrong. The law of polarity points to the dual nature of everything and how balance should be sought between opposites.

Greater than the individual, the law of gravitation in the limit of a weak gravitational field underlines the universal principle of attraction between objects, echoing the law of God consciousness that emphasizes the necessity to direct us to something higher.

The principles of rhythm or cyclicity teach us to trust in the natural ebbs and flows in life's rhythms. The law of pure potential reminds us about our infinite capacity to learn and create while the law of unity reminds us of our connectedness to the larger cosmos, reinforcing the law of mentalism—just how much our thoughts affect reality.

Coherence among these laws therefore allows us to lead our lives in a more conscious and intentional way-as indeed the law of reversibility states that we have the power through acting with intent to turn any situation into a positive one.

What these universal laws fundamentally do is provide spiritual and philosophical guidance, besides practical insights on how to live consciously and intentionally. These inculcated principles make people use their inherent power to bring reality into the realms of making aspirations an accomplished fact. They keep reminding one that by putting thought, belief, and action together with positive intention, ripples of positivity can be created not only within but also in the outside world.

It can be a transformation in itself as one puts these principles into practice. The following steps are helpful in inculcating these principles within you, aligned with your daily routine:

1. Mindfulness and awareness: In the first place, be more considerate of your thoughts, beliefs, and actions; the energy you emit into the atmosphere does a great deal in influencing events in life.

2.  POSITIVE AFFIRMATIONS: Positive affirmations will help in the change of thoughts and beliefs.

3.  VISUALIZE AND REALIZE: Practice your visualization techniques, and see your desires and goals as crystal clear.

4.  Gratitude practice: Establish a daily practice of gratitude that will further integrate you into the law of unity and the law of pure potential. Practicing gratitude for what you already have may even attract more positive experiences to your life.

5.  Correction of self: Take time to reflect on yourself, to look into your inner self. Reflect upon how the law of cause and effect and the law of correspondence are operating in your life and how you may change things for the better.

6.  Balancing: Apply the law of polarity in life, finding your balance in everything. Remember, like all things, through challenges and difficulties, this too shall pass and can be an opportunity for growth and evolution.

7.  Allowing the God consciousness: If this is a law that resonates with you, find time to pray, meditate, or connect with nature.

8.  Compassion and understanding: Apply the law of relativity with compassion and understanding for different perspectives. Do not judge; instead, try to understand the experiences of others.

9.  Taking inspired action: To this powerhouse of thought, add inspired action. The law of cause and effect reminds you that you must take purposeful steps in the direction of your desires intentionally.

10. Harmony and flexibility: Flow along with life's ebbs and
    flows. Life moves in rhythms; hence, believe in the law
    of rhythm or cyclicity. Keep flexible yet coherent in your
    thoughts, beliefs, and actions.

Keep in mind that this is a personal journey, and finding the right
balance for yourself is key. It would also be beneficial to seek guidance
regarding mentors, spiritual leaders, and like-minded people who can
support you on this path.

You are doing fabulous, and I'm so proud of all that you've
accomplished to date. For the next few moments, focus on being a
success. Great, let's get into the final chapter of my book!

# CHAPTER 13

## TRUE MEASURE OF POWER

In the silence of the mind, you can hear the voice of the divine.

—Deepak Chopra

The real true measure of power lies in our ability to create and manifest anything we want and desire. This extends beyond mere physical and monetary strength or wealth. It stems from a profound connection with the universe and one's spiritual inner being is the process of turning thoughts and ideas into tangible reality, showcasing our innate creative potential.[119] This power isn't limited to material possessions but encompasses intangible desires like love, happiness, and success, reflecting our capacity to shape our external world through focused thoughts, emotions, and actions.

Joseph Murphy's insights in *The Power of the Subconscious Mind* underscore how our mind shapes health and well-being, emphasizing the transformative power of positive thinking in maintaining vitality.[120] By harnessing this power through practice techniques such

119  Goddard, *Feeling is the Secret*, 22.

120  Murphy, *The Power of Your Subconscious Mind*, 87.

as visualization and even through prayer, we align our desires with internal, universal energies, paving the way for a life of abundance and fulfillment.[121]

This perspective refutes the shallow consciousness that conventional science attempts to install in us and demands of us an awareness of ourselves as spiritual beings. As individuals, the more we tend to our spiritual well-being, the happier we become and help create a kinder world.

"This path is a reminder of who we truly are in our divine essence, and to push the limiting containers that haunt us all."

As powerful as these tools are, they allow us to manifest what our hearts desire and enable each individual to change their life and the world around us.

Guided visualization and prayer visualization are potent tools for manifesting desires and fostering positive change in our lives and the world. These practices tap into our spirituality, connecting us with our true selves and radiating compassion, positivity, and love.

Guided visualization allows introspection, unveiling truths and accessing inner wisdom.

Consistent practice empowers us to achieve fulfillment and contribute to a better world.

These practices not only benefit individuals but also catalyze collective shifts toward a more peaceful, loving environment. By embracing our inherent power and channeling it for the greater good, we influence tomorrow positively. The journey of self-transformation demands delving deep within, discovering our potential, and evolving into our best selves.

---

121  Murphy, Joseph, *The Power of Your Subconscious Mind*, 112.

Belief in the power of our inner mind is crucial. The concept that "seeing is believing" underscores the importance of unwavering faith in our potential; without it, achieving our desired life remains out of reach. Our beliefs and internal programming shape our journey toward realizing our goals.

This journey, while challenging, offers purpose and fulfillment. Overcoming limiting beliefs and perceiving beyond our immediate senses can be difficult, yet surrendering our desires to the universe and practicing preemptive gratitude enhances our ability to realize our goals.

Such belief fosters a fulfilling life by alleviating fear and doubt, emphasizing joy, and appreciating the journey. Trusting that the universe aligns with our desires can speed up the process of achieving our goals, making the attraction of these desires more straightforward. Ultimately, having confidence in our co-creative abilities nurtures peace and fulfillment. We become the conscious architects of our reality, taking responsibility for our own happiness.

The belief in relinquishing control and trusting in the process of life allows us to shape our destiny intentionally and abundantly. By embracing the power to choose our beliefs, we pave the way for a more fulfilling life.

This process involves observing our environment, identifying triggers, accepting uncomfortable beliefs, tracing their origins, and challenging their validity with logic and evidence. We then replace limiting beliefs with positive ones aligned with our goals.

Understanding the influence of our thoughts and beliefs on our lives allows us to shape a more intentional future aligned with our potential. Self-discovery and growth help us break free from limitations.

Abraham Hicks emphasizes the certainty and confidence needed to manifest our desires. Believing, proclaiming, and acting in alignment with our goals lead to their fulfillment.

Recognizing that some things are beyond our control and trusting the universe's timing allows us to find peace. True happiness lies not in controlling everything but in embracing life's journey, knowing that every experience serves a purpose.

Peace and contentment are found in the flow of life now, relieving us from the need to carve a future that is inherently insecure. In releasing the desire for control and manipulation, we allow ourselves to experience the beauty of life, which unfolds spontaneously.

It is, in fact, through the releasing of our need to be in control that we learn to appreciate the beauty of life and all those beautiful, unexpected moments. As human beings, we have a very strong urge to regulate our environment and determine the outcomes of our lives, but it is this same preoccupation with being in control that binds us.

We learn to love the world for its imperfections and chaos rather than struggle to make our life perfect. It is only when one ceases trying to forge one's own path and opens up to the journey called life that the real meaning of spontaneity can be fully embraced.

The role of life is not to forcefully make our desires come true but to have faith in the journey and be brave enough to open the doors leading toward them.

By pursuing what inspires us, we can inspire others and help lift the veil that may be obscuring their vision. The need for control often arises from fear and attachment to a specific outcome, as if we always know what is best for ourselves.

Releasing control means ceasing to struggle against ourselves and the universe. In that process, we release many unnecessary battles.

This release enables us to ride the wave of positivity and be an inspiration for others along the way. Losing control frees us from our struggles to achieve more.

It is said that gratitude is the key to happiness. That means whatever we have, we need to be thankful for and appreciate, cherish it, and not take it for granted.

We must be thankful yet take inner action toward our desires. This means maintaining a positive attitude, setting intent, and moving in the direction of our desires. In that way, our desires manifest, and fulfillment is experienced.

Through embracing this release, we realize true freedom. Growth and expansion into all of life's experiences are the results. Releasing one's grip and allowing life to unfold without control takes courage and trust.

Freeing ourselves from the need for control releases us from limitations and fears, opening our road to growth, expansion, and eventually to freedom. The process requires courage, trust, positivity, gratitude, and action.

## Transformative Belief Statements: Shaping Identity and Purpose

Belief statements are guiding principles that shape an individual's thoughts, actions, and decision-making processes, influenced by personal experiences, cultural background, and environmental factors. Acting as a moral compass, they aid in navigating life's complexities and ensuring that choices align with personal values.

These statements not only shape perception and behavior but also provide purpose and motivation during challenges. Regular reflection on belief statements ensures alignment with core values, fostering personal growth and authenticity. They play a pivotal role in defining identity, guiding relationships, and offering clarity in uncertain times, grounding individuals in what truly matters most to them.

## Strength of Positive Inner Dialogue

Positive self-talk has transformative power, helping you avoid self-sabotaging emotions and negative beliefs. By consciously replacing negative thoughts with affirming statements, you create a supportive inner dialogue that fosters resilience and encourages personal growth. This shift in mindset empowers you to face challenges with confidence and optimism, diminishing feelings of anxiety, fear, and hopelessness.

Through positive self-talk, you actively challenge limiting beliefs that might hold you back. For instance, when feelings of frustration or shame arise, affirming phrases can redirect your focus toward your strengths and abilities. This approach not only reduces negative emotions but also nurtures a sense of accountability and empowerment, reinforcing your ability to move forward with confidence.

Create a habit of positive self-talk.

## Positive Words for Manifestation

Here's a list of positive words and phrases that can deeply impact your inner consciousness, aiding in the manifestation of your desired lifestyle and satisfaction:

- I can.

- I am capable.

- I deserve success.

- I am worthy.

- I embrace challenges.

- I choose positivity.

- I believe in myself.

- I am resilient.

- I attract abundance.

- I learn and grow.

- I am grateful.

- I create my reality.

- I have the power to change.

- I trust the process.

- I can overcome obstacles.

- I am surrounded by plenty.

- I am chosen by God, and I am abundance.

- I am chosen to receive extraordinary favor.

## Positive Affirmations

1. I am capable. Deserving of success. No matter my past. No matter my current circumstances.

2. My talents are unique. My experiences are valuable. They can help me reach my goals.

3. The power to overcome fear is within me. I can surpass limiting beliefs that restrain me.

4. I deserve financial freedom. I Have the ability to enhance my financial status.

5. My age does not define me. My appearance does not determine me. My mistakes do not label me. I can grow. I can learn at any age.

6. I'm capable of embracing flaws. They act as opportunities—opportunities for development and self-improvement.

7. I am capable of creating change—positive change. I can achieve greatness. It happens through self-belief, through perseverance.

## Unlimited Negative Beliefs

Unhealthy negative beliefs create an all-encompassing cycle of self-doubt, with fear and pessimism often rooted in past experiences, societal pressures, or personal insecurities. These beliefs erode confidence and block personal growth and success.

Eradicating deep-seated negative beliefs requires self-awareness, patience, and a commitment to challenging these thoughts. It also involves replacing them with positive affirmations that foster self-love, confidence, and growth.

In doing so, individuals can reclaim control over their thoughts, steer their actions, and pave the way for significant personal growth and satisfaction.

*Negative Beliefs*

1. I am incapable of achieving success due to my past failures and current limitations.

2. My talents and experiences are worthless and will never help me achieve my goals.

3. I am powerless against the fears and limiting beliefs that continually hold me back.

4. I do not deserve financial freedom and am doomed to remain in my current financial situation.

5. I am defined by my age, appearance, and past mistakes; and I am incapable of growth or learning.

6. My imperfections are permanent flaws that prevent me from growing or improving.

7. I lack the ability to create positive change and achieve greatness because I don't truly believe in myself.

These negative beliefs reflect deep-seated doubts and obstacles that can hinder personal growth and success. Recognizing and challenging them are crucial steps in overcoming barriers and shifting toward a more empowering mindset.

## Income Streams That Make Millionaires Rich

There are various wealth-building income streams that have the potential to make aspiring millionaires rich. One of the most popular sources of income for millionaires is entrepreneurship. Many millionaires find success in entrepreneurship by building their wealth through creating and growing their own businesses, whether through innovative products or services or by investing in real estate. Another lucrative income stream is investing. By carefully selecting and diversifying their investments, millionaires can generate significant returns and grow their wealth over time.

Additionally, most millionaires pursue high-salary positions in finance, tech, or entertainment industry as well as acquiring new knowledge or expertise in technology, which can also be major sources of income for millionaires, leveraging specialized skills and knowledge to command substantial salaries and bonuses. Lastly, passive income streams such as rental properties, royalties from intellectual property, and dividends from stocks also contribute to millionaire wealth.

Capital gains from appreciated assets like real estate, stocks, bonds, and currency provide both passive and recurring income. Passive and residual income streams encompass various sources, including ATMs, vending machines, eBooks, livestock, and laundromats. Dividend income, paid out of a corporation's profits to stockholders, is another significant source.

Rental income from properties or equipment, like housing, appliances, and vehicles, constitutes another vital income source. Business income derived from launching and managing successful ventures represents another form of earned income. Royalties and selling rights can yield income from creative works such as graphic design, writing, music, or web development.

Nursing professionals may consider launching home care services or health counseling practices. Lucrative avenues include coaching, public speaking, and motivational services aimed at transformational growth. Launching laundromats, transportation services, or car detailing and repair ventures also holds strong potential for profitability. Digital marketing offers lucrative prospects for those with the requisite skills.

Nurse Next Door, a compassionate home care service, draws inspiration from the dedication of nurses. As the husband of a nurse, I've witnessed firsthand the profound impact they have, which motivated my wife to become a nursing consultant. Personally, I dedicate my time to expanding my knowledge in nurse life coaching and transformational life coaching, guiding individuals toward personal growth.

My ultimate aspiration is to become a published author, sharing insights on goal setting and career development. Passionate about personal and financial growth, I strive to positively impact lives by helping individuals lay a solid foundation for their future.

## How to Perfect the Art of Manifestation: Steps and Techniques

Manifestation is a potent process. It has the power to convert thoughts, desires, and dreams into an existing reality. It all starts by recognizing that we are conscious beings. We cultivate a positive self-image by seeing ourselves as capable, competent, and confident individuals.

On the flip side, a negative self-image and doubts about our abilities can hinder our actions and interactions, which is crucial because they directly impact our energy levels and how we present ourselves.

Clearly defining our goals and believing wholeheartedly in their possibility is another essential step. Visualizing ourselves already living our desired reality helps align our thoughts and energy toward its manifestation.

Our self-image and beliefs have a great impact on our realization of possibilities that will keep us living a rewarding, rich, financially fit life, or burden us with poverty and a paycheck-to-paycheck lifestyle. Even in adversity and discouragement, commitment and progress toward what is wanted are paramount.

Whether material possessions, career, or relationship goals, having a clear idea of what one is seeking is essential to realization.

Let me remind you: This is not a magic formula that grants your wishes the moment you want them. Achieving your desires requires a combination of hard work, self-belief, and faith in life.

With a positive mindset and gratitude, we naturally attract more abundance into our lives. Regularly evaluating our goals keeps us aligned and moving in the right direction.

Realization isn't a magic trick that happens overnight; it's a journey that requires dedication and perseverance to create the life we truly desire.

Self-hypnosis can also be a powerful tool for overcoming limiting beliefs and developing a mindset that attracts abundance.

Developing the qualities and characteristics of the person you wish to become, even if they haven't manifested yet, is an essential step in achieving your desires.

Awareness of the mind's power and practical steps toward our goals enable us to bring our envisioned life into being.

Mastery of realization requires gratitude, being thankful for what we already have and for future blessings.

Realization is not about commanding the universe but about aligning our thoughts and actions with its flow to create the life we desire.

Writing down what we desire has a powerful effect on the process of realizing our goals because it clearly defines and focuses our intentions. Speaking our desires aloud not only gives them tangible form but also specifies what we want the universe to work with.

Bruce Lee, the legendary martial artist and actor, deeply believed in the power of the mind. He regularly wrote down his goals and dreams, understanding that doing so would help him visualize and focus on them with greater clarity and intention.

Meditation is also a beneficial tool. It aids in releasing distractions, centering our thoughts, and allowing us to focus on our goals fully.

Our thoughts and intentions are powerful forces that shape our reality. Writing down our desires serves as both an affirmation and a visualization, making our goals more tangible and achievable.

By committing our desires to paper, we maintain motivation and commitment, creating a clear intention and a strong signal to the universe.

As a result, the universe responds, aligning circumstances and opportunities to help us attain our true desires.

Napoleon Hill famously said, "Thoughts become things." When we commit our desires to paper, we set events in motion, moving closer to their manifestation in reality.

The more regularly we revisit and refine our written goals, the stronger this alignment becomes, attracting the resources and opportunities necessary for manifestation. Writing down our desires is a crucial step toward their materialization.

To manifest our desires, we can follow five key steps.

Letting go of our old ideal self can be challenging but is essential for growth.

To facilitate this transformation, find a quiet space with members of your mastermind group and share your vision as if you were already living it, using the present tense.

You may experience moments of laughter and excitement, which are signs of genuine connection with your vision. However, be mindful of any negative emotions that arise, as they can indicate deep-seated beliefs and doubts about your commitment to this new lifestyle.

Such feelings often surface when your deeper mind is not fully aligned with your goals.

Immerse yourself in positive influences and consistently visualize abundance to strengthen your belief in financial prosperity.

## Awareness of Abundance Expressing Itself Back at Itself

Every desire, experience, imagination, and manifestation framework is awareness expressing itself through its own conscious creation.

Even every experience we have, a person's desire, perception, belief, activation, challenge, and imagination realized in reality, is the movement of awareness, the Source Creator. Every thought, intention, emotion, action, and belief arises from within awareness itself.

# CHAPTER 14

## THE ABUNDANCE MINDSET

In the silence of the mind, you can hear the voice of the divine.

—Deepak Chopra

To cultivate an abundance mindset requires a deliberate shift in perspective, supported by consistent and intentional action. One of the most powerful places to begin is with gratitude, choosing to focus on what is already present rather than on what appears to be lacking. This practice heightens awareness of abundance that already exists and gently redirects attention away from scarcity. Equally important is belief in your own worth and capability, as these beliefs form the foundation for releasing self-doubt and limiting thoughts.

Inspired action begins with clarity of desire, but it is sustained by self-belief. Many people struggle to experience abundance not because opportunity is absent, but because self-doubt convinces them they are undeserving. When limiting beliefs are released, space opens for growth, confidence, and expansion. By recognizing your inherent worthiness to receive, you naturally align with abundance and allow it to flow more freely into your life.

This is so important—being among people who encourage and inspire—to keep the positive attitude going and to be motivated. Put your concentration on your own track without comparing your life with that of others.

As you open up to balance and well-being, you attract much more positivity and abundance into every area of your life.

## Cultivate a Mindset of Abundance

One powerful method to transform a scarcity mindset into one of abundance is by embodying a conscious attitude of thankfulness. Gratitude deepens this mindset. By reflecting daily on progress, small victories, and existing blessings, abundance becomes a lived experience rather than an abstract concept. This awareness creates momentum, allowing abundance to compound naturally over time.

Keep your mind focused on the life you desire—one fully endowed with everything you want. Affirm abundance by saying, "I am abundant" or "I live in a world of plenty."

To ingrain this attitude even further, develop the habit of reflecting on the positive features in your life. By becoming more conscious and appreciative of little successes, a positive snowball effect will be created, hence increasing this perception of abundance.

Environment and influence matter. Surrounding yourself with people who encourage growth strengthens your mindset while comparison weakens it. Focusing on your own path, practicing generosity, and prioritizing self-care through rest, nourishment, and balance reinforce abundance on both mental and physical levels.

As balance and well-being increase, so does the ability to attract positivity across all areas of life. An abundance mindset is not wishful thinking, it is disciplined awareness, intentional belief, and consistent alignment.

## Inspired Action

It would also be of essence to clarify your intentions by explaining what abundance personally means and state exactly what you want to manifest. Break those desires down into smaller, achievable goals and define what steps will be taken to accomplish them-making a clearly defined life plan and financial plan as a road map toward the fulfillment of your abundance vision. Consistent forward movement is key in taking steps that will move you closer to your vision of abundance.

Abundance requires more than belief; it demands action that aligns with intention. Inspired action begins with clarity. Defining what abundance personally means allows goals to become specific rather than abstract. When desires are clearly identified, they can be broken into achievable steps that move vision into reality.

Aside from clearly setting goals, review your plans regularly to keep pace with evolving aspirations. A practical plan provides direction. Clear financial and life goals function as a roadmap, offering structure while allowing flexibility. Progress is sustained through consistent forward movement, not perfection. Each step, no matter how small, builds momentum and reinforces belief.

Flexibility strengthens progress. Remaining open to new opportunities allows growth without rigidity. Celebrating milestones, even modest ones, reinforces confidence and motivation. Acknowledging progress prevents discouragement and keeps momentum alive.

You also want to surround yourself with tools and resources that support your journey toward abundance: things like books, courses, or mentors that inspire and provide guidance.

## Practice Detachment and Acceptance

Let go of fear and release any doubts that may hold you back from believing in abundance. Trust the process and understand that abundance doesn't happen overnight; have patience and believe that the universe is supporting you. Accept your current reality while working toward your long-term goals and avoid dwelling on what you lack.

Fear often emerges when action begins. While natural, fear should not control direction. When approached with awareness, fear becomes a guide rather than a restraint. Stepping beyond comfort builds resilience and expands capacity. Progress accelerates when fear is faced rather than avoided.

Detachment sustains inspired action. Trusting the process allows movement without anxiety over immediate results. When action is aligned with purpose and supported by patience, progress becomes steady and sustainable.

Other Techniques

Feng shui is a valuable tool for creating an empowering environment by organizing your space to facilitate positive energy. Meditate and visualize regularly to align with your inner abundance, manifesting into your physical reality what you want to see.

Additional Tips

No love equals the love I give myself—a love grounded in boundless wisdom. In a universe filled with constant expectations and demands, it's easy to neglect our own well-being, often prioritizing others instead. Yet true self-love means acknowledging our worth and elevating ourselves to a priority.

Guidance is essential, and infinite intelligence helps us access vast knowledge. We can use it to nurture ourselves and appreciate who we are. Here, love is not rooted in others' validation; it springs from within and then shines outward.

Infinite intelligence is our ally on this journey. Through this alliance, we grow and evolve in our self-love, always connected to an infinite source of unconditional love.

Indeed, there's no love superior to the love we extend ourselves. This comes with assistance from infinite intelligence.

Altering Mindset for Financial Prosperity

Changing one's mindset to financial abundance helps greatly in reaching the set financial goals. It allows you to visualize the outcome you want, believe in your worthiness, set clear goals, take inspired action, develop a growth mindset, apply gratitude, let go of attachment to the outcome, connect with positive influences, and regularly visualize abundance.

Start by creating a vivid mental image of your desired outcome, engaging all your senses in this vision. Believe that you are capable, worthy and deserving of achieving your financial goals.

Develop a growth mindset: Challenges, therefore, are opportunities for growth. Practice gratitude daily, which shifts perception from lack to abundance.

By shifting your mindset and taking aligned actions toward your goals, you can manifest the financial abundance you desire.

## Shifting Your Mindset for Financial Abundance

1. Visualize your desired outcome.

    - Picture yourself living in your dream home on 10 acres, earning $150,000 annually.

    - Engage all your senses: See it, hear it, smell it, feel it.

2. Believe in your worthiness.

    - Know you're capable and deserving of your financial goals.

    - Replace negative self-talk with affirmations like, "I am worthy of abundance."

3. Set clear goals.

    - Be specific: a $250,000 home on 10 acres, $150,000 annual income.

    - Break these down into smaller, doable steps.

4. Take inspired action.

    - Find activities that align with your goals.

    - Explore new careers, start a business, or invest smartly.

    - Seek guidance from mentors or financial advisors.

5. Cultivate a growth mindset.

    - Embrace challenges as chances to learn and grow.

    - See setbacks as temporary and refine your strategies.

    - Focus on constant improvement.

6. Practice gratitude.

   - Daily gratitude shifts your perspective from lack to abundance.

   - Recognize and appreciate what you already have.

7. Detach from outcomes.

   - Trust the process and let go of anxiety about results.

   - Take aligned actions without stressing over the outcome.

8. Yourself with positivity.

   - Seek out people who believe in you and support your financial goals.

   - Limit time with negative or pessimistic individuals.

9. Visualize abundance.

   - Regularly visualize yourself by wealth and prosperity.

   - Use affirmations and meditation to reinforce these images.

10. Celebrate your progress; acknowledge achievements.

   - Be it big or small, celebrate!

   - Embrace your progress. It will boost your confidence and nourish your motivation.

   - Changing your mindset is tough—it takes time and effort. But remember to stay committed to your goals and embrace positivity.

Financial abundance may seem impossible, but it is within reach. With perseverance and belief, you can manifest the abundance you desire.

Some people seem to have all the luck. They achieve success in their careers, see boosts in their finances, and experience fulfillment in their personal relationships. But why does this happen?

A few key factors may contribute to their success. First, these individuals often have access to opportunities that others might not, whether due to their social connections, education, financial resources, or simply being in the right place at the right time. They are also more willing to take risks that others shy away from.

One's outlook on life plays a big role. People who seem lucky often have a positive attitude. They have a strong belief in their abilities.

It can create a kind of self-fulfilling prophecy too. Perseverance is also crucial.

Having a solid support system is the key—family, friends, and mentors all play a part. These networks provide encouragement and valuable advice.

Now, luck does play a part. But there is more to remember. Fortunate people often create their own luck.

How to up the luck quotient? Take advantage of opportunities when they arrive. Also take calculated risks. Stay Positive through this. Get past obstacles. Build a sturdy support system. Lastly, recognize the role of luck.

Luck is neither fixed nor predetermined. It's moldable. It's something we can shape. Put in effort. Cultivate an appropriate mindset. Then, it's for the taking opportunities present themselves. Good fortune is sure to follow.

# Elara's Journey to Abundance

Elara yearned for profound transformation in her life amid an ambitious metropolis. She envisioned prosperity that went beyond material wealth, seeing abundance as inseparable from joy and fulfillment. Yet despite her perseverance, she felt confined, caught in the repetitive routine of striving for an elusive richness.

She understood that true change required more than surface-level adjustments; something within her needed to shift. Elara began by embracing humility and gratitude, learning to value simple blessings, the warmth from a morning coffee, a kind smile, and moments of peace. These small acknowledgments gradually reshaped her awareness, allowing her to recognize abundance already present in her life.

As her awareness grew, Elara confronted lingering self-doubt. Through reflection, affirmation, and visualization, she strengthened her belief in her worth and potential. This internal alignment created the confidence needed to move forward with intention rather than hesitation.

Determined to act on her new mindset, Elara took the time to define her deepest desires and set achievable goals. She pursued them with daily commitment, viewing each challenge as an opportunity to grow. She also incorporated innovative techniques into her routine, transforming her life one step at a time.

These techniques included harnessing the power of sound healing, practicing dynamic breathwork, and applying cutting-edge neurolinguistic programming. These innovative methods strengthened Elara's mindset and accelerated her journey toward abundance. She also honed her skills in detachment, accepting her present reality while steadily working toward her goals. She understood that creating abundance was not instantaneous, so she persevered with patience and trust.

Elara immersed herself in her progress, consciously avoiding thoughts of lack. She explored multiple methods to reinforce her mindset, including feng hui, which optimized her environment, and crystal healing with stones like citrine and green aventurine, known to enhance abundance. Regular meditation and visualization practices further helped her connect with her inner wealth. Gratitude journaling became a daily ritual, reinforcing a mindset of appreciation.

She surrounded herself with positive, supportive people who believed in her vision. Elara chose to focus on her unique journey, avoiding comparisons. Embracing generosity, she shared her blessings openly, giving more of herself and keeping her heart open. By prioritizing self-care and making healthy choices, she supported her well-being and strengthened her path forward.

Elara continued her journey, realizing that true abundance was about more than external achievements; it was rooted in inner transformation. She embraced personal growth, with self-awareness as the key. As a result, her external successes became more meaningful and fulfilling.

Elara's story illustrates how mindset shifts can lead to financial abundance. She manifested her financial dreams by visualizing her goals and believing in her worth. By setting clear objectives and taking inspired action, she demonstrated that those who attract fortune create their own luck through their actions and attitudes. They seize opportunities, take risks, and maintain a positive outlook, all while supported by a network of encouraging individuals.

By nurturing gratitude, prioritizing self-care, and surrounding herself with supportive people, Elara experienced a deeper sense of balance. She understood that abundance was not something to acquire, but something to allow. Her journey revealed that true abundance begins within and radiates outward into every area of life.

A select group of individuals appears to have all the luck, continually hitting it big in their careers, finances, or personal relationships. But what's the reason behind this? A few key factors often contribute to their good fortune.

First, these individuals have access to opportunities, opportunities that others might not, often due to social connections, education, financial resources, or simply being in the right place at the right time. They are also more willing to take risks, even those others are hesitant about. While taking risks can sometimes lead to failure, it can also bring about great rewards.

Another major factor is their outlook on life. People who seem lucky often maintain a positive attitude and a strong belief in their abilities.

An optimistic mindset can attract opportunities and create self-fulfilling prophecies. Perseverance is crucial, as they don't give up easily, tackling challenges with determination. Equally important is having a strong support system, family, friends, and mentors who offer both emotional encouragement and valuable advice.

While luck plays a role, it's important to remember that fortunate people often make their own luck through their actions and attitudes. So how can you boost your chances of being "lucky"? Seize opportunities when they arise, take calculated risks, and maintain a positive attitude. Power through challenges, build a strong support network, and recognize the role of luck in your journey.

Fortune is neither fixed nor predetermined; it's something you can cultivate. All it takes is the right mindset, a clear vision, and the emotional drive to manifest your goals. Ava lived in the heart of New York City, driven by ambition and dreams of financial success. Despite working tirelessly, she felt trapped in a cycle of effort without fulfillment. One quiet evening, she experienced a pivotal realization: Imagination was the missing link between desire and reality.

Despite her tireless efforts, Ava often felt trapped in a cycle of unfulfilled potential. A critical realization dawned on her: Knowledge alone wasn't enough to break free. She needed something profound, powerful enough to ignite her path to financial freedom.

Late one evening, as she sat quietly in her apartment, gazing out at the city lights, Ava had a life-changing moment of clarity. She understood that the key to unlocking her true potential lay in her imagination. It wasn't just about having a vision; it was about deeply immersing herself in that vision and allowing it to guide her actions.

Ava understood that vision required emotional engagement, not passive thought. She created a vivid picture of her ideal life, immersing herself in the feelings of success, joy, and purpose as if they already existed. This vision became her anchor.

Embracing this newfound understanding, Ava embarked on a transformative journey. The first step was crafting a vivid and dynamic vision for her life, image by image. In her mind, she created a vibrant, lively scene: herself achieving financial success and a life filled with purpose and joy. This vision wasn't a fleeting thought; it was a detailed, immersive experience that began to shape her path forward.

In this vision, each aspect of her life thrived. She linked her dreams, and her deepest passions were connected. The vision became reality. She started a vision board with images of wealth and symbols of her passions and values. Each morning, she would spend time in front of this board, allowing herself to fully engage with the emotions of her future success. She aligned her daily actions with this newly clarified purpose by feeling the excitement and joy of her envisioned achievements. Ava made a series of steadfast commitments to herself:

1.   She decreed that she deserved abundance. This was not just a belief but a fundamental assertion of her self-worth.

2.   She acknowledged that her passions were the driving force behind her success.

3.   She reinforced her confidence in her abilities and skills.

4.   She vowed to practice daily gratitude for the progress she made.

5.   She promised to remain excited about her goals, allowing this positive emotion to propel her.

With each of these decrees, Ava began to shift her mindset. She recognized the key to her success lay not just in establishing goals; it resided also in personifying the feelings linked with achieving them too. She submerged herself in the awaited sentiments of success. As she did, she started attracting opportunities. Her encounters led her to make choices. These choices were in sync with her vision.

Ava never waned. She continued to reside in a profound sense of emotional engagement. Seemingly magical transformations began to unfold in her life. Doors opened up that had earlier appeared unattainable. Her passions and objectives began colliding. They did so in poignant manners. They steered her toward a more gratifying and affluent existence. Ava's vision transformed. No longer was It a nebulous dream. It was a tangible reality. This reality took form before her eyes. A powerful reminder. envisioning unlimited possibilities

Crafting. Imagining. Creating. Ava embarked on a journey with a vivid dynamic vision. This ideal lifestyle was hers. The journey had begun.

Ava investigated various avenues. They assured a rich and varied lifestyle. Options were abundant. She could envisage a fulfilling professional life. Relationships, too, seemed ripe and vibrant. Health held a high priority. Every element was smoothened. Progress was led by a keen interest in personal growth. The canvas of her life's vision was rich and varied. Each aspect is painted with intricacy. Professional goals included aspects of creativity and growth. The landscape of relationships held stories of friendship and love. Health and wellness were the focus of her physical goals. Ava's future was a tapestry. And she was its artist.

Mapping a tangible plan, she built the blueprint of her envisioned life. Each step was calculated—be it education, career path or personal growth. Ava's journey was guided by her vision. In her hands lay the paintbrush of her future. She painted bold strokes. The hues of success and fulfillment on her canvas. Scenes of her life unfolded before her eyes. They resonated with a vibrant tempo. Accomplishments and growth were her companions. Personal and professional success formed a melody she hummed while financial independence was her rhythm. Partnerships and relationships were in harmony.

The vision of the life she wanted began to influence the life she lived. Ava was living her vision. The line between dreams and reality blurred. The frame that held her vision was expanding. She saw unlimited possibilities before her.

Ava visualized the life she wanted. She created a vision board. The board was a collage of her aspirations. The visual reminders kept her focused and on track. The dreams were now tangible. Ava was living an envisioned reality. The journey had found its way. Unleashed potential. The possibilities had no end.

Ava's journey illustrates that imagination, when paired with belief and emotion, becomes a powerful force. Vision is not wishful thinking; it is disciplined focus supported by feeling and action.

Success was no longer a distant picture. The painted canvas was her life. Inspired. She had bridged the gap between the dream and the reality. Ava had unlocked unlimited possibilities.

Her journey was a testament to the power of imagination, showing how it unleashes potential when connected to sincere emotion. The story of Ava showed that financial freedom and personal fulfillment require more than knowledge and labor, they demand deep engagement with one's vision and unwavering belief in the possibility of it turning real. Ava's experience clarifies the path to success. It is dreaming big and feeling joy. The excitement of those dreams is equally vital, feeling as if they are already fulfilled is crucial. Her imagination was integrated with her core passions and deeper emotions. Through this union, Ava transformed mere aspirations into reality. The reality outpaced initial expectations. Her story is a strong reminder. It reminds us of the transforming force of vision. Emotion also plays a significant role. Vision and emotion are integral in materializing a rich and satisfying life.

## Unleashing Unlimited Possibilities

Ava began by crafting a vivid, dynamic vision. It was a vision of her perfect life. She viewed her existence as a canvas. Each color and brushstroke symbolized an aspect of her desired future vision that was not static. It was vibrant and continuously unfolding. It was bubbling with endless possibilities. Ava grasped that she had to fasten this vision to her core passions. She had to materialize her wants.

This connection was not just about setting goals. It was about indwelling her vision into her inherent self. This vision became her very essence, bold, stirring, and alive.

## Linking Vision to Passion

With unwavering determination, Ava connected her vision to her passions. She created a vision board that featured images of material wealth and symbols of her passions and values. Each morning, she immersed herself in this vision board, allowing her imagination to breathe life into her goals. She visualized the excitement of her achievements, felt the joy of success, and immersed herself in the emotions associated with her ideal lifestyle. This daily ritual of envisioning her future became a powerful tool for aligning her actions with her dreams.

## The Five Decrees

To solidify her commitment, Ava made five powerful decrees to herself:

1. I am abundant: Ava declared she was worthy of abundance and prosperity. She affirmed her belief in her capacity to achieve great things.

2. I am passionate: She acknowledged that her passions were the driving force behind her success and that they would guide her toward her goals.

3. I am capable: Ava reinforced her belief in her skills and talents, recognizing that she had everything she needed to achieve her dreams.

4.  I am grateful: She promised to practice gratitude daily, appreciating the steps she had already taken and the progress she had made.

5.  I am excited: Ava vowed to anticipate the excitement of her achievements, allowing this positive emotion to fuel her journey.

These decrees were not mere words but powerful affirmations that shaped her mindset and actions. Ava understood that anticipation and excitement were not just fleeting feelings but integral parts of her manifestation process.

## Believing in the Anticipated Emotion

Ava knew that the true power of her vision lay in the emotions she cultivated. She believed that immersing herself in the anticipated feelings of success would align her reality with her dreams. Each day, she practiced feeling the joy, satisfaction, and exhilaration of her future achievements as if they were happening in the present moment. This emotional resonance became the secret to her manifestation process, turning her imagination into a tangible reality.

## From Imagination to Reality

As Ava continued to embody her vision, she noticed profound changes taking shape in her life. The more she embraced her imagined future, the more her reality shifted. Opportunities that aligned with her goals presented themselves, and her passions guided her actions with a newfound sense of purpose.

Ava realized that she had transformed her vision into reality by becoming the embodiment of her ideal self. Her journey demonstrated that imagination, when coupled with emotion and passion, is a powerful force for manifesting financial freedom and purpose. Ava unlocked her potential and achieved the lifestyle she had always dreamed of by fully engaging her vision and aligning her emotions with her goals.

Ava's story is a testament to the power of imagination and emotion in the manifestation process. It shows that when one truly becomes the ideal they envision, the imagined future seamlessly merges with reality. Embracing unlimited possibilities and connecting them to one's deepest passions can lead to extraordinary transformation, turning dreams into achievable and fulfilling outcomes.

## Embracing Your Path to Financial Freedom

Achieving financial freedom and leading a purposeful life requires more than mere desire; it demands a wholehearted commitment to engaging fully with your journey. Embracing your path involves stepping into your potential with bravery, confronting your fears directly, and transforming anxieties into opportunities. By facing these fears head-on, you can convert them from barriers into stepping stones that propel you forward.

To navigate your path effectively, taking intentional action is crucial. Although fear is a natural response, it should not immobilize you. Instead, harness it as a source of motivation. Step beyond your comfort zone, treating each action as a chance to build momentum, and surround yourself with a support network of individuals who uplift and inspire you. Their encouragement and guidance will strengthen your resolve and help you confidently tackle challenges.

Perfectionism often serves as a major roadblock to progress. Embrace and accept your imperfections instead of chasing an unattainable ideal. Recognize that imperfections are not flaws but valuable lessons. Rejection and criticism should be viewed constructively, serving as tools for refinement and growth rather than discouragement.

Finding joy in your journey is vital to achieving financial freedom. Celebrate your milestones and take pride in your progress. Don't let the pursuit for perfection overshadow your achievements. Allow yourself to feel good about your successes and practice positive self-talk. Negative words can diminish the positive energy essential for driving you forward—whether from yourself or others.

Maintaining a positive outlook means breaking free from the need for constant external validation. Resist the urge to seek continual praise or affirmation. Instead, concentrate on turning your aspirations into tangible results. Acquiring specialized knowledge pertinent to your field is crucial to achieving financial success. This expertise will be vital in delivering value and securing your desired wealth.

Your journey toward financial freedom encompasses more than merely accumulating wealth; it involves mastering your path's internal and external elements. Confronting fears, taking decisive action, and moving past perfectionism are the foundations to building success. A strong support network, a positive mindset, and specialized knowledge are essential for turning your dreams into reality.

Engagement with your goals should be proactive and purposeful. Each step you take must be deliberate, with the understanding that challenges are an integral part of growth. Your support team serves as a crucial source of strength and inspiration, helping you stay focused and motivated as you pursue your financial and personal objectives.

Release the notion that perfection is required for success. Embrace your journey, with all its imperfections, and view them as learning opportunities. Feedback and criticism should be regarded as opportunities for growth rather than setbacks. By adopting this perspective, you continually refine your approach and move closer to your goals.

Celebrate your progress and acknowledge your achievements. Feeling satisfied with your current status and accomplishments is essential for maintaining a positive mindset. Allow yourself to enjoy your successes, and be mindful of negative influences that may undermine your self-belief. Break free from the cycle of seeking constant validation. Focus instead on intrinsic motivation and the practical steps that will lead you toward your goals. Specialized knowledge about your service, product, or profession will be crucial to your success. This expertise enhances your value and distinguishes you in your field.

The path to financial freedom is multifaceted, involving both internal and external efforts. Embrace this journey with courage, intentional action, and a readiness to learn. Build a supportive network, foster a positive outlook, and gain the specialized knowledge necessary to achieve your ambitions.

Mastering these elements lays a solid foundation for translating your dreams into concrete results. Your dedication to confronting fears, taking action, and accepting imperfections will guide you toward a successful and fulfilling life. Pursuing financial freedom is as much about personal development as it is about reaching financial milestones.

You can unlock your full potential with unwavering commitment and the right mindset. Embrace every step of your journey, knowing that each challenge and success contributes to your ultimate growth and fulfillment. Your path to financial freedom exemplifies your resilience and the power of transforming aspirations into reality.

Achieving financial freedom and a purposeful life requires more than mere desire; it demands a wholehearted commitment to actively engaging in your life's journey. Embracing your path means stepping into your full potential with courage, confronting your fears, and transforming anxieties into opportunities. By directly addressing these fears, you can turn them from obstacles into powerful stepping stones that propel you toward success.

Consider the story of Jessica, a young entrepreneur from a bustling city. Jessica's life was marked by relentless ambition and dreams of financial success. Despite her tireless efforts and numerous ventures, she was in a cycle of unmet potential. She knew that knowledge alone was insufficient; she needed something more profound, a force that transcended mere information and ignited her path to both financial freedom and purpose.

One evening, while reflecting on her ambitions, Jessica experienced a profound revelation: The power of imagination was the key to unlocking her true potential. She envisioned a life overflowing with abundance and purpose, one where her passions aligned with her financial goals. With renewed clarity, Jessica decided to capture this vision in a form that would reshape her reality and guide her path toward success.

It was essential for Jessica to take deliberate action as she navigated her journey, fear, while a natural response, should not hinder progress. Instead, Jessica learned to harness fear as a potent motivator. She took steps beyond her comfort zone and viewed each action as an opportunity to build momentum. Establishing a support network of uplifting and inspiring individuals gave Jessica the encouragement and guidance to overcome challenges confidently.

Jessica also discovered that perfectionism was a significant barrier to her progress. Embracing her imperfections rather than striving for an unattainable ideal became essential to her growth. She realized that imperfections were not flaws but valuable opportunities for learning and self-improvement. Rejection and criticism, she learned, were not deterrents but powerful tools for refinement and personal growth.

Finding joy in the journey was another critical aspect of Jessica's path to financial freedom. She celebrated her achievements and remained content with her progress, refusing to let the pursuit of perfection overshadow her successes. By allowing herself to feel good about her accomplishments, Jessica recognized the importance of positive self-talk and the impact of maintaining a positive mindset.

She maintained a positive outlook, which meant breaking free from the need for constant external validation. Jessica resisted the temptation to seek constant praise or approval. Instead, she focused on turning her aspirations into tangible achievements. Jessica knew she needed specialized knowledge about her service, product, or profession to achieve financial success. This expertise became instrumental in providing value and securing the fortune she desired. Jessica's journey toward financial freedom extended beyond merely accumulating wealth; it involved mastering both internal and external aspects of her path. Facing fears, taking decisive actions, and rejecting perfectionism were key foundations  of lasting success. Her robust support system, positive mindset, and in-depth knowledge equipped her to transform her dreams into reality.

Every step Jessica took was intentional, grounded in the understanding that challenges were integral to her growth. Her support team played a crucial role in providing strength and inspiration, helping her remain focused and motivated as she pursued her financial and personal goals.

Jessica learned to embrace the idea that perfection was not a prerequisite for success. By accepting her journey with all its imperfections, she used them as valuable learning experiences. Feedback and criticism, rather than setbacks, were opportunities for growth and improvement. Jessica celebrated her journey and acknowledged her progress, recognizing the importance of being satisfied with her achievements. She allowed herself to enjoy her successes and remained vigilant against negative influences that might undermine her self-belief.

Breaking free from the cycle of seeking constant validation, Jessica focused on cultivating intrinsic motivation and taking the concrete steps necessary to achieve her goals. Specialized knowledge about her field played a vital role in her success, enhancing her value and setting her apart from others in her industry.

The path to financial freedom is multifaceted, encompassing internal and external efforts. By embracing the journey with courage, action, and a willingness to learn, Jessica built a strong foundation for success. Her support network, positive outlook, and specialized knowledge were essential to her journey.

Jessica's dedication to facing her fears, taking action, and embracing her imperfections paved the way for a successful and fulfilling life. Her story exemplifies that the journey to financial freedom is as much about personal growth as it is about attaining financial success.

With unwavering commitment and the right mindset, Jessica unlocked her full potential. Each challenge and accomplishment contributed to her overall success. Her path to financial freedom is a testament to the resilience and power of transforming aspirations into reality.

# From Adversity to Achievement -
# A Journey To Financial Success.

In the relentless quest for financial freedom, many find themselves on the edge of transformation, only to fall short of true success. Achieving our dreams requires more than mere ambition; it demands an unwavering commitment to our path. So how do we bridge the gap between dreaming and achieving? Here's a powerful guide to unlocking your inner potential and realizing the life you've always envisioned beyond the usual clichés.

## From Pressure to Purpose

Meet Marcus Whitaker—a figure who defies the typical success story. Marcus faced mounting financial strain during an economic downturn. Overwhelmed by bills, workplace pressure, and uncertainty, he felt trapped by circumstances that seemed beyond his control.

Marcus's breakthrough occurred on what seemed like an ordinary day. Seated in his cramped, cluttered apartment, overwhelmed by overdue bills and shattered dreams, he experienced a profound realization: the key to change lay in facing his struggles directly. Marcus recognized that fear and adversity were not barriers but signals for change. Rather than retreat, he chose deliberate action. Each step beyond his comfort zone became momentum toward stability and growth.

Determined to turn his life around, Marcus embarked on bold and deliberate actions. Recognizing that fear was an inevitable companion, he chose to use it as a driving force rather than letting it paralyze him. Each step he took outside his comfort zone became a building block for lasting momentum.

Marcus surrounded himself with mentors and supportive peers who reinforced accountability and perspective. He rejected perfectionism, understanding that progress required action, not flawless execution. Mistakes became feedback, not failure.

One major hurdle Marcus encountered was overcoming the paralyzing grip of perfectionism. He confronted the reality that perfection was both an illusion and an obstacle to progress. Instead of being discouraged by imperfections in his plans and execution, Marcus embraced them as valuable learning experiences. This shift in perspective allowed him to view rejection and criticism as constructive feedback rather than setbacks.

Marcus's journey also involved finding joy in celebrating small victories. He realized that true fulfillment comes from appreciating the present moment and acknowledging progress. By focusing on his achievements rather than an unattainable ideal of perfection, Marcus maintained a positive outlook that kept him motivated.

By managing distractions, refining priorities, and celebrating incremental progress, Marcus regained control over his direction. His persistence transformed pressure into purpose, proving that resilience and action can reshape even the most challenging circumstances.

Marcus's story is not just about individual success; it offers a blueprint for anyone navigating the challenges of a post-recession world. It demonstrates that financial freedom is not a distant dream but an attainable reality when approached with the right mindset and strategies. His journey highlights the importance of connecting with one's inner self, embracing imperfections, and finding lasting fulfillment.

One of humanity's greatest flaws is our comfort with the term *impossible*. Many are familiar with all the failed methods and tasks deemed unachievable. This narrative is for those seeking the principles that have guided others to success and are ready to fully commit to those principles.

Marcus's story demonstrates that abundance is built through courage, discipline, and consistent effort. Success is not accidental; it is cultivated through choice and action.

Over the past twenty-five years, countless individuals have turned adversity into achievement. Marcus's story exemplifies how personal transformation can lead to extraordinary success. It shows that you don't have to sacrifice your life, time, or relationships to achieve your goals.

The path to financial freedom does not involve chasing unrealistic promises of a four-hour workweek or instant success. Instead, it requires connecting with your higher self, tapping into your passion, and adopting a mindset that embraces both challenges and opportunities. Belief lies at the core of this journey. Your beliefs about money shape your financial reality. These beliefs evolve and can be intentionally changed. Developing beliefs that attract money while discarding those that repel it is essential.

Although underlying beliefs can be challenging to pinpoint, this journey will help you develop new foundational beliefs that support your financial objectives. Managing your inner mindset is crucial for attracting wealth. Desire is the catalyst for action. To enhance your financial success, amplify your desire for greater prosperity. Emotion fuels movement, so the stronger your desire for wealth, the more power you'll have to attract it. Your desire for more money has already prompted you to take action. Desire breeds action, and that action, in turn, fuels desire. As you push yourself to start this process, it will propel you forward, helping you achieve the financial abundance you seek.

Marcus's journey illustrates that success is not about working harder but working smarter. It involves making deliberate choices, seeking support, and consistently pushing beyond your comfort zone. His experience demonstrates that by focusing on your passions and taking actionable steps, you can achieve the financial freedom and fulfillment you've always desired. In conclusion, this is more than just a call to action; it's an invitation to rethink your approach to success. Embrace your journey with all its imperfections, celebrate your progress, and maintain an unwavering focus on your goals. By following Marcus's example and connecting with your higher self, you'll discover that success is not merely a possibility but a certainty as well.

Step into your potential with courage and conviction. Harness your fears, take decisive actions, and reject the constraints of perfectionism. Your path to financial freedom is not a distant dream but a vivid reality waiting for you to seize it. Marcus's story stands as a testament to what is possible when you approach your journey with unwavering determination and a passion for success.

## The Secret Sauce of Digital Success Is Passion

In the fast-paced world of digital entrepreneurship, one factor consistently distinguishes those who succeed from those who falter: passion. Passion isn't just a fleeting feeling; it's the driving force behind every digital success story. But how do you channel this passion into tangible results? The secret lies in mastering the art of "completion consciousness" and embracing the five Ds of manifestation. In this section, we explore how passion, when combined with deliberate actions and strategic planning, can transform your digital ventures from mere ideas into thriving realities.

To begin, let's discuss the fundamental role of decision-making. Achieving success in the digital world starts with the strength of a decision. Whether launching a new app, creating content, or starting an online business, you must commit to your goal. This decision acts as the foundation upon which everything else is built. For instance, consider Lisa, who decided to pivot her blog into a full-scale digital marketing agency. Her decision wasn't merely a casual choice but a dedicated commitment to her vision, which set the stage for all subsequent actions.

Next comes the concept of completion. Completing is more than simply finishing tasks—it's about creating a sense of closure and readiness for new endeavors. It's the difference between a half-baked idea and a polished project. Take Jake, a software developer who worked on a project for months without completing it. Once he embraced the idea of completion, he launched his app successfully, making space for innovations. This process involves not just finishing what you start but also ensuring that you wrap up projects in a way that allows you to move forward unburdened.

Planning is another crucial step. Without a clear plan, even the most passionate ideas can lose momentum. Crafting a detailed roadmap helps you navigate the path to success. Consider Samantha, who planned every step meticulously before launching her e-commerce store. Her detailed plan included market research, budget allocation, and a marketing strategy, ultimately leading to a successful launch. Planning transforms abstract passion into actionable steps, ensuring your efforts are directed toward achieving specific goals.

Once you have a plan, the next step is to execute it fully. This involves not just starting but following through to completion. It's about finishing what you've begun. For example, an aspiring YouTuber, Alex, started creating content enthusiastically but struggled with consistency. By focusing on completing each video and implementing feedback, he developed a steady content flow that significantly grew his channel's audience significantly.

Continuing the momentum is equally vital. Digital success isn't a sprint; it's a marathon. After completing one project, it's essential to keep the momentum going. A digital artist, Emily continuously releases new work and engages with her audience, maintaining her visibility and relevance in a competitive field. Her ability to keep creating and sharing her art was crucial in building a loyal following and achieving long-term success.

Getting into completion consciousness is about understanding the importance of finishing tasks and projects with intention and clarity. This mindset helps you stay focused and avoid starting numerous projects without bringing any to fruition. John, a digital entrepreneur, practiced completion consciousness by setting clear goals and ensuring each project was finished before moving on to the next. This approach prevented him from becoming overwhelmed and ensured consistent progress.

Creating room for new opportunities involves finishing existing projects to shift your focus to fresh possibilities. This principle is about clearing the old to make room for the latest. For instance, a content creator, Mia, archived her outdated courses to concentrate on developing new, more relevant material. By doing so, she ensured that her energy and resources were directed toward creating content that resonated with her audience.

The five Ds of manifestation are essential tools in this process: decide, dream, design, do, and deliver. First, decide on your goal with clarity. Then dream about the possibilities and visualize your success vividly. Design a plan to achieve your vision and take consistent actions to do what's necessary. Finally, deliver your project with excellence. For example, if you're developing a digital product, these steps help transform your vision into a reality by providing a clear, structured approach.

Transcending limiting beliefs is a critical aspect of achieving digital success. Many people sabotage their progress by holding onto beliefs that undermine their efforts. These beliefs can manifest as fears of failure or self-doubt. Consider Tom, who initially doubted his ability to succeed in digital marketing due to his lack of experience. He achieved notable success in his field by overcoming these limiting beliefs and focusing on his strengths.

Combining passion with these strategies transforms potential into performance. Passion fuels your drive, but without completion consciousness, planning, and execution, it remains a spark. By integrating decision-making, completion, planning, execution, and continued effort, you turn passion into tangible results. This process requires a commitment to your goals and a strategic approach to overcoming obstacles and maximizing opportunities.

To illustrate this further, consider Anna, who started a digital consulting business. Her passion for helping others succeed drove her to make decisive choices, complete her certifications, plan her services, and execute her marketing strategy with precision. She continued to evolve by embracing new challenges and learning from each experience, ultimately achieving significant success in her field.

Your journey to digital success hinges on embracing passion and translating it into deliberate actions. By following these principles, you establish a clear roadmap for achieving your goals. Passion alone is not enough; it must be paired with a commitment to completion, strategic planning, and ongoing effort. This approach ensures that your dreams are not only envisioned but also realized. In conclusion, the secret sauce of digital success is passion, but it's passion coupled with the right strategies. Decide, complete your tasks with purpose, plan effectively, finish your projects, and continue building on your success. By making space for new opportunities and transcending limiting beliefs, you harness the true power of your passion and turn it into lasting digital achievement.

## The Hall of Mirrors: Understanding Reality and Consciousness

In the grand theater of existence, the world often resembles a hall of mirrors, where every reflection manifests our consciousness. What we perceive in the physical realm is a projection of our inner self. This "reality" is akin to a 3D printing of our desires, inner thoughts, and energy. The true essence of our desires, inner thoughts, and energy. The true essence of what is real lies in the "I AM" consciousness, the core of our being that transcends physicality.

Our ideal self exists in its complete form from the moment of our birth. It's as if we are continually reborn into a higher level of consciousness. This transformation requires shedding old self-deceptions and outdated identities. We must let go of the past and embrace a new self to evolve from our current reality and create a new one. This means cultivating a mindset and consciousness that align with our ideal self, leading us to a new reality.

Many individuals attempt to alter their external circumstances without addressing their internal perceptions and self-image. Actual change begins from within. By delving into the sanctuary of our inner self, often described as the "Holy of holies," we can initiate a profound transformation. From this sacred seat of consciousness, we can manifest a new version of ourselves and, consequently, a new world.

To clarify these concepts further:

- Spirit vs. World

Spirit represents the immaterial essence of being, the source of awareness beyond physical form.

World refers to the tangible environment shaped by perception and experience. While the world appears external, it is interpreted through consciousness.

- Consciousness vs. Conscience

*Consciousness* is awareness of existence, thought, and perception.

*Conscience* functions within this awareness as a guide for ethical judgment and decision making. Both influence behavior, but consciousness determines perception while conscience directs choice.

- Eternal vs. Time vs. Infinity vs. Space

The eternal exists beyond sequence and limitation.

Time measures change within physical experience. Infinity represents boundlessness without restriction.

Infinity represents something without limits, extending beyond time and space constraints.

Space provides the structure in which physical events occur. Together, these concepts frame the relationship between perception and reality.

- I AM vs. Ego vs. Knowledge

I AM reflects pure awareness, independent of identity.

Ego is the psychological construct of self, encompassing identity, personality, and individual experiences. It is distinct from the pure essence of the "I AM."

Knowledge is the understanding gained through experience, education, or insight. When awareness is anchored in the "I AM," ego and knowledge serve growth rather than control it.

• Perception vs. Unchanging vs. Changing

Perception is the subjective process of interpreting sensory information can differ according to individual perspectives and experiences.

Unchanging refers to something constant and unaffected by external influences or the passage of time.

Changing describes the dynamic aspect of reality, where conditions and states evolve.

• Love vs. Fear

Love is a profound emotional state characterized by affection, care, and connection, and it is associated with unity and compassion.

Fear is  an emotional response to perceived threats linked to avoidance, anxiety, and a sense of separation.

Understanding the distinctions of these concepts deepens awareness and strengthens alignment between consciousness and experience. When inner awareness is clarified, external circumstances respond accordingly.

# CHAPTER 15

# THE ULTIMATE INSIGHT: YOUR PATH TO MANIFESTATION MASTERY

Philippians 4:19 declares, *"My God shall supply all your needs according to His riches in glory by Christ Jesus."* This verse affirms the faithfulness of the Divine and reassures us that both material and spiritual needs are met through God's boundless grace and abundance. It speaks to a promise that extends beyond circumstance, grounding trust in a source that is constant and sufficient.

This assurance reminds us that infinite intelligence is fully capable of providing for every need in our lives. By understanding and embracing this promise, we can move forward on our spiritual journey with confidence, trusting that our needs will be met in divine timing and in the way that serves our highest good.

By understanding this promise, we can approach our spiritual journey with confidence, trusting that our needs will be met in divine timing and in the best possible way.

## Key Insights from the Verse

1.  Affirms the Divine's willingness to provide: The Divine is a loving source eager to bless and attend to our needs.

2.  Declares the abundance of Divine resources: The richness of the Divine is infinite and generously shared with us.

3.  Connects us to the Divine through Christ: We access divine grace and favor through our connection with Christ.

4.  Sets a clear expectation: We can confidently anticipate that our needs will be met, both physically and spiritually.

## The 41-word prayer

I am open and ready to accept the cup of blessing that the universe holds for me. I am worthy of expanding my steps. I am deserving of an abundance of wealth and prosperity. This abundance should come in all areas of my life.

The affirmation can be a potent instrument for realizing one's desires. Also, by ascertaining one's worthiness by setting clear intentions and fostering a positive mindset. These actions can draw abundance into life. When repeated daily with gratitude and a clear vision, it strengthens belief and supports the manifestation process.

Trust that the universe is actively working to bring your desires to you. Stay connected to the abundance that already exists within you and allow that trust to guide your journey.

## How to Use This Insight in Your Spiritual Practice

1.  Pray regularly: Add this verse to your regular prayers, especially during challenging times.

2.  Customize your prayer: Insert your individual wants or needs into your prayer. Make your prayer personal and poignant.

3.  Believe in God's timing: Know that the infinite intelligence is listening. It will supply answers at its perfect moment.

4.  Show gratitude: Develop gratitude for the Divine's provision. Do this even before your desires are met.

Prayer is not a magic Band-Aid. It is a way of deepening your connection to the Divine. Align your intentions with the Divine will, this allows you to receive guidance and support. When you weave verse into your spiritual practice, you open to abundance and await blessings.

## Manifesting Your Desires:
## A Guide to the "Ask, Believe, Receive" Principle

**Ask with clarity and specificity.**

Define precisely what you desire by being clear about your intentions and specific outcomes. Avoid vague requests, as clarity strengthens focus and improves manifestation results.

**Trust the process.**

Have unwavering faith that your requests will come to fruition, even when results are not immediately visible.

**Open yourself to receive**

Embrace what you've asked for. Show gratitude to the universe—be thankful for what you have and what's yet to come. Welcome the joy and abundance that are flowing into your life with an open heart.

**Take action toward your goals.**

Manifestation requires active effort; it's not a passive process. Be alert to the opportunities that present themselves along the way.

**Maintain a positive mindset.**

Clear your mind of negative thoughts, as they can block manifestation. Accept challenges while keeping your focus on positive outcomes, maintaining a clear vision and persevering through setbacks.

**Visualize and affirm daily.**

Spend time each day visualizing your desired outcome. See yourself already in possession of what you want.

**Be patient and persistent.**

Manifestation takes time—it's not always immediate and patience is essential.

*The Secret's* **"Ask, Believe, Receive"** framework is a powerful method that uses the law of attraction to manifest your desires. To effectively use this system, you need to be both clear and specific.

**Ask:** Clearly define what you want, including all the details and reasons behind your desires. For example, instead of saying, "I want a better job," say, "I want a graphic designer position in Los Angeles with a salary of $70,000 a year."

**Believe:** Cultivate an unwavering belief in the universe's power.

**Receive:** Be open to opportunities and abundance.

**Take inspired action:** Don't just passively wait for your desires to appear—actively pursue them.

## Practice self-love and acceptance.

Clear negative energy by nurturing self-love and acceptance. Visualization and affirmations are also key in the manifestation process. Dedicate time each day to visualize yourself enjoying your desires, and use affirmations to reinforce your beliefs and counter any limiting thoughts.

## Patience and Persistence

Trust that your desires will manifest at the perfect time. Ensure that your desires align with your highest good and the greater good.

The law of attraction works best when your goals are aligned with your true purpose.

When manifesting something specific, like a house worth $1,500,000 on 27 acres, be precise. This level of precision sends a clear message to the universe about what you truly desire.

This same attention to detail applies to other areas of your life. For instance, if you're starting a consulting business, companies like Vision Quest Consulting specialize in crafting customized business plans for entrepreneurs and established businesses alike. They transform visions into actionable strategies.

Likewise, when setting goals for publishing books, be specific. Choose your target audience, define the success you envision for your business, and avoid vague language. By doing so, you enhance your ability to clarify and manifest your desires.

## Manifesting Every Day: How to Align Your Reality with Your Desires

Manifesting is something we do every day, often without realizing it. Our thoughts, beliefs, language, and actions all play a role in shaping our reality.

### How We Manifest Daily

### Negative Manifestation

Examples of negative manifestation include focusing on financial worry or repeatedly voicing health concerns, both of which reinforce unwanted outcomes.

**Positive Manifestation**

Positive manifestation includes focusing on gratitude, health, and meaningful relationships, which strengthens positive outcomes.

**Tips for Conscious Manifestation**

1.  Identify your desires:

    Clearly define what you want to manifest in your life. Be specific and detailed.

2.  Visualize and affirm:

    Regularly visualize yourself already possessing or experiencing what you desire. Use affirmations to reinforce your belief and maintain a positive mindset.

3.  Take inspired action:

    Engage in activities that align with your goals and bring you closer to your desired outcome. Act on opportunities that come your way.

4.  Release resistance:

    Let go of negative thoughts, beliefs, or emotions that block your manifestation. Practice forgiveness, self-love, and acceptance.

5.  Be patient and persistent:

    Manifestation takes time and effort. Stay consistent with your practices and trust in the universe's perfect timing.

# Common Misconceptions About Manifestation

- **Misunderstanding:** Some think manifestation is about controlling the universe or getting things without effort, leading to unrealistic expectations.

- **Lack of belief:** Others may view manifestation as wishful thinking or superstition.

- **Negative experiences:** Past disappointments with manifestation can cause skepticism.

- **Religious beliefs:** Some may feel manifestation conflicts with their faith or view it as trying to control outcomes.

- **Cultural influences:** Manifestation might be seen as selfish or arrogant in some cultures.

- **Fear of failure:** Fear of not achieving goals can discourage people from trying.

- **Focus on lack:** Those who focus on what they lack may find it hard to believe in the manifestation's power.

## Aligning Your Morning Routine with Manifestation

Our morning routines significantly impact our ability to manifest our desires. Using this time to set intentions and visualize goals helps direct focus throughout the day.

**Incorporate manifestation into your morning routine.**

1. **Set intentions:** Set clear intentions for your day upon waking.

2. **Visualize your desires**: Visualize yourself already experiencing your desired outcomes.

3. **Use affirmations**: Use affirmations that reinforce intention and belief.

4. **Practice gratitude**: Begin the day by acknowledging what you are grateful for.

Integrating these practices into your daily routine aligns your thoughts, words, and actions with your desires.

Starting your day with practices such as meditation, visualization, gratitude, and affirmations helps align your energy with your desires.

Taking tangible steps toward finding love is also crucial. Whether it's joining a new social group or exploring dating apps, showing the universe that you're ready to receive love can make a big difference. Creating a vision board can further support your manifestation efforts. By displaying images and words that represent your dream relationship, you keep your desires in focus and stay motivated. It's equally important to let go of any attachments or rigid expectations, as these can block the flow of love into your life. Trust the process and believe that the universe will bring you the perfect partner at the right time. Regular practices of self-love and self-care also play a key role in ensuring that you are in a healthy state of mind to welcome your soulmate.

By integrating these practices into your daily routine, you can manifest the love of your life and build a beautiful, fulfilling relationship that aligns with your deepest desires.

By integrating these affirmations into your daily routine, you align your thoughts, beliefs, and actions with the powerful forces of manifestation. Embrace them with an open heart and watch as your reality transforms into alignment with your deepest desires.

More tips….

## A Game-changing Financial Strategy

Bob Proctor's insights emphasize the importance of prioritizing your financial well-being. A transformative approach is to pay yourself first before tackling other expenses.

### Why pay yourself first?

1. Financial Prioritization: By setting aside money for savings and investments right away, you prioritize your own financial goals and future security.

2. Healthy Balance: This strategy ensures a balance between immediate needs and future financial aspirations, promoting proactive financial management.

### A Simple Formula to Implement Bob's Advice

Calculate Your Savings
*Example:*
- Hourly wage: $15.50
- Hours per week: 40
- Pay periods per year: 26

Gross Pay Per Paycheck:

$15.50 × 40 hours = $620

Savings Per Paycheck (One Day of Pay):
$15.50 × 8 hours = $124

If you save $124 from each of the 26 annual paychecks:

Annual Savings:
$124 × 26 = $3,224

Every year you save $3,224 when you take $124 out twice a month across the 26 paychecks.

**Plan for Your Future with a Savings Formula**

To save for larger goals, the formula is:
$$F = (G - B(1 + t)^p) / (((1 + t)^p - 1)/t)$$

Where:
F = amount to be vested annually
G = target of financial goal
B = already saved funds
t = interest rate (decimal) per annum
p = time (in years) for which goal is to be reached

*Example Goal*

Goal: $1,000,000
Our current savings amount will be $50,000
10% Interest Rate
Years to Goal – 5

Calculate
$$F = (1,000,000 - 50,000(1 + 0.10)^5) / (((1 + 0.10)^5 - 1) / 0.10)$$
F = $148,000

To achieve a goal of $1,000,000 in less than 5 years with a 10% return per year means one has to invest around $148,000 per annum.

**So here is what makes this realistic**

Now here is how this example shows that saving alone at $3,224/ year will not create $1,000,000 in 5 years.

However, if the savings discipline is mixed with:
- Business income
- Brand monetization
- Sales of products
- Distribution of stores
- Scale social media
- Investments with higher returns

Then hitting $1,000,000 in less than 5 years is mathematically possible, not guaranteed but achievable with scale and execution.

## How Rich People Use Debt to Create Wealth

*Leverage: Amplify Your Gains*

Wealthy individuals use debt to magnify their investments. By borrowing to invest, they increase potential returns.

*Tax Benefits: Reduce Your Tax Burden*

Interest on debt can often be tax deductible, reducing taxable income.

*Asset Acquisition: Invest in Growth*

Debt can be used to acquire assets that generate income or appreciate over time. For instance, borrowing money to purchase real estate or stocks can yield long-term gains.

*Business Expansion: Fuel Growth*

Debt helps finance business expansion, leading to increased profits. Wealthy individuals use loans to invest in equipment, new locations, or additional staff, thereby boosting their income and wealth.

*Estate Planning: Preserve Wealth*

Debt can also aid in estate planning by reducing the taxable value of an estate, helping to minimize estate taxes and preserve wealth for heirs.

*Risks and Considerations*

Using debt involves risks, including potential financial loss if investments don't perform well or if interest rates rise. It's crucial to assess these risks carefully before leveraging debt.

*Examples of Debt in Wealth Creation*

- **Real estate investing:** Using debt to purchase rental properties can generate rental income and long-term appreciation.

- **Stock market investing:** Borrowing to buy stocks on margin allows for greater potential returns.

- **Private equity:** Debt-financed investments in companies can lead to higher returns.

- **Business ventures:** Financing new business projects with debt can yield significant profits if successful.

Debt, when used wisely, can be a powerful tool for creating wealth. However, it's essential to use it carefully and understand the associated risks.

Prayer is an essential part of my daily routine. At the end of each day and after every workshop or seminar, I pray to break free from limiting beliefs and fears. One powerful prayer I use is the following:

*Dear infinite, intelligent universe, god of consciousness, higher power within me, I release all limiting beliefs and fears that have held me back from living to my fullest potential. I surrender my doubts and worries to you, knowing that you have the power to guide me toward a life of love, abundance, and fulfillment. I trust in your divine guidance and ask for the strength and courage to let go of any negative thoughts or beliefs that no longer serve me. I am ready to step into my true power and embrace all that I am capable of. Thank you for helping me break free from my subconscious limitations and allowing me to live a life of joy and abundance.*

*Amen/So it is.*

This prayer acknowledges the higher power's role in guiding us to a life free from limiting beliefs, expressing gratitude for the opportunity to release negativity and embrace a positive mindset. By surrendering our fears, we open ourselves to divine guidance and step into our true potential.

*Then the nations that are left all around you shall know that I am the Lord; I have rebuilt the ruined places and replanted that which was desolate. I am the Lord; I have spoken, and I will do it.* (Ezekiel 36:36)

# The Secret to Manifestation:
# Repetition, Duration, and Emotions

The law of attraction, popularized in Rhonda Byrne's *The Secret*,[122] proposes that we attract into our lives whatever our attention is focused on.

**Repetition is like walking a path**; with each step, it cuts a groove. Repeated affirmations on a regular basis strengthen the neural pathways in the brain.

**Time:** Manifestation takes time.

**Emotions:** Gratitude and joy are some of the positive emotions that align our energies to a frequency that is on par with what we want to bring forth.

**Overcoming limiting beliefs**: Core beliefs shape the reality we experience. Breaking down negative beliefs and implanting positive affirmations helps modify our mental settings and open up avenues to actual change.[123]

**The magical trio of the trinity**: Repetition, duration, and emotion come together in an unbeatable formula for change.

**Example**: In order to attract financial abundance, one must daily affirm something like "I am a magnet for wealth and prosperity,"[124] visualize financial success, and cultivate feelings of joy and gratitude. With time, this will help reprogram deeper mental frameworks and may help in enhancing the present financial situation.[125]

---

122  Byrne, *The Secret*.

123  Samso, *The Manifestation Code*.

124  Schwartz, *The Magic of Thinking Big*.

125  Jack Canfield, *The Success Principles: How to Get from Where You Are to Where You Want to Be* (HarperCollins, 2005).

**What's more...**

### Transcending Health Excuses and Unlocking Financial Abundance: A Journey Through Conscious Manifestation

Integrate these four transformative steps into your daily practice to align with higher consciousness and manifest optimal health and financial abundance. These steps will help you harness the power of **"I am"** and create a life of profound fulfillment and prosperity.

### Shift Your Focus from Health Complaints to Positive Vibration

**Illustration:** Imagine someone constantly discussing their minor health issues with friends and family. Each conversation amplifies their discomfort and reinforces negative energy, trapping them in a cycle of health complaints. Now, picture this person redirecting their focus toward positive and constructive conversations, engaging in activities that uplift their spirits.

**Step-by-step demonstration:**

- Identify negative focus: Observe when your thoughts or conversations revolve around health complaints.

- Redirect your attention: Discuss uplifting topics or engage in activities that bring joy and satisfaction.

- Cultivate positivity: Surround yourself with positive influences and practices that enhance your well-being.

- Align with universal energy: By consistently focusing on positivity, you align with the universal energy, which attracts health and financial abundance.

## Transform Excessive Health Worry into Spiritual Awareness

**Illustration:** Consider someone who obsessively schedules medical tests out of fear, creating unnecessary anxiety.

**Step-by-step demonstration:**

- Recognize excessive worry: Notice when your health concerns overwhelm your peace.

- Practice mindfulness: Engage in meditation or deep breathing to center yourself.

- Trust in higher intelligence: Develop faith in the natural order of life and your body's ability to heal.

- Foster inner peace: By shifting your focus to spiritual awareness, you reduce anxiety and align with the higher consciousness necessary for manifesting health and financial success.

### Embrace Deep Gratitude for Your Current Health

**Illustration:** Reflect on the saying, "I once felt sorry for myself because I had ragged shoes until I met a man with no feet."

**Step-by-step demonstration:**

- Acknowledge current health: Take time each day to recognize and appreciate your current state of health.

- Reflect on gratitude: Consider the blessings in your life and express heartfelt thanks for them.

- Enhance your vibration: Use gratitude to raise your vibrational frequency, making you more receptive to attracting financial abundance and overall well-being.

- Strengthen resilience: By fostering appreciation, you build resilience and create a more positive life experience.

## Adopt the Philosophy of Vibrant Engagement Over Passive Limitation

**Illustration:** Picture a person who, despite having health concerns, actively engages in life's activities and pursues their passions. Contrast this with someone else who allows health issues to limit their participation in life.

**Step-by-step demonstration:**

- Assess your engagement: Evaluate whether health concerns are causing you to live a limited or sedentary life.

- Embrace active participation: Seek out and engage in activities that excite and fulfill you.

- Foster a dynamic approach: Focus on energetic involvement rather than passive existence.

- Align with spiritual fulfillment: By living fully and actively, you align with spiritual fulfillment and pave the way to health and financial prosperity.

**To unlock your purpose and achieve financial freedom, consider these four key strategies:**

## Leverage Your Unique Skills and Passion

**Illustration:** Imagine someone who loves personal development and uses their passion to offer coaching services or create valuable content.

**Step-by-step demonstration:**

- Identify your skills: Recognize your unique talents and passions.

- Align your work: Tailor your business or career to match what you love and excel at.

- Attract opportunities: Focus on areas where your enthusiasm aligns with your skills to draw in opportunities and clients.

- Create resonance: Offer services or products that align with your passions, such as personal development coaching or relevant content creation.

# Create Multiple Income Streams

**Illustration:** Visualize a person selling books who also creates online courses and workshops.

**Step-by-step demonstration:**

- Explore diversification: Identify potential additional income sources related to your primary business.

- Expand offerings: Develop complementary products or services, like online courses or workshops.

- Invest in passive income: Consider investments that generate passive income.

- Monitor and adjust: Regularly assess and adjust your income streams to ensure financial stability.

## Adopt a Growth Mindset and Continuous Learning

**Illustration:** Consider someone who remains current with industry trends and invests in their personal development.

**Step-by-step demonstration:**

- Embrace growth: Adopt a mindset that's focused on personal and professional development.

- Seek knowledge: Stay updated on industry trends and continuously seek new learning opportunities.

- Invest in development: Engage in courses or workshops that enhance your expertise.

- Position yourself as a leader: Use your knowledge to establish yourself as a thought leader and attract more opportunities.

## Practice Generosity and Networking

**Illustration:** Picture a person actively participating in industry events and building meaningful connections.

**Step-by-step demonstration:**

- Engage in networking: Attend industry events and connect with peers.

- Offer value: Contribute to discussions and offer assistance to others.

- Build relationships: Cultivate meaningful connections that can lead to new opportunities.

- Collaborate: Look for ways to collaborate and partner with others in your industry.

*Understanding the Nature of Miracles*

Miracles arise from elevated consciousness rather than personal effort alone.

*Applying the Miracle Process for Manifestation*

**To effectively manifest your desires, apply the miracle process through these three critical steps:**

## Declare "I Am" as the Presence

**Illustration:** Envision yourself acknowledging your true, unbounded identity through meditation or affirmations. This recognition aligns you with your infinite essence and removes past limitations.

**Step-by-step demonstration:**

- Acknowledge your identity: Engage in practices that reveal your authentic self.

- Embrace "I am": Recognize that past self-concepts do not define your true essence.

- Elevate your mindset: Use the "I am" power to redefine your reality and align with your higher self.

## Immerse in the Expectation of Achievement

**Illustration:** Imagine fully immersing yourself in the belief that your desires are already fulfilled. This emotional state accelerates the manifestation process by aligning your mindset with your goals.

**Step-by-step demonstration:**

- Cultivate certainty: Develop a deep belief that your desires are already on their way.

- Embrace emotional fulfillment: Fully experience the emotions of having achieved your goals.

- Align with your desires: Immerse yourself in the anticipation of fulfillment to align with the manifestation process.

## Express Gratitude and Let Go

**Illustration:** Picture yourself proactively expressing gratitude for the realization of your desires while releasing control over the details of their manifestation. This approach allows the process to unfold naturally.

**Step-by-step demonstration:**

- Surrender control: Trust in universal intelligence to handle the details of manifestation.

- Express gratitude: Offer thanks in advance for the fulfillment of your desires.

- Release attachment: Let go of any attachment to outcomes and allow the natural flow of manifestation.

*Final Reflections*

As Neville emphasizes, your assumed identity reflects the power of "I am." Trust in your true essence to guide your path to your desires. By focusing on inner transformation and embracing the miracle process, you will discover that your goals are achieved effortlessly, guided by higher wisdom and a profound sense of inner alignment.

# STILL HUNGRY FOR MORE?

# HERE ARE A FEW TASKS TO COMPLETE

Clemer Leggett: Cosmic consciousness is the deep realization that your desires are already fulfilled because you are intricately connected to infinite intelligence. When you are crystal clear about what you wish to manifest, you intuitively understand that it has already come to fruition. This is not about blind faith but rather a profound inner wisdom that arises from aligning your thoughts, emotions, and actions with limitless energy within, fully embracing your divine essence.

With this unwavering certainty, doubt and hesitation dissolve, giving way to a confident magnetism that effortlessly attracts your desired outcomes. Successful individuals often speak of a relentless inner fire, an unwavering determination that their dreams will materialize despite any obstacles or skeptics.

To nurture this profound knowledge, delve into your intuition, heed the whispers of your soul, and forge a deep connection with your higher self, the source of infinite wisdom within. By quieting external distractions and turning inward, one can access a reservoir of unwavering certainty. Maintaining a positive mindset is crucial—embrace thoughts and emotions that reinforce your steadfast belief in your desires and vividly visualize yourself as already embodying the person you aspire to be.

This transformative practice not only amplifies your personal power but also aligns with the cosmic forces that work to manifest the deepest aspirations into reality. Achieving financial success involves adopting the mindsets and behaviors of successful individuals. Envision yourself as someone who has achieved their goals and let this vision guide your decisions. Prioritize long-term investments over quick, high-risk gains.

Cultivate an ideal identity that embodies success—dress with clarity and confidence, speak with authority, and act professionally. Set clear, attainable goals, such as saving a portion of your income or investing in growth opportunities. Develop disciplined daily rituals as a priority, rising early, working with focus, and investing in personal development. Assess your progress and adjust your strategies as needed. Stay enthusiastic and motivated by tracking your achievements and visualizing your goals.

By aligning your actions with those of successful individuals, you will pave the way to achieving your financial objectives.

## Unfold Your Potential: How to Realize Your Highest Self

1. Conceptualize your ideal self.

   How can I idealize myself?

   Reflect on your personal and professional self on an emotional and spiritual level. What characteristics and accomplishments, and actions do you want to possess and master? How can I conceptualize clear goals?

   Now, transform your vision into concrete, quantifiable, and feasible goals. Examples include career milestones, personal development, and lifestyle changes.

2. Know thyself and reflect.

   How do I evaluate my present self?

Reflect on where your current reality stands compared to the ideal self. List your strengths and weaknesses.

Why reflect on values and passions?

It enables you to set meaningful goals and act on things that are authentic and important to you.

3. Develop a growth mindset.

How should I perceive challenges?

Challenges should be seen as opportunities to grow, not as obstacles. This helps foster a learning attitude and resilience.

Why is it important to celebrate your progress?

Celebrating minor achievements keeps you motivated, maintains a positive outlook, and encourages you to work further toward improvement.

4. Create a personal development plan.

How do I identify the gap in my skills and knowledge?

Identify what skills or knowledge you need to acquire in order to move closer to your ideal self.

What are some good ways of seeking learning opportunities?

Enroll in courses, workshops, or experiences that target these gaps to promote continuous learning in the process of personal growth.

5. Developing positive habits.

How do I set up routines that help me in realizing my goals?

Design daily or weekly routines that move you closer to your goals; this could include exercising, meditating, or managing time more effectively.

Why is discipline worth practicing?

Consistency breeds momentum and moves you closer to your ideal self.

6. Surround yourself with support.

   Seek out mentors who possess the qualities you wish to acquire, as well as the knowledge and experience from which you can learn and take advice.

7. Tap into the power of visualization.

   How does visualization help me in achieving success?

   Close your eyes and visualize yourself achieving success while embodying all the qualities of this ideal self. This helps maintain motivation and focus on the top level.

   How about affirmations?

   Create positive affirmations and repeat them to yourself, declaring your goals and the qualities that you want to attain.

8. Practice mind management and emotional control.

   How can mindfulness benefit me?

   Be more mindful and practice meditation to become more self-aware and balanced with your emotions.

   How should I handle negative self-talk?

Recognize and question any thoughts that are negative, or self-doubting. After recognizing these doubts replace them with empowering beliefs.

9.  Take inspired action.

    How can I break down my goals into smaller manageable tasks?

    Take big goals and divide them into smaller tasks; apply consistent effort to achieve them.

    Why would I want to learn to be adaptable?

    Be flexible, and as you go along, make changes that will realign with your ideal self.

10. Review and adjust.

    How often should I check my progress?

    Periodically, review your progress and reflect on what's working and what may need adjustment.

    When should I change my goals?

    Alter goals or methods according to how you feel about what you are achieving and is the shift in your aspirations.

    By following these steps, you can progressively align with your ideal self, unlocking your full potential and leading a more fulfilling and authentic life.

# Beyond the Surface: A Bonus Thought to Ponder

In this world where financial freedom seems so elusive, *Get Rich Like Instant Coffee: Unlocking Your Purpose for Financial Freedom* offers a different perspective. The powerful manifestation principles and awareness of self-explored in this guide will lead you to your desired destination in achieving your financial goals are concerned.

Here's how it can change your life: manifestation.

The foundation of this book is the core power of manifestation. You will learn how to channel your thoughts and beliefs toward attracting wealth and success. Just as the external world reflects the internal, you will come to understand how to shift your mindset to manifest your goals. It is not about mere positive thinking; rather, it is about truly confronting the subconscious mind to make a reality of deep desires.

*Spiritual Growth and Consciousness*

This guide explores how one can expand their consciousness to connect with higher awareness in order for one's personal and financial growth. You will dive deep into the concept of infinite intelligence and how to tap into this creative wisdom. Through spiritual practice and release from beliefs that constrain you, a higher level of comprehension and direction awaits.

*Practical Strategies for Financial Freedom*

Rich in philosophical underpinnings, the book nonetheless offers concrete ways to achieve financial freedom. You'll be guided through practical exercises, journaling questions, and reflective tasks that clarify your vision and provide an action plan to overcome obstacles. Whether you're starting a business, seeking a different path, or just simply trying to make your financial circumstances better, this advice will get you on your journey and help you move forward with confidence and purpose.

Self-discovery has been the major theme depicted in this guide. This will inspire you toward self-discovery about your identity, strengths, and passions, which, in turn, will take you to your true purpose. The workbook section of the book offers an interactive set of exercises that reveal your potential and help align your actions with your aspirations, ensuring they remain in sync. A deeper understanding of yourself will enable you to make better decisions and live with greater clarity and purpose.

*Success Stories and Practical Applications*

The book also seeks to provide evidence of the discussed principles through testimonials and real-life examples of individuals who transformed their lives using these teachings. Their stories are a source of inspiration and demonstrate that manifestation and consciousness principles can result in tangible success.

*Get Rich Like Instant Coffee* is more than a how-to guide to financial success; it's a comprehensive roadmap to a more empowered and fulfilling life. Putting together the power of manifestation, consciousness, and real-world strategy, this guide offers an integrated approach toward both personal and financial goals. Take the first step on this transformational journey today and unlock your true potential.

# EPILOGUE

-----------

As I look back on my journey, I'm reminded that the path to success is rarely straightforward. It is filled with moments of doubt, trials, and unexpected twists. Yet these very moments define us: They shape our character, resilience, and ultimately, our purpose. Through the lessons learned, I discovered that true success isn't just about financial independence or business achievements; it's about aligning with your higher self, finding joy in every step, and giving back to the world that shaped you.

This journey is not mine alone. It belongs to every person who dares to dream, those who strive in spite of obstacles, and to all who believe that their best self is yet to be uncovered. The wisdom gained through hardships and triumphs has only deepened my gratitude for life's experiences, and I am more certain than ever that the most powerful tool we possess is our mind. By nurturing our inner world, we manifest abundance in our external reality.

In the end, it's about growth—intentional and continuous growth. Whether you're seeking success in business, love, or spirituality, the principles of this journey remain the same: faith, discipline, and an unwavering belief in the power of the subconscious. You, too, have the ability to reshape your life, step into your greatness, and to inspire those around you. May my story serve as a testament to the extraordinary power within each of us, waiting to be awakened.

# BIBLIOGRAPHY


Allen, James. *As a Man Thinketh.* Arc Manor, 1903.

Bernstein, Gabrielle. *The Universe Has Your Back: Transform Fear to Faith.* Hay House, 2016.

Britton, Scott. "Understanding the Map of Consciousness." Accessed December 9, 2024. [Provide full URL or publication details].

Byrne, Rhonda. *The Secret.* Atria Books/Beyond Words, 2006.

Canfield, Jack. *The Success Principles: How to Get from Where You Are to Where You Want to Be.* HarperCollins, 2005.

Douglass, Frederick. *Narrative of the Life of Frederick Douglass, an American Slave.* Anti-Slavery Office, 1845.

Du Bois, W. E. B. *The Souls of Black Folk.* A. C. McClurg & Co., 1903.

Eker, T. Harv. *Secrets of the Millionaire Mind: Mastering the Inner Game of Wealth.* Harper Business, 2005.

Goddard, Neville. *Feeling is the Secret.* Martino Publishing, 2012. Originally published in 1944.

Hawkins, David R. *Power vs. Force: The Hidden Determinants of Human Behavior.* Hay House, 1995.

Hicks, Esther, and Jerry Hicks. *Ask and It Is Given: Learning to Manifest Your Desires.* Hay House, 2004.

Hill, Napoleon. *Think and Grow Rich.* The Ralston Society, 1937.

Kiyosaki, Robert T. *Rich Dad Poor Dad.* TechPress, 1997.

Micheaux, Oscar. *The Conquest: The Story of a Negro Pioneer.* The Western Book Supply Company, 1913.

Murphy, Joseph. *The Power of Your Subconscious Mind.* Prentice Hall, 1963.

Nightingale, Earl. *The Strangest Secret.* NightingaleConant, 1956.

Samso, Raimon. *The Manifestation Code.* Self-published, 2016.

Schwartz, David J. *The Magic of Thinking Big.* New York: Simon and Schuster, 1959.

Shakespeare, William. *Hamlet.* Various editions (circa 1600).

The Holy Bible. King James Version (KJV).

The Holy Bible. English Standard Version (ESV).

Tolstoy, Leo. *The Kingdom of God Is Within You.* Dodd, Mead, 1894.

Wheatley, Phillis. *Poems on Various Subjects, Religious and Moral.* Archibald Bell, 1773.